CHOCTAW BY BLOOD

ENROLLMENT CARDS

1898-1914

VOLUME IV

TRANSCRIBED BY

JEFF BOWEN

NATIVE STUDY
Gallipolis, Ohio
USA

Originally published:
Baltimore, Maryland
2015

Reprinted by:

Native Study LLC
Gallipolis, OH
www.nativestudy.com

Library of Congress Control Number: 2020911767

ISBN: 978-1-64968-007-5

Made in the United States of America.

This series is dedicated to
Mike Marchi,
who keeps my spirits up.

CREEK CENSUS.

SECOND NOTICE.

Members of the Dawes Commission will be present at the following times and places for the purpose of enrolling Creek citizens, as required by Act of Congress of June 10, 1896:

At Muskogee, Nov. 8 to 30, 1897, inclusive.
At Wagoner, Nov. 8 to 13, " inclusive.
At Eufaula, Nov. 8 to 13, " inclusive.
At Sapulpa, Nov. 15 to 20, " inclusive.
At Wetumpka, Nov. 15 to 20, " inclusive.
At Okmulgee, Nov. 22 to 30, " inclusive.

All persons who have not heretofore enrolled before the Dawes Commission should appear and enroll. Parents and guardians can enroll their families and wards.

TAMS BIXBY,
FRANK C. ARMSTRONG,
A. S. McKENNON,
THOS. B. NEEDLES,
Commissioners.

The above illustration is similar in nature to what was found throughout Indian Territory for different tribes as far as postings on bulletin boards, public centers, or wherever they could be read so people would be notified of where and when they needed to be for enrollment with the Dawes Commission.

This is a picture of the Dawes Commission at Camp Jones in Stonewall, Indian Territory on September 8, 1898.

The images below are of two of the original cards given on the microfilm. The cards given in this book have been formatted to fit on one page and still give all the information found on the original cards.

Introduction

This series of Choctaw Enrollment Cards for the Five Civilized Tribes 1898-1914 has been transcribed from National Archive Film M-1186 Rolls 39-46.

The series contains more than 6100 Choctaw enrollment cards. All of the cards list age, sex and degree of blood, the parties' Dawes Roll Numbers, and date of enrollment by the Secretary of Interior for each person. The contents also give the enrollee's parents' names as well as miscellaneous notes pertaining to the enrollee's circumstances, when needed. Most entries indicate whether or not a spouse is an Intermarried White, with the initials I.W.

Enrollment wasn't as simple a process as most would think just by going through these pages. The relationships between the Five Tribes and the Dawes Commission were weak at best. There were political battles going on between the tribes and the U.S. Government as it was, but the struggles didn't stop there. Each tribe had its own political factions pulling it from every direction. On top of everything else, people from every corner of the United States were trying to figure how to get in on the spoils (Money and Land Allotment) by means of political favor. Kent Carter, author of *The Dawes Commission*, describes the continuous effort required to enroll the different tribes and the pressure the Commission incurred from people all over the country who tried to insinuate themselves into the equation:

"In May 1896 the Dawes Commission Returned To Indian Territory for its third visit, establishing its headquarters at Vinita in the Cherokee Nation. It now had to process applications for citizenship in addition to negotiating allotment agreements; these circumstances make the narrative of events more confusing because the commission attempted the two tasks concurrently. The commissioners resumed making their usual speeches to tribal officials and public gatherings to promote negotiations, but now they inevitably had to respond to questions about how the application process for citizenship would work. They also began receiving letters from people all over the United States asking how they could 'get on the rolls' so they could 'get Indian land'."[1]

For the actual process of Choctaw enrollment, "A commission was appointed in each county of the Choctaw Nation under an act of September 18 to make separate rolls of citizens by blood, by intermarriage, and freedmen; it was to deliver them to recently elected Chief Green McCurtain by October 20, but he rejected them even before they were completed because of charges that people were being left off for political reasons. On October 30, the National Council authorized establishment of a five-member

---

[1] *The Dawes Commission* by Kent Carter, page 15, para. 1

ix

commission to revise the rolls within ten days and then directed McCurtain to turn them over to the Dawes Commission on November 11, 1896. The Choctaws hired the law firm of Stuart, Gordon, and Hailey, of South McAlester to represent the tribe at all proceedings held by the Dawes Commission,"[2] another indication that throughout the Commission's efforts there was always controversy between the tribes and the negotiators.

When completed, this multi-volume series will contain thousands of names, all of them accounted for in the indexes carefully prepared by the author. Hopefully this work will help many researchers find their ancestors and satisfy the questions that so many have had about their Native American heritage.

Jeff Bowen
Gallipolis, Ohio
NativeStudy.com

---

[2] *The Dawes Commission* by Kent Carter, page 16, para. 5

Choctaw By Blood Enrollment Cards 1898-1914

RESIDENCE: Eagle   COUNTY.   **Choctaw Nation**   **Choctaw Roll** (Not Including Freedmen)   CARD NO.
POST OFFICE: Eagletown, I.T.   FIELD NO. **901**

Dawes' Roll No.	NAME		Relationship to Person First Named	AGE	SEX	BLOOD	TRIBAL ENROLLMENT		
							Year	County	No.
2408	1 Tonihka Susan	39	First Named	36	F	Full	1893	Eagle	P.R. 587
2409	2 " Sylvester	15	Son	12	M	"	1893	"	588
2410	3 " Sallie	13	Dau	10	F	"	1893	"	589
2411	4 " Eusie	6	Dau	3	F	"	1896	"	12227
	5								
	6								
	7								
	8								
	9								
	10								
	11								
	12								
	13								
	14								
	15								
	16								
	17								

ENROLLMENT
OF NOS. 1 2 3 and 4 HEREON
APPROVED BY THE SECRETARY
OF INTERIOR Dec 12, 1902

TRIBAL ENROLLMENT OF PARENTS

	Name of Father	Year	County	Name of Mother	Year	County
1	Davis Colbert	Dead	Eagle	Unknown	Dead	Eagle
2	Silan Tonihka	"	"	No 1		
3	Silan Tonihka	Dead	"	No 1		
4	Silan Tonihka	Dead	"	No 1		
5						
6	No1 on 1893 Pay roll Eagle Co. No 587, Page 63 as Susan Toneka					
7	No2 " " " " " No 588 " 63 " Sylvester "					
8	No3 " " " " " No 589 " 63 " Sonli "					
	No1 also on 1896 Roll Page 318 No 12226					
9	No4 Identified from 1896 Roll Page 318 No 12227					
10	No2 probably duplicate of Watson Tonihka – a – 13477					
11						
12						
13						
14					Date of Application for Enrollment.	
15					April 26/99	
16						
17						

1

Choctaw By Blood Enrollment Cards 1898-1914

RESIDENCE: **Nashoba**   COUNTY.   **Choctaw Nation**   **Choctaw Roll** *(Not Including Freedmen)*   CARD NO. FIELD NO. **902**

POST OFFICE: **Alikchi, I.T.**

Dawes' Roll No.	NAME		Relationship to Person First Named	AGE	SEX	BLOOD	TRIBAL ENROLLMENT		
							Year	County	No.
2412	1 Noah, Johnson	49	First Named	46	M	Full	1896	Nashoba	9706
2413	2 " Esian	47	Wife	44	F	"	1896	"	9707
1414	3 " Joseph	17	Son	14	M	"	1896	"	9709
2415	4 " Colbertson	15	"	12	"	"	1896	"	9710
2416	5 " Littie	13	Dau	10	F	"	1896	"	9712
2417	6 " Mary	8	"	5	"	"	1896	"	9712
2418	7 " Magdalene	6	"	3	"	"	1896	"	9713
2419	8 " Christopher	3	Son	5mo	M	"			
	9								
	10								
	11	ENROLLMENT OF NOS. 1234567and8 HEREON APPROVED BY THE SECRETARY OF INTERIOR							
	12								
	13								
	14								
	15								
	16								
	17								

TRIBAL ENROLLMENT OF PARENTS

	Name of Father	Year	County	Name of Mother	Year	County
1	Charles Noah	Dead	Nashoba	Ematona Noah	Dead	Nashoba
2	Kana-lit-ubbee	"	Wade	Un-te-ma-hoke	"	Wade
3	No 1			No 2		
4	No 1			No 2		
5	No 1			No 2		
6	No 1			No 2		
7	No 1			No 2		
8	No 1			No 2		
9						
10						
11						
12						
13						
14				No 8 enrolled Nov 24/99		
15				Date of Application for Enrollment. April 26/99		
16				1 to 7 inc		
17						

2

Choctaw By Blood Enrollment Cards 1898-1914

RESIDENCE: Towson COUNTY.	POST OFFICE: Alikchi I.T.

Choctaw Nation

Choctaw Roll *(Not Including Freedmen)*

CARD NO. FIELD NO. **903**

Dawes' Roll No.	NAME		Relationship to Person First Named	AGE	SEX	BLOOD	TRIBAL ENROLLMENT		
							Year	County	No.
2420	1 Peter Simon	53	First Named	50	M	Full	1896	Towson	10342
2421	2 " Salena	39	Wife	36	F	"	1896	"	1102
2422	3 " Mary	15	Dau	12	F	"	1896	"	10344
2423	4 " Sarah	11	"	8	F	"	1896	"	10345
2424	5 Bond Emma	17	Step Dau	14	F	"	1896	"	1103
	6								
	7								
	8								
	9								
	10								
	11	ENROLLMENT							
	12	OF NOS. 1 2 3 4 and 5 HEREON APPROVED BY THE SECRETARY							
	13	OF INTERIOR Dec. 12, 1902							
	14								
	15								
	16								
	17								

TRIBAL ENROLLMENT OF PARENTS

	Name of Father	Year	County	Name of Mother	Year	County
1	Martin Peter	Dead	Cedar	Salina Peter	Dead	Towson
2	Unknown	"	Mississippi	Sallie ----	"	"
3	No 1	1896	Towson	Mariah Peter	Dead	"
4	No 1	1896	"	" "	"	"
5	Fred Bond	Dead	"	No 2	1896	
6						
7						
8						
9						
10	No 2 enrolled as Salena Bond					
11	For child of No5 see N.B. (March 3, 1905) #844					
12						
13						
14						
15					Date of Application for Enrollment.	
16					April 26/99	
17						

3

Choctaw By Blood Enrollment Cards 1898-1914

RESIDENCE: Cedar COUNTY.
POST OFFICE: Doaksville I.T.

Choctaw Nation

Choctaw Roll *(Not Including Freedmen)*

CARD NO.
FIELD NO. **904**

Dawes' Roll No.	NAME	Relationship to Person First Named	AGE	SEX	BLOOD	TRIBAL ENROLLMENT		
						Year	County	No.
2425	1 Tom Morris ⁴¹	First Named	38	M	Full	1896	Cedar	12082
2426	DIED PRIOR TO SEPTEMBER 25, 1902 ₂ Sukey	Wife	33	F	"	1896	"	12083
	3							
	4							
	5							
	6							
	7							
	8							
	9							
	10							
	11							
	12							
	13							
	14							
	15							
	16							
	17							

ENROLLMENT
OF NOS. 1 and 2 HEREON
APPROVED BY THE SECRETARY
OF INTERIOR Dec 12 1902

TRIBAL ENROLLMENT OF PARENTS

Name of Father	Year	County	Name of Mother	Year	County
1 Isom Tom	Dead	Cedar	Silly Tom	Dead	Cedar
2 Bob Nehka	1896	"	Pis-a-ho-toma	"	"
3					
4					
5					
6					
7	No.1 is now the husband of Mary Fletcher Choctaw No.1030				11/25, '02
8	No.2 died Dec 3, 1901: proof of death filed Dec 3, 1902				
9					
10	No.2 died December 3, 1901: Enrollment cancelled by Department May 2, 1906.				
11					
12					
13					
14					
15					
16			Date of Application for Enrollment.		April 26/99
17					

Choctaw By Blood Enrollment Cards 1898-1914

	RESIDENCE:	Cedar	COUNTY.

RESIDENCE: Cedar COUNTY. **Choctaw Nation** **Choctaw Roll** CARD NO.
POST OFFICE: Doaksville, I.T. *(Not Including Freedmen)* FIELD NO. **905**

Dawes' Roll No.	NAME	Relationship to Person First Named	AGE	SEX	BLOOD	TRIBAL ENROLLMENT		
						Year	County	No.
2427	1 Solomon, Cephus 48	First Named	45	M	Full	1896	Cedar	11345
2428	2 " Criston 45	Wife	42	F	"	1896	"	11346
2429	3 " Willie 15	Son	12	M	"	1896	"	11348
2430	4 " Dickson 12	"	9	"	"	1896	"	11349
2431	5 " Thompson 7	"	4	"	"	1896	"	11350
	6							
	7							
	8							
	9							
	10							
	11	ENROLLMENT						
	12	OF NOS. 1 2 3 4 and 5 HEREON APPROVED BY THE SECRETARY						
	13	OF INTERIOR Dec 12 1902						
	14							
	15							
	16							
	17							

TRIBAL ENROLLMENT OF PARENTS

	Name of Father	Year	County	Name of Mother	Year	County
1	E-ya-hubbee	Dead	Cedar	Martha	Dead	Atoka
2	Gibson	"	"	Ma-hin-t[?]-na	"	Cedar
3	No. 1			No 2		
4	No. 1			No 2		
5	No. 1			No 2		
6						
7						
8						
9						
10						
11						
12						
13						
14						
15						
16				Date of Application for Enrollment	April 26/99	
17						

Choctaw By Blood Enrollment Cards 1898-1914

RESIDENCE: Cedar COUNTY. **Choctaw Nation** **Choctaw Roll** CARD NO.

POST OFFICE: Doaksville, I.T. *(Not Including Freedmen)* FIELD NO. **906**

Dawes' Roll No.	NAME	Relationship to Person First Named	AGE	SEX	BLOOD	TRIBAL ENROLLMENT		
						Year	County	No.
2432	1 McFarland, Daniel *DIED PRIOR TO SEPTEMBER 25, 1902*		24	M	Full	1896	Cedar	9254
	2							
	3							
	4							
	5							
	6							
	7							
	8							
	9							
	10							
	11							
	12							
	13							
	14							
	15							
	16							
	17							

ENROLLMENT OF NOS. ~ 1 ~ HEREON APPROVED BY THE SECRETARY OF INTERIOR Dec 12 1902

TRIBAL ENROLLMENT OF PARENTS

	Name of Father	Year	County	Name of Mother	Year	County
1	Sam McFarland	Dead	Nashoba	Criston Solomon	1896	Cedar
2						
3						
4						
5						
6						
7	No.1 died January 22, 1901; Proof of death filed Dec. 30, 1902					
8	No.1 died Jan 22, 1901; Enrollment cancelled by Department July 8 1904					
9						
10						
11						
12						
13						
14						
15						
16					Date of Application for Enrollment.	April 26/99
17						

6

Choctaw By Blood Enrollment Cards 1898-1914

RESIDENCE: Eagle   COUNTY.
POST OFFICE: Lukfata, I.T.

Choctaw Nation

Choctaw Roll
(Not Including Freedmen)

CARD NO.
FIELD NO. **907**

Dawes' Roll No.	NAME	Relationship to Person First Named	AGE	SEX	BLOOD	TRIBAL ENROLLMENT Year	County	No.
2433	1 McKinney, Jackson 38	First Named	35	M	Full	1896	Eagle	9299
2434	2 " Cristin 25	Wife	22	F	"	1896	"	9300
2435	3 " Green 16	Son	13	M	"	1896	"	9302
2436	4 " Joseph 6	"	3	"	"	1896	"	9305
2437	5 ~~DIED PRIOR TO SEPTEMBER 25, 1902~~ Sweeney	"	2mo	"	"			
	6							
	7							
	8							
	9							
	10							
	11	ENROLLMENT						
	12	OF NOS. 1 2 3 4 and 5 HEREON APPROVED BY THE SECRETARY						
	13	OF INTERIOR Dec 12 1902						
	14							
	15							
	16							
	17							

TRIBAL ENROLLMENT OF PARENTS

Name of Father	Year	County	Name of Mother	Year	County
1 Lewis McKinney	Dead	Eagle	Frances McKinney	1896	Eagle
2 Nelson Tonihka	"	"	Ilsie Tonihka	Dead	"
3 No. 1			Stea-he-ma	1896	"
4 No. 1			No.2		
5 ~~No.1~~			~~No.2~~		
6					
7		No.2 on 1896 roll as Istea McKinney			
8		No.4 " 1896 " " Joe "			
9		For child of nos. 1&2 see NB (March 3,1905) #1162			
10		~~No5 died July 15, 1900: proof of death filed Dec 12, 1902~~ ~~No.5 died July 15, 1900. Enrollment cancelled by Department July 8, 1904~~			
11					
12					
13					
14				Date of Application for Enrollment.	
15					
16				April 26/99	
17					

Choctaw By Blood Enrollment Cards 1898-1914

RESIDENCE: Bok Tuklo   COUNTY.   **Choctaw Nation**   Choctaw Roll   CARD No.

POST OFFICE: Alikchi, I.T.   *(Not Including Freedmen)*   FIELD NO.   **908**

Dawes' Roll No.	NAME	Relationship to Person First Named	AGE	SEX	BLOOD	TRIBAL ENROLLMENT Year	TRIBAL ENROLLMENT County	TRIBAL ENROLLMENT No.
2438	1 Peter, Lina ⁵⁸	First Named	55	F	Full	1896	Bok Tuklo	10389
2439	2 Noah, Foster ²⁹	Son	26	M	"	1893	" "	P.R. 211
	3							
	4							
	5							
	6							
	7							
	8							
	9							
	10							
	11	ENROLLMENT OF NOS. 1 and 2 HEREON						
	12	APPROVED BY THE SECRETARY						
	13	OF INTERIOR Dec 12, 1902						
	14							
	15							
	16							
	17							

TRIBAL ENROLLMENT OF PARENTS

Name of Father	Year	County	Name of Mother	Year	County
1 Dixon Peter	Dead	Towson	Dora Peter	Dead	Towson
2 Nicholas Noah	"	"	No 1		
3					
4					
5					
6					
7	No 1 on 1896 roll as Leimey Peter				
8					
9	No 2 on 1893 Pay roll as Foster Nowa				
10	For child of No2 see N.B. (March 3,1905) #844				
11					
12					
13					
14				Date of Application for Enrollment.	
15					
16				April 26/99	
17					

8

Choctaw By Blood Enrollment Cards 1898-1914

Choctaw Nation

Choctaw Roll (Not Including Freedmen)

CARD NO.
FIELD NO. **909**

Dawes' Roll No.	NAME		Relationship to Person	AGE	SEX	BLOOD	TRIBAL ENROLLMENT		
							Year	County	No.
2440	₁ Ontontabi, Isin	33	First Named	30	F	Full	1893	Red River	P.R. 534
2441	₂ Wesley, Colbert	11	Son	8	M	"	1893	" "	783
14612	₃ James, Ada	1	Dau	1	F	"			
	₄								
	₅								
	₆								
	₇								
	₈								
	₉								
	₁₀								
	₁₁								
	₁₂								
	₁₃								
	₁₄								
	₁₅								
	₁₆								
	₁₇								

ENROLLMENT OF NOS. 1 and 2 HEREON APPROVED BY THE SECRETARY OF INTERIOR Dec. 12, 1902

ENROLLMENT OF NOS. 3 HEREON APPROVED BY THE SECRETARY OF INTERIOR May 20, 1903

TRIBAL ENROLLMENT OF PARENTS

	Name of Father	Year	County	Name of Mother	Year	County
₁	On-ton-tabi	Dead	Bok Tuklo	Me-ha-te-ma	Dead	Bok Tuklo
₂	Sam Wesley	1896	Jacks Fork	No 1		
₃	Willie James		Choctaw Roll	No 1		
₄						
₅						
₆						
₇	No1 on 1893 Pay roll as Aison Ontontaby					
₈	No1 Correct surname is Ontontubbee					
₉	No3 born May 27, 1901: enrolled Dec. 2, 1902.					
	No1 is now wife of Willie James on Choctaw #873 11/25/02					
₁₀						
₁₁						
₁₂						
₁₃						
₁₄					#1&2 Date of Application for Enrollment.	
₁₅						
₁₆					April	26/99
₁₇						

Choctaw By Blood Enrollment Cards 1898-1914

RESIDENCE: Red River   COUNTY. **Choctaw Nation**   **Choctaw Roll**   CARD NO.

POST OFFICE: Garvin, I.T.   *(Not Including Freedmen)*   FIELD NO. **910**

Dawes' Roll No.	NAME		Relationship to Person First Named	AGE	SEX	BLOOD	TRIBAL ENROLLMENT		
							Year	County	No.
2442	1 Willie, William A	29	First Named	26	M	Full	1896	Red River	13655
2443	2 " Sina	30	Wife	27	F	"	1893	" "	P.R. 518
2444	3 McAfee, Allen	10	SSon	7	M	"	1893	" "	519
2445	4 " Netsey	7	SDau	4	F	"	1896	" "	9324
2446	5 Willie, Hodges	1	Son	3mo	M	"			
2447	6 " Thomas	3	"	34mo	M	"			
	7								
	8								
	9								
	10	ENROLLMENT							
	11	OF NOS. 1 2 3 4 5 and 6 HEREON APPROVED BY THE SECRETARY							
	12	OF INTERIOR Dec 12, 1902							
	13								
	14								
	15								
	16								
	17								

TRIBAL ENROLLMENT OF PARENTS

	Name of Father	Year	County	Name of Mother	Year	County
1	Williamson Willie	Dead	Red River	Ansie Willie	1896	Red River
2	Elum Taylor	"	Towson	Bickie Taylor	Dead	Towson
3	Frank McAfee	1896	Red River	No2		
4	" "	1896	" "	No2		
5	No1			No 2		
6	No1			No 2		
7						
8	No1 on 1896 roll as Wm Amos Willie					
9	No2 " 1893 " " Siney McAffie					
10	No4 " 1896 " " Nancy McField					
	No2 also on 1896 roll as Sina McField					
11	Page 234, No. 9323 Red River Co.					
12	No3 on 1893 Roll as Allen McAffe					
13	No5 Born Feby 24, 1902: Enrolled June 13, 1902					
14	No6 Born Nov. 21, 1899. Evidence of birth filed April 21, 1900 and May 26, 1900. Name of [sic]					
	No6 enrolled on this card Sept. 18, 1902				Date of Application for Enrollment.	
15						
16					April 26/99	
17	P.O. Idabel I.T.					

Choctaw By Blood Enrollment Cards 1898-1914

RESIDENCE: **Red River** COUNTY. **Choctaw Nation** **Choctaw Roll** CARD NO.
POST OFFICE: **Kully Tuklo, I.T.** *(Not Including Freedmen)* FIELD NO. **911**

Dawes' Roll No.	NAME		Relationship to Person First Named	AGE	SEX	BLOOD	TRIBAL ENROLLMENT		
							Year	County	No.
2448	1 Stewart, Semie	49	First Named	46	F	Full	1896	Red River	11436
2449	2 " , Rise	29	Son	26	M	"	1896	" "	11435
2450	3 " , Levi	27	"	24	M	"	1896	" "	11455
2451	4 " , Ilis	21	Dau	18	F	"	1896	" "	11437
2452	5 " , Silison	13	"	10	F	"	1896	" "	11438
	6								
	7								
	8								
	9								
	10								
	11	ENROLLMENT							
	12	OF NOS. 1 2 3 4 and 5 HEREON APPROVED BY THE SECRETARY							
	13	OF INTERIOR Dec 12, 1902							
	14								
	15								
	16								
	17								

TRIBAL ENROLLMENT OF PARENTS

	Name of Father	Year	County	Name of Mother	Year	County
1	Iba-fo-ka	Dead	Eagle	Unknown	Dead	Eagle
2	Adam Stewart	"	"	No 1		
3	" "	"	"	No 1		
4	Isom Stewart	"	"	No.1		
5	" "	"	"	No.1		
6						
7	No1 enrolled as Simmie Steward					
8	No3 " " Levi Stuart					
9	No4 " " Elise Steward					
	No5 " " Sillisson "					
10	No3 is the husband of Annie Collins on Choctaw card #1099 – Dec24 – 1902					
11	For child of No3 see NB (Apr 26-1906) Card No. 139.					
12	" " " " (Mar 3, 1905) " " 883.					
13						
14					Date of Application for Enrollment.	
15						
16					April 26/99	
17						

11

Choctaw By Blood Enrollment Cards 1898-1914

RESIDENCE: Cedar COUNTY.
POST OFFICE: Doaksville, I.T.

Choctaw Nation

Choctaw Roll *(Not Including Freedmen)*

CARD NO.
FIELD NO. **912**

Dawes' Roll No.	NAME	Relationship to Person First Named	AGE	SEX	BLOOD	TRIBAL ENROLLMENT Year	TRIBAL ENROLLMENT County	TRIBAL ENROLLMENT No.
2453	1 Thomas, Joseph 28	First Named	25	M	Full	1896	Cedar	12099
2454	2 " , Sinie 28	Wife	25	F	"	1896	"	12100
2455	3 ~~DIED PRIOR TO SEPTEMBER 25, 1902~~ Daniel	Son	4	M	"	1896	"	12101
2456	4 ~~DIED PRIOR TO SEPTEMBER 25, 1902~~ Osborne	Son	1	M	"			
14643	5 " , Harrison J. 1	Son	3mo	M	"			
	6							
	7							
	8	ENROLLMENT OF NOS. 1 2 3 and 4 HEREON APPROVED BY THE SECRETARY OF INTERIOR Dec. 12, 1902						
	9							
	10							
	11	ENROLLMENT OF NOS. 5 HEREON APPROVED BY THE SECRETARY OF INTERIOR APR 20, 1903						
	12							
	13							
	14							
	15							
	16							
	17							

TRIBAL ENROLLMENT OF PARENTS

Name of Father	Year	County	Name of Mother	Year	County
1 Seman Thomas	Dead	Cedar	Silon Thomas	1896	Nashoba
2 Jackson Henderson	Dead	Jack Fork	Unknown	Dead	Nashoba
3 ~~No 1~~			~~No 2~~		
4 ~~No 1~~			~~No 2~~		
5 No 1			No 2		
6					
7					
8					
9					
10 No5 Born June 26, 1902: enrolled Oct. 15, 1902.					
11 No3 died - - ,1900: No4 died - -,1900: Enrollment cancelled by Department July 8, 1904.					
12					
13					
14				#1 to 4 Date of Application for Enrollment.		
15						
16				April 26/99		
17						

Choctaw By Blood Enrollment Cards 1898-1914

RESIDENCE: Bok Tuklo   COUNTY. **Choctaw Nation**   **Choctaw Roll**   CARD No.
POST OFFICE: Lukfata, I.T.   (Not Including Freedmen)   FIELD No. **913**

Dawes' Roll No.	NAME	Relationship to Person	AGE	SEX	BLOOD	TRIBAL ENROLLMENT Year	County	No.
2457	1 Dennis, Thompson ⁵⁹	First Named	56	M	Full	1896	Bok Tuklo	3392
2458	2 " , Silway ³⁸	Wife	35	F	"	1896	" "	3393
	3							
	4							
	5							
	6							
	7							
	8							
	9							
	10							
	11							
	12							
	13							
	14							
	15							
	16							
	17							

ENROLLMENT OF NOS. 1 and 2 HEREON APPROVED BY THE SECRETARY OF INTERIOR Dec. 12, 1902

TRIBAL ENROLLMENT OF PARENTS

Name of Father	Year	County	Name of Mother	Year	County
1 Cham-pa-la-by	Dead	Bok Tuklo	Yo-tah	Dead	Bok Tuklo
2 Jack Wilson	"	Towson	Ann-ua-tey	"	Towson
3					
4					
5					
6					
7	No1 on 1896 roll as Thompson Dines				
8	No2 " 1896 " " Silway	"			
9					
10					
11					
12					
13					
14					
15					
16			Date of Application for Enrollment.	April 26/99	
17					

Choctaw By Blood Enrollment Cards 1898-1914

RESIDENCE: Towson COUNTY.

POST OFFICE: Alikchi I.T.

Choctaw Nation

Choctaw Roll
(Not Including Freedmen)

CARD No.

FIELD No. 914

Dawes' Roll No.	NAME	Relationship to Person First Named	AGE	SEX	BLOOD	TRIBAL ENROLLMENT Year	County	No.
2459	1 James, Milan 53	First Named	50	F	Full	1896	Towson	6795
	2							
	3							
	4							
	5							
	6							
	7							
	8							
	9							
	10							
	11	ENROLLMENT OF NOS. 1 HEREON						
	12	APPROVED BY THE SECRETARY						
	13	OF INTERIOR DEC 12 1902						
	14							
	15							
	16							
	17							

TRIBAL ENROLLMENT OF PARENTS

Name of Father	Year	County	Name of Mother	Year	County
1 Nakishtubbee	Dead	Towson	I-loi-ahin hona	Dead	Towson
2					
3					
4					
5					
6					
7	No 1 enrolled as Maelin James				
8					
9					
10					
11					
12					
13					
14					
15					
16			DATE OF APPLICATION FOR ENROLLMENT.	April 26/99	
17					

Choctaw By Blood Enrollment Cards 1898-1914

RESIDENCE: Towson COUNTY.
POST OFFICE: Doaksville I.T.

Choctaw Nation

Choctaw Roll (Not Including Freedmen)

CARD NO.
FIELD NO. 915

Dawes' Roll No.	NAME		Relationship to Person First Named	AGE	SEX	BLOOD	TRIBAL ENROLLMENT		
							Year	County	No.
2460	1 Jackson Lizzie	36	First Named	33	F	Full	1896	Towson	6777
2461	2 " Albert	8	Son	5	M	"	1896	"	6778
14614	3 Wesley Moses	1	Son	1	M	"			
	4								
	5								
	6								
	7	ENROLLMENT OF NOS. 1 and 2 HEREON							
	8	APPROVED BY THE SECRETARY							
	9	OF INTERIOR DEC 12 1902							
	10								
	11	ENROLLMENT OF NOS. 3 HEREON							
	12	APPROVED BY THE SECRETARY							
	13	OF INTERIOR MAY 20 1903							
	14								
	15								
	16								
	17								

TRIBAL ENROLLMENT OF PARENTS

	Name of Father	Year	County	Name of Mother	Year	County
1	Nicholas Noah	Dead	Towson	Sa-ho-ta-ma	Dead	Towson
2	Jesse Jackson	Dead	"	No.1		
3	Edward Wesley		Choctaw Roll	Nº1		
4						
5						
6						
7	Nº1 is now the wife of Edward Wesley on Choctaw card #1226. Evidence					
8	of marriage filed Oct. 15, 1902					
9	No3 Enrolled Dec. 5, 1902: born Nov 4, 1901					
10						
11						
12						
13						
14					#1&2	
15					Date of Application for Enrollment.	
16					April 26/99	
17						

15

Choctaw By Blood Enrollment Cards 1898-1914

RESIDENCE: Bok Tuklo   COUNTY.   **Choctaw Nation**   **Choctaw Roll**   CARD NO.
POST OFFICE: Luk-Fa-Ta I.T.   *(Not Including Freedmen)*   FIELD NO.   916

Dawes' Roll No.	NAME	Relationship to Person First Named	AGE	SEX	BLOOD	TRIBAL ENROLLMENT Year	County	No.
DEAD.	1 Anderson Houston		30	M	Full	1896	Bok Tuklo	248
2462	2 Charley Ester ³³	Wife	30	F	"	1896	" "	249
2463	3 Anderson Alex ⁸	Son	5	M	"	1896	" "	259
2464	4 " Byington ⁸	Son	5	M	"	1896	" "	250
2465	5 Crosby Sarah ²	Dau of No 2	7m	F	"			
	6							
	7							
	8 ENROLLMENT							
	9 OF NOS. 2 3 4 and 5 HEREON APPROVED BY THE SECRETARY							
	10 OF INTERIOR DEC 12 1902							
	11							
	12 No. 1 HEREON DISMISSED UNDER							
	13 ORDER OF THE COMMISSION TO THE FIVE CIVILIZED TRIBES OF MARCH 31, 1905.							
	14							
	15							
	16							
	17							

TRIBAL ENROLLMENT OF PARENTS

	Name of Father	Year	County	Name of Mother	Year	County
1	John Anderson	Dead	Red River	Susie Watkin	1896	Bok Tuklo
2	Nelson Ishkana	"	Bok Tuklo	Ishtoke	Dead	" "
3	No 1			No. 2		
4	No 1			No 2		
5	Josiah Crosby	1896	Bok Tuklo	No.2		
6						
7	No2 enrolled as Hestor Anderson					
8	No5 Enrolled May 11,1901. Illegitimate child See letter of					
9	H.L. Fowler Notary public filed herein May 13,1901					
	No2 Is now the wife of Elain Charley Choctaw Card #1071. Evidence of marriage requested May 11"					
10	No1 Said to be Dead Blank for Proof of death sent to HL Fowler N.P. May 13" 1901					
11						
12	Nº 1 Died April 24, 1898. proof of death filed Oct. 24, 1902.					
13						
14						
15					Date of Application for Enrollment.	
16					April 26/99	
17						

Choctaw By Blood Enrollment Cards 1898-1914

RESIDENCE: Bok Tuklo   COUNTY.   **Choctaw Nation**   **Choctaw Roll**   CARD NO.
POST OFFICE: Luk-Ta-Ta IT.   *(Not Including Freedmen)*   FIELD NO.   917

Dawes' Roll No.	NAME	Relationship to Person First Named	AGE	SEX	BLOOD	TRIBAL ENROLLMENT		
						Year	County	No.
2466	1 Watkins Susan 63	First Named	60	F	Full	1893	Bok Tuklo	P.R. 8
	2							
	3							
	4							
	5							
	6							
	7							
	8							
	9							
	10							
	11	ENROLLMENT OF NOS. 1 HEREON APPROVED BY THE SECRETARY OF INTERIOR DEC 12 1902						
	12							
	13							
	14							
	15							
	16							
	17							

TRIBAL ENROLLMENT OF PARENTS

	Name of Father	Year	County	Name of Mother	Year	County
1	Unknown		Mississippi	Annie	Dead	Red River
2						
3						
4						
5						
6	No 1 on P 1 No.8 Bok Tuklo Co 1893 Pay roll as Susan, also					
7	on 1896 roll as Susan Jones, Page 170, No 6923 Bok Tuklo Co					
8						
9						
10						
11						
12						
13						
14						
15						
16				Date of Application for Enrollment	April 26/99	
17						

Choctaw By Blood Enrollment Cards 1898-1914

RESIDENCE: Towson   COUNTY.   **Choctaw Nation**   Choctaw Roll *(Not Including Freedmen)*   CARD NO.

POST OFFICE: Fowlerville, I.T.   FIELD NO. 918

Dawes' Roll No.	NAME	Relationship to Person First Named	AGE	SEX	BLOOD	TRIBAL ENROLLMENT		
						Year	County	No.
I.W. 990	1 Garrison, LaFayette O⁴²	First Named	39	M	I.W.			
2467	2 " Effie M ²⁴	Wife	21	F	Full	1896	Towson	8608
2468	3 " David C ¹	Son	2mo	M	1/2			
	4							
	5							
	6							
	7 ENROLLMENT							
	8 OF NOS. 2 and 3 HEREON							
	APPROVED BY THE SECRETARY							
	9 OF INTERIOR DEC 12 1902							
	10							
	11 ENROLLMENT							
	12 OF NOS. ~~ 1 ~~ HEREON							
	APPROVED BY THE SECRETARY							
	13 OF INTERIOR OCT 21 1904							
	14							
	15							
	16							
	17							

TRIBAL ENROLLMENT OF PARENTS

	Name of Father	Year	County	Name of Mother	Year	County
1	David C. Garrison	1896	Non Citz	Sarah E. Garrison	Dead	Non Citz
2	Tom Haley	Dead	Towson	Betsey Haley	"	Towson
3	No 1			No 2		
4						
5						
6	No2 on 1896 roll as Effie Mahaley					
7	No.3 Enrolled Aug 13, 1901					
8	Correct name of No2 is Effie Mary Garrison See letter filed Aug 28,1901					
	For child of Nos1&2 see NB (March 3,1905) #895					
9						
10						
11						
12						
13						
14				Date of Application for Enrollment.		
15						
16	P.O. Idabel IT 4/11/05			April 26/99		
17	P.O. Shawneetown I.T.					

18

Choctaw By Blood Enrollment Cards 1898-1914

Tuklo
ukfata, I.T.   COUNTY.   **Choctaw Nation**   Choctaw Roll *(Not Including Freedmen)*   CARD No.   FIELD No. 919

Dawes' Roll No.	NAME		Relationship to Person First Named	AGE	SEX	BLOOD	TRIBAL ENROLLMENT		
							Year	County	No.
DEAD. Dead	1 Willis, Sabail DEAD.			27	F	Full	1896	Bok Tuklo	13434
2469	2 " Louisa	9	Dau	6	"	"	1896	" "	13441
2470	3 " Kitsy	1	Dau	4mo	F	"			
	4								
	5								
	6								
	7								
	8								
	9 ENROLLMENT								
	10 OF NOS. 2 and 3 HEREON								
	11 APPROVED BY THE SECRETARY OF INTERIOR DEC 12 1902								
	12								
	13 No. 1 HEREON DISMISSED UNDER								
	14 ORDER OF THE COMMISSION TO THE FIVE CIVILIZED TRIBES OF MARCH 31, 1905.								
	15								
	16								
	17								

TRIBAL ENROLLMENT OF PARENTS

	Name of Father	Year	County	Name of Mother	Year	County
1	Thompson Dennis	1896	Bok Tuklo	Mary Dennis	Dead	Bok Tuklo
2	Wilson Willis	Dead	" "	No 1		
3	Unknown			No 1		
4						
5						
6						
7	No2 on 1896 roll as Louisie Willis					
8	No1 " 1896 " " Sabel "					
9	No3 Born 4 Feb 18' 1902 Enrolled June 23rd 1902. (Ilegitimate[sic])					
10	No1 Died Feby 18, 1902, evidence of death filed Sept 30, 1902.					
11	No3 See Choctaw Card No 479 –					
12						
13						
14				Date of Application for Enrollment.		
15						
16				April 26/99		
17						

19

Choctaw By Blood Enrollment Cards 1898-1914

RESIDENCE: Red River COUNTY. **Choctaw Nation** Choctaw Roll CARD NO.
POST OFFICE: Garvin, I.T. (Not Including Freedmen) FIELD NO. 920

Dawes' Roll No.	NAME			Relationship to Person	AGE	SEX	BLOOD	TRIBAL ENROLLMENT		
								Year	County	No.
2471	1	Taylor, Robert	48	First Named	45	M	Full	1896	Red River	12280
2472	2	" Bicey	48	Wife	45	F	"	1896	" "	12281
2473	3	" Elsie	17	Dau	14	"	"	1896	" "	12282
2474	4	" Sylvester	14	Son	11	M	"	1896	" "	12283
2475	5	" Rosa	12	Dau	9	F	"	1896	" "	12284
2476	6	" Icy	7	"	4	"	"	1896	" "	12285
	7									
	8									
	9									
	10									
	11									
	12									
	13									
	14									
	15									
	16									
	17									

ENROLLMENT
OF NOS. 1 2 3 4 5 and 6 HEREON
APPROVED BY THE SECRETARY
OF INTERIOR DEC 12 1902

TRIBAL ENROLLMENT OF PARENTS

	Name of Father	Year	County	Name of Mother	Year	County
1	E-ma-ha-na	Dead	Red River	Fannie	Dead	Red River
2	Thomas Ronkin	"	" "	Wa-hu-na	"	" "
3	No 1			No 2		
4	No 1			No 2		
5	No 1			No 2		
6	No 1			No 2		
7						
8						
9	No5 on 1896 roll as Lucy Taylor					
10						
11						
12						
13						
14						
15					Date of Application for Enrollment.	
16					April 26/99	
17						

20

Choctaw By Blood Enrollment Cards 1898-1914

RESIDENCE: Cedar COUNTY. **Choctaw Nation** **Choctaw Roll** CARD NO.
POST OFFICE: Doaksville, I.T. *(Not Including Freedmen)* FIELD NO. 921

Dawes' Roll No.	NAME	Relationship to Person First Named	AGE	SEX	BLOOD	TRIBAL ENROLLMENT		
						Year	County	No.
2477	1 Home, Alixen	*DIED PRIOR TO SEPTEMBER 25, 1902*	26	M	Full	1896	Cedar	5456
2478	2 Fannie	*DIED PRIOR TO SEPTEMBER 25, 1902* Wife	21	F	"	1896	"	5457
	3							
	4							
	5							
	6	ENROLLMENT						
	7	OF NOS. 1 and 2 HEREON APPROVED BY THE SECRETARY						
	8	OF INTERIOR DEC 12 1902						
	9							
	10							
	11							
	12							
	13							
	14							
	15							
	16							
	17							

TRIBAL ENROLLMENT OF PARENTS

	Name of Father	Year	County	Name of Mother	Year	County
1	Dixon Home	Dead	Cedar	Elizabeth Nehka	1896	Cedar
2	Lije Holman	"	"	Jeneey Holman	Dead	"
3						
4						
5						
6	No1 on 1896 roll as Alexander Holmes					
7	No2 " 1896 " " Fannie Holmen					
8						
9	No1 died in 1900: No2 died in 1901: Enrollment cancelled by Department May 2 1906					
10						
11						
12						
13						
14						
15						
16				Date of Application for Enrollment	April 26/99	
17						

Choctaw By Blood Enrollment Cards 1898-1914

RESIDENCE: Cedar   COUNTY.   **Choctaw Nation**   Choctaw Roll (Not Including Freedmen)   CARD NO.
POST OFFICE: Doaksville, I.T.   FIELD NO. 922

Dawes' Roll No.	NAME	Relationship to Person First Named	AGE	SEX	BLOOD	TRIBAL ENROLLMENT Year	County	No.
2479	1 Nehka, Sam ⁵¹	First Named	48	M	Full	1896	Cedar	9631
2480	2 " Sina ⁴³	Wife	40	F	"	1896	"	9632
2481	3 " Lena ²¹	Dau	18	"	"	1896	"	P.R. 346
15567	4 Hopson, Johney ¹	Son of N°3	2	M	"			
	5							
	6							
	7	ENROLLMENT OF NOS. 1 2 and 3 HEREON						
	8	APPROVED BY THE SECRETARY						
	9	OF INTERIOR DEC 12 1902						
	10							
	11	ENROLLMENT						
	12	OF NOS. ~~ 4 ~~ HEREON APPROVED BY THE SECRETARY						
	13	OF INTERIOR SEP 22 1904						
	14							
	15							
	16							
	17							

TRIBAL ENROLLMENT OF PARENTS

	Name of Father	Year	County	Name of Mother	Year	County
1	Neh-ka	Dead	Nashoba	Pisa-hu-na	Dead	Cedar
2		"	Bok Tuklo		"	Bok Tuklo
3	Reason Hopson	1896	Cedar	N°3		
4						
5						
6						
7						
8	No2 on 1896 roll as Sainey Nehka					
9	No3 " 1893 Pay roll as Lumsey Nehka					
10	No.3 is now the wife of Reason Hopson, Choctaw Card #920 12/2 ⁰²					
11	Names of parents of No2 waived by Commissioner Needles					
12	N°4 Born Feby 28, 1902. Application first received May 18, 1902. Enrolled May 13, 1904					
13	For child of No.3 see NB (March 3 1905) #1093					
14						
15					#1 to 3	
16					Date of Application for Enrollment	April 26/99
17						

Choctaw By Blood Enrollment Cards 1898-1914

RESIDENCE: Nashoba COUNTY. **Choctaw Nation** Choctaw Roll CARD NO.
POST OFFICE: Alikchi, I.T. *(Not Including Freedmen)* FIELD NO. **923**

Dawes' Roll No.	NAME		Relationship to Person First Named	AGE	SEX	BLOOD	TRIBAL ENROLLMENT		
							Year	County	No.
2482	1 Cephus, Wilbon	37	First Named	34	M	Full	1896	Nashoba	2514
2483	2 " , Elmesa	23	Wife	20	F	"	1896	"	2515
2484	3 " , Minnie	15	Dau	12	"	"	1896	"	2516
2485	4 DIED PRIOR TO SEPTEMBER 25, 1902 , Jonnie		"	2	"	"			
2486	5 DIED PRIOR TO SEPTEMBER 25, 1902 , Florance		"	2mo	"	"			
	6								
	7								
	8								
	9								
	10								
	11								
	12								
	13								
	14								
	15								
	16								
	17								

ENROLLMENT
OF NOS. 1 2 3 4 and 5 HEREON
APPROVED BY THE SECRETARY
OF INTERIOR Dec 12, 1902

TRIBAL ENROLLMENT OF PARENTS

	Name of Father	Year	County	Name of Mother	Year	County
1	Kone-monteby	Dead	Nashoba	Sha-te-ma	Dead	Nashoba
2	Lake John	"	"	Ickine John	"	"
3	No 1			Annie Cephus	1896	"
4	No 1			No 2		
5	No 1			No 2		
6						
7	No2 on 1896 roll as Artimissie					
8	No5 enrolled May 24, 1901					
9	Given name of No1 is Wilbon. See his letter filed July 13, 1901.					
10	No4 died Nov.20,1899: Proof of death filed Dec.3, 1901. No5 " Aug.24,1902: " " " " " "					
11	No4 died Nov.20,1899: No5 died Aug.24,1902: Enrollment cancelled by Department July 8,1904.					
12	No3 is now wife of Isham Baker on Choctaw card #632					
13	For child of No3 see N.B. (Apr 26-06) Card #605 " " " " " (Mar 3-05) " #950					
14						
15				Date of Application for Enrollment.		
16				April 26/99		
17	No3 P.O. Bethel I.T. 4/5/05					

23

Choctaw By Blood Enrollment Cards 1898-1914

RESIDENCE: Nashoba	COUNTY.	**Choctaw Nation**	**Choctaw Roll** (Not Including Freedmen)	CARD NO.
POST OFFICE: Alikchi, I.T.				FIELD NO. **924**

Dawes' Roll No.	NAME	Relationship to Person First Named	AGE	SEX	BLOOD	TRIBAL ENROLLMENT		
						Year	County	No.
2487	1 Battiest, Colbert 25	First Named	22	M	Full	1896	Nashoba	1220
DEAD	2 " , Nisa DEAD	Wife	21	F	"	1896	"	7541
	3							
	4							
	5							
	6	ENROLLMENT						
	7	OF NOS. 1 HEREON						
	8	APPROVED BY THE SECRETARY OF INTERIOR Dec. 12, 1902						
	9							
	10							
	11							
	12	No2 hereon dismissed under order of						
	13	the Commission to the Five Civilized Tribes of March 31, 1905.						
	14							
	15							
	16							
	17							

TRIBAL ENROLLMENT OF PARENTS

	Name of Father	Year	County	Name of Mother	Year	County
1	Cason Battiest	Dead	Nashoba	Sis Battiest	Dead	Nashoba
2	Allington King	1896	"	Mary King	1896	"
3						
4						
5						
6	No2 on 1896 roll as Naisie King.					
7	No1 is now the husband of Enettie Baker on Choctaw Card #539.					
8						
9	No2 died Dec. 15, 1899: Proof of death filed Dec. 13, 1901.					
10						
11	For children of No1 see N.B. (Apr. 26'06) #606					
12						
13						
14						
15						
16					Date of Application for Enrollment April 26/99	
17						

Choctaw By Blood Enrollment Cards 1898-1914

RESIDENCE: Cedar COUNTY. **Choctaw Nation** Choctaw Roll CARD NO.

POST OFFICE: Doaksville, I.T. *(Not Including Freedmen)* FIELD NO. 925

Dawes' Roll No.	NAME		Relationship to Person First Named	AGE	SEX	BLOOD	TRIBAL ENROLLMENT		
							Year	County	No.
2488	1 Hopson, Reason	32	First Named	29	M	Full	1896	Cedar	5415
Dead	2 " Lena DEAD.		Wife	25	F	"	1896	"	5416
DEAD.	3 " William DEAD.		Son	7	M	"	1896	"	5417
2489	4 " Cornelius	8	"	5	"	"	1896	"	5418
DEAD.	5 " Eli DEAD.		"	1	"	"			
2490	6 " Julius	16	Ward	13	"	"	1896	Cedar	5464
2491	7 " Martha	8	"	5	F	"	1896	"	5465
	8								
	9		ENROLLMENT						
	10		OF NOS. 1 4 6 and 7 HEREON						
	11		APPROVED BY THE SECRETARY OF INTERIOR DEC 12 1902						
	12								
	13		No. 2-3 and 5 HEREON DISMISSED UNDER						
	14		ORDER OF THE COMMISSION TO THE FIVE CIVILIZED TRIBES OF MARCH 31, 1905						
	15								
	16								
	17								

TRIBAL ENROLLMENT OF PARENTS

	Name of Father	Year	County	Name of Mother	Year	County
1	William Hopson	Dead	Cedar	Elizabeth Hopson	1896	Cedar
2	Moses Wesley	"	"	Konchee Wesley	Dead	"
3	No 1			No 2		
4	No 1			No 2		
5	No 1			No 2		
6	John Hopson	Dead	Cedar	Jinsey Hopson	Dead	Cedar
7	" "	"	"	" "	"	"
8						
9	No6 on 1896 roll as Julius Hohnan					
10	No3 died July 14,1900. Proof of death filed July 18,1901.					
11	No2 died in September 1900. Proof of death filed July 18,1901.					
	No5 died in September 1900. Proof of death filed July 18,1901					
12	For child of No.1 see NB (March3,1905) #1093					
13						
14						
15					Date of Application for Enrollment.	
16					April 26/99	
17						

Choctaw By Blood Enrollment Cards 1898-1914

RESIDENCE: Eagle COUNTY. **Choctaw Nation** Choctaw Roll CARD NO.

POST OFFICE: Lukfata, I.T. (Not Including Freedmen) FIELD NO. **926**

Dawes' Roll No.	NAME	Relationship to Person First Named	AGE	SEX	BLOOD	TRIBAL ENROLLMENT		
						Year	County	No.
2492	DIED PRIOR TO SEPTEMBER 25, 1902 1 Ka nim ubbe		59	M	Full	1896	Eagle	7556
2493	DIED PRIOR TO SEPTEMBER 25, 1902 2 Mollie	Wife	45	F	"	1896	"	7557
	3							
	4							
	5							
	6							
	7	ENROLLMENT						
	8	OF NOS. 1 and 2 HEREON APPROVED BY THE SECRETARY						
	9	OF INTERIOR DEC 12 1902						
	10							
	11							
	12							
	13							
	14							
	15							
	16							
	17							

TRIBAL ENROLLMENT OF PARENTS

	Name of Father	Year	County	Name of Mother	Year	County
1	Ka-ne-chee	Dead	Eagle	Lo-sho-mat-ema	Dead	in Mississippi
2	To-chan-eby	"	"	Betsey Wilson	1896	Eagle
3						
4						
5						
6	Surnames on 1896 roll as Kanimmubbe					
7	No1 died Jan'y 25 1901: proof of death filed Dec 15, 1902					
	No2 " Jan'y 4, 1902: " " " " " "					
8	No1 died Jan 25 1901: No2 died Jan 1 1902: Enrollment cancelled by Department July 8, 1904					
9						
10						
11						
12						
13						
14						
15						
16				Date of Application for Enrollment		April 26/99
17						

26

Choctaw By Blood Enrollment Cards 1898-1914

RESIDENCE: Cedar COUNTY.
POST OFFICE: Doaksville, I.T.

Choctaw Nation

Choctaw Roll (Not Including Freedmen)

CARD NO.
FIELD NO. 927

Dawes' Roll No.	NAME		Relationship to Person	AGE	SEX	BLOOD	TRIBAL ENROLLMENT		
							Year	County	No.
2494	1 Gabel, William	24	First Named	21	M	Full	1896	Cedar	4720
2495	2 " Nancy		Wife	17	F	"	1896	"	7899
14885	3 " Jincie	2	Dau	2 2/3	F	"			
	4								
	5								
	6								
	7								
	8	ENROLLMENT							
	9	OF NOS. 1 and 2 HEREON APPROVED BY THE SECRETARY							
	10	OF INTERIOR DEC 12 1902							
	11								
	12	ENROLLMENT							
	13	OF NOS. 3 HEREON APPROVED BY THE SECRETARY							
	14	OF INTERIOR MAY 21 1903							
	15								
	16								
	17								

DIED PRIOR TO SEPTEMBER 25, 1902

TRIBAL ENROLLMENT OF PARENTS

	Name of Father	Year	County	Name of Mother	Year	County
1	Gabel	Dead	Cedar	Susie Gabel	Dead	Cedar
2	Edmund LeFlore	1896	"	Mary LeFlore	"	"
3	Nº1			Nº2		
4						
5			No2 on 1896 roll as Nancy LaFlore			
6						
7			No2 died March 2, 1901: proof of death filed Dec. 15, 1902.			
8			No.1 is now husband of No.1 on Choctaw Card #989 12/10 '02			
9			Nº3 Born April 9 1900: application made Dec.10,1902. Proof of birth filed March 10,1903.			
10			No2 died March 2, 1902: Enrollment cancelled by Department July 8, 1904			
11						
12			For child of No1 see NB (Mar 3rd 1905) Card #97			
13						
14					#1&2	
15					Date of Application for Enrollment.	
16					April 26/99	
17	P.O. Spencerville Okla					

Choctaw By Blood Enrollment Cards 1898-1914

RESIDENCE: Bok Tuklo   COUNTY.   **Choctaw Nation**   Choctaw Roll *(Not Including Freedmen)*   CARD NO.

POST OFFICE: Lukfata, I.T.   FIELD NO. **928**

Dawes' Roll No.	NAME	Relationship to Person First Named	AGE	SEX	BLOOD	TRIBAL ENROLLMENT Year	County	No.
2496	1 Anderson, Silas ⁵⁹		56	M	Full	1896	Bok Tuklo	238
2497	2 " , Jinsey ³⁹	Wife	36	F	"	1896	" "	239
2498	3 DIED PRIOR TO SEPTEMBER 25, 1952 Elizabeth	Dau	12	"	"	1896	" "	240
2499	4 " , Moses ¹⁰	Son	7	M	"	1896	" "	241
2500	5 DIED PRIOR TO SEPTEMBER 25, 1952 Rose	Dau	3	F	"	1896	" "	242
	6							
	7							
	8							
	9							
	10							
	11	ENROLLMENT						
	12	OF NOS. 1 2 3 4 and 5 HEREON APPROVED BY THE SECRETARY						
	13	OF INTERIOR Dec 12, 1902						
	14							
	15							
	16							
	17							

TRIBAL ENROLLMENT OF PARENTS

	Name of Father	Year	County	Name of Mother	Year	County
1	Ok-li-o-bey	Dead	Bok Tuklo	Pisa-ha-ma	Dead	Bok Tuklo
2	Wilson Thomas	"	" "	Maley Cornelius	1896	" "
3	No 1			No 2		
4	No 1			No 2		
5	No 1			No 2		
6						
7			Proof of death filed Dec 3, 1902.			
8	No3 died Feb 22,1902:					
	No5 " March25,1901: " " " " " " "					
9	No3 died Feb.22,1902:No5 died March25,1901:Enrollment cancelled by Department July 8, 1904					
10						
11						
12						
13						
14					Date of Application for Enrollment.	
15						
16					April 26/99	
17						

Choctaw By Blood Enrollment Cards 1898-1914

RESIDENCE: Red River   COUNTY. **Choctaw Nation**   Choctaw Roll   CARD NO.
POST OFFICE: Garvin, I.T.   *(Not Including Freedmen)*   FIELD NO. 929

Dawes' Roll No.	NAME		Relationship to Person	AGE	SEX	BLOOD	TRIBAL ENROLLMENT		
							Year	County	No.
2501	1 Taylor, Ben	24	First Named	21	M	Full	1896	Red River	12286
	2								
	3								
	4								
	5								
	6								
	7	ENROLLMENT							
	8	OF NOS. 1 HEREON APPROVED BY THE SECRETARY							
	9	OF INTERIOR DEC 12 1902							
	10								
	11								
	12								
	13								
	14								
	15								
	16								
	17								

TRIBAL ENROLLMENT OF PARENTS

	Name of Father	Year	County	Name of Mother	Year	County
1	Billy Taylor	Dead	Red River	Bicey Taylor	Dead	Red River
2						
3						
4						
5						
6						
7						
8						
9						
10						
11						
12						
13						
14						
15						
16				Date of Application for Enrollment		April 26/99
17						

Choctaw By Blood Enrollment Cards 1898-1914

RESIDENCE: Bok Tuklo   COUNTY.   **Choctaw Nation**   **Choctaw Roll** (Not Including Freedmen)   CARD NO.
POST OFFICE: Lukfata, I.T.   FIELD NO. **930**

Dawes' Roll No.	NAME	Relationship to Person First Named	AGE	SEX	BLOOD	TRIBAL ENROLLMENT Year	County	No.
15568	1 Charley, Willie	First Named	39	M	Full	1896	Bok Tuklo	2556
15781	2 Eliza	Wife	27	F	"	1896	" "	2557
2502	3 " Mary 16	Dau	13	"	"	1896	" "	2558
	4							
	5 ENROLLMENT							
	6 OF NOS. 3 HEREON APPROVED BY THE SECRETARY							
	7 OF INTERIOR Dec 12, 1902							
	8							
	9 ENROLLMENT							
	10 OF NOS. ~1~ HEREON APPROVED BY THE SECRETARY							
	11 OF INTERIOR Sep 22, 1904							
	12							
	13 ENROLLMENT							
	14 OF NOS. 2 HEREON APPROVED BY THE SECRETARY							
	15 OF INTERIOR Mar. 15, 1904							
	16							
	17							

DIED PRIOR TO SEPTEMBER 25, 1902 (on lines 1, 2)

TRIBAL ENROLLMENT OF PARENTS

Name of Father	Year	County	Name of Mother	Year	County
1 Charlie Ukatubbee	Dead	Bok Tuklo	Sallie Ukatubbee	Dead	Bok Tuklo
2 Bill Anderson	"	" "	La-ho-na	"	" "
3 No 1			Alice Charley	"	" "
4					
5					
6					
7 For child of No3 see N.B. (Apr 26-06) Card #833					
8					
9 No1 died in 1900; Enrollment cancelled by Department March 4, 1907					
10 No2 died in 1901 Enrollment cancelled by Department December 22, 1906					
11					
12					
13					
14					
15					
16			Date of Application for Enrollment		
17			April 26/99		

30

Choctaw By Blood Enrollment Cards 1898-1914

RESIDENCE: Cedar COUNTY. **Choctaw Nation** Choctaw Roll CARD NO.
POST OFFICE: Doaksville, I.T. *(Not Including Freedmen)* FIELD NO. 931

Dawes' Roll No.	NAME		Relationship to Person First Named	AGE	SEX	BLOOD	TRIBAL ENROLLMENT		
							Year	County	No.
2503	1 Billy, Lyman	29	First Named	26	M	Full	1896	Cedar	1080
2504	2 " Susan	24	Wife	21	F	"	1896	"	1081
	3								
	4								
	5								
	6								
	7								
	8								
	9								
	10								
	11	ENROLLMENT OF NOS. 1 and 2 HEREON APPROVED BY THE SECRETARY OF INTERIOR DEC 12 1902							
	12								
	13								
	14								
	15								
	16								
	17								

TRIBAL ENROLLMENT OF PARENTS

	Name of Father	Year	County	Name of Mother	Year	County
1	John Billy	Dead	Cedar	Ko-yon-ho-tema	Dead	Cedar
2	Ona-hubbee	"	"	Elizabeth	1896	"
3						
4						
5						
6						
7						
8						
9						
10						
11						
12						
13						
14						
15						
16					Date of Application for Enrollment	April 26/99
17						

Choctaw By Blood Enrollment Cards 1898-1914

RESIDENCE: Red River	COUNTY.						CARD NO.	
POST OFFICE: Kullituklo, I.T.		Choctaw Nation			Choctaw Roll *(Not Including Freedmen)*		FIELD NO. 932	

Dawes' Roll No.	NAME	Relationship to Person First Named	AGE	SEX	BLOOD	TRIBAL ENROLLMENT		
						Year	County	No.
2505	1 Wakaya, Simon ⁴³	First Named	40	M	Full	1896	Red River	13576
2506	2 " Nancy ³⁷	Wife	34	F	"	1896	" "	13577
	3							
	4							
	5							
	6							
	7							
	8							
	9							
	10							
	11	ENROLLMENT OF NOS. 1 and 2 HEREON APPROVED BY THE SECRETARY OF INTERIOR DEC 12 1902						
	12							
	13							
	14							
	15							
	16							
	17							

TRIBAL ENROLLMENT OF PARENTS

	Name of Father	Year	County	Name of Mother	Year	County
1	Wa-ka-ya	Dead	Red River	Siney Wakaya	Dead	Red River
2	Wᵐ Tuckoby	"	Bok Tuklo	Sabie Tuckoby	"	Bok Tuklo
3						
4						
5						
6						
7						
8						
9						
10						
11						
12						
13						
14						
15						
16				Date of Application for Enrollment April 26/99		
17						

Choctaw By Blood Enrollment Cards 1898-1914

RESIDENCE: Eagle COUNTY. **Choctaw Nation** Choctaw Roll CARD NO.
POST OFFICE: Eagletown, I.T. *(Not Including Freedmen)* FIELD NO. 933

Dawes' Roll No.	NAME	Relationship to Person First Named	AGE	SEX	BLOOD	TRIBAL ENROLLMENT Year	County	No.
2507	1 Jefferson, Simeon 55	First Named	52	M	Full	1896	Eagle	6962
2508	2 " Elliston 13	Son	10	"	"	1896	"	6958
	3							
	4							
	5							
	6							
	7							
	8							
	9							
	10							
	11	ENROLLMENT						
	12	OF NOS. 1 and 2 HEREON APPROVED BY THE SECRETARY						
	13	OF INTERIOR DEC 12 1902						
	14							
	15							
	16							
	17							

TRIBAL ENROLLMENT OF PARENTS

	Name of Father	Year	County	Name of Mother	Year	County
1	Ha-la-la-chubbee	Dead	Eagle	Ka-ne-ya-huna	Dead	Bok Tuklo
2	No 1			Mary Jefferson	"	Eagle
3						
4						
5						
6						
7						
8						
9						
10						
11						
12						
13						
14					Date of Application for Enrollment.	
15						
16					April 26/99	
17						

Choctaw By Blood Enrollment Cards 1898-1914

RESIDENCE: Nashoba COUNTY. **Choctaw Nation** **Choctaw Roll** CARD No.
POST OFFICE: Alikchi, I.T. (Not Including Freedmen) FIELD No. 934

Dawes' Roll No.	NAME	Relationship to Person First Named	AGE	SEX	BLOOD	TRIBAL ENROLLMENT		
						Year	County	No.
2509	1 Hicks, Cephus 35	First Named	32	M	Full	1896	Nashoba	5526
	2							
	3							
	4							
	5							
	6							
	7							
	8							
	9							
	10							
	11	ENROLLMENT OF NOS. 1 HEREON APPROVED BY THE SECRETARY OF INTERIOR DEC 12 1902						
	12							
	13							
	14							
	15							
	16							
	17							

TRIBAL ENROLLMENT OF PARENTS

	Name of Father	Year	County	Name of Mother	Year	County
1	Adam Hicks	Dead	Nashoba	Ouahima Hicks	Dead	Nashoba
2						
3						
4						
5		On 1896 roll as Cephus Hayes				
6						
7		For child of No1 see NB (Apr 26 '06) No 1297				
8		" " " " " " (March3 '05) " 907				
9						
10						
11						
12						
13						
14						
15						
16				Date of Application for Enrollment April 26/99		
17						

Choctaw By Blood Enrollment Cards 1898-1914

RESIDENCE: Cedar COUNTY.
POST OFFICE: Doaksville, I.T.

Choctaw Nation

Choctaw Roll
(Not Including Freedmen)

CARD NO.
FIELD NO. 935

Dawes' Roll No.	NAME		Relationship to Person First Named	AGE	SEX	BLOOD	TRIBAL ENROLLMENT		
							Year	County	No.
2510	1 Nehka, Robert	59	First Named	56	M	Full	1896	Cedar	9652
2511	2 " Elizabeth	65	Wife	62	F	"	1896	"	9653
	3								
	4								
	5								
	6								
	7								
	8								
	9								
	10								
	11	ENROLLMENT OF NOS. 1 and 2 HEREON APPROVED BY THE SECRETARY OF INTERIOR DEC 12 1902							
	12								
	13								
	14								
	15								
	16								
	17								

TRIBAL ENROLLMENT OF PARENTS

	Name of Father	Year	County	Name of Mother	Year	County
1	Ka-me-tubbee	Dead	Cedar	Pisa-ho-na	Dead	Cedar
2	Pisa-mock-lun-tubbee	"	Towson		"	
3						
4						
5						
6						
7						
8						
9						
10						
11						
12						
13						
14						
15						
16				Date of Application for Enrollment		April 26/99
17						

Choctaw By Blood Enrollment Cards 1898-1914

RESIDENCE: Red River   COUNTY.   **Choctaw Nation**   **Choctaw Roll** (Not Including Freedmen)   CARD NO.

POST OFFICE: Garvin, I.T.   FIELD NO. 936

Dawes' Roll No.	NAME		Relationship to Person First Named	AGE	SEX	BLOOD	TRIBAL ENROLLMENT		
							Year	County	No.
2512	1 Taylor, Simon	29		26	M	Full	1896	Red River	12255
2513	" Melvina	21	Wife	18	F	"	1896	" "	13615
2514	" Frances	4	Dau	4mo	"	"			
DEAD.	" James Woods		Son	3mo	M	"			
	5								
	6	ENROLLMENT							
	7	OF NOS. 1 – 2 and 3 HEREON APPROVED BY THE SECRETARY							
	8	OF INTERIOR DEC 12 1902				No			
	9								
	10								
	11	No. 4 HEREON DISMISSED UNDER ORDER OF THE COMMISSION TO THE FIVE							
	12	CIVILIZED TRIBES OF MARCH 31, 1905.							
	13								
	14								
	15								
	16								
	17								

TRIBAL ENROLLMENT OF PARENTS

	Name of Father	Year	County	Name of Mother	Year	County
1	Robert Taylor	1896	Red River	Bicey Taylor	1896	Red River
2	Daniel Wilson	Dead	" "	Siney Wilson	Dead	" "
3	No 1			No.2		
4	No.1			No.2		
5						
6						
7		No2 on 1896 roll as Melvina Wilson				
8						
9		No.4 Enrolled March 7th, 1901				
10						
11		Nº4 Died Feby 9,1902, proof of death filed Oct 13, 1902				
12		For children of Nos 1&2 see NB (March 3 1905) #714				
13						#1 to 3
14						Date of Application for Enrollment.
15						
16					April	26/99
17						

Choctaw By Blood Enrollment Cards 1898-1914

RESIDENCE: Nashoba COUNTY. **Choctaw Nation** Choctaw Roll CARD No.
POST OFFICE: Alikchi, I.T. *(Not Including Freedmen)* FIELD NO. **937**

Dawes' Roll No.	NAME			Relationship to Person First Named	AGE	SEX	BLOOD	TRIBAL ENROLLMENT		
								Year	County	No.
2515	1	Williams, Thomas	47	First Named	44	M	Full	1896	Nashoba	13303
2516	2	" Lucy	37	Wife	34	F	"	1896	"	13304
2517	3	" Edward	15	Son	12	M	"	1896	"	13305
2518	4	" Billy	12	"	9	"	"	1896	"	13306
2519	5	" Mike	10	"	7	"	"	1896	"	13307
2520	6	" Osby	7	"	4	"	"	1896	"	13308
2521	7	" Lonena	5	Dau Son	2	"	"			
2522	8	" Levicy	2	Dau	1	F	"			
	9									
	10									
	11									
	12									
	13									
	14									
	15									
	16									
	17									

ENROLLMENT OF NOS. 1234567and8 HEREON APPROVED BY THE SECRETARY OF INTERIOR Dec 12 1902

TRIBAL ENROLLMENT OF PARENTS

	Name of Father	Year	County	Name of Mother	Year	County
1	John Williams	Dead	Nashoba	Sophie Williams	Dead	Nashoba
2	Umpson Takoby	1896	Sans Bois	Inie Takoby	"	"
3	No.1			Sillen Williams	"	Cedar
4	No.1			" "	"	"
5	No.1			No.2		
6	No.1			No.2		
7	No.1			No.2		
8	No.1			No.2		
9						
10	No3 on 1896 roll as Edmund Williams					
11	No6 " 1896 " " Ansby "					
12	No8 Born March 16, 1901: enrolled June 2, 1902					
	For child of Nos. 1 and 2 see NB. (March 3, 1905) #1236.					
13						#1to7
14					Date of Application for Enrollment.	
15						
16					April 26/99	
17	P.O. Bethel, I.T.					

P.O. Noah, I.T. 4/17/05

Choctaw By Blood Enrollment Cards 1898-1914

RESIDENCE: Red River COUNTY. **Choctaw Nation** **Choctaw Roll** CARD NO.
POST OFFICE: Garvin, I.T. *(Not Including Freedmen)* FIELD NO. 938

Dawes' Roll No.	NAME	Relationship to Person First Named	AGE	SEX	BLOOD	TRIBAL ENROLLMENT		
						Year	County	No.
2523	1 Wright, Crockett 21	First Named	18	M	1/2	1896	Nashoba	13224
	2							
	3							
	4							
	5							
	6							
	7	ENROLLMENT						
	8	OF NOS. 1 HEREON APPROVED BY THE SECRETARY						
	9	OF INTERIOR DEC 2 1902						
	10							
	11							
	12							
	13							
	14							
	15							
	16							
	17							

TRIBAL ENROLLMENT OF PARENTS

	Name of Father	Year	County	Name of Mother	Year	County
1	William Wright	Dead	Red River	Cissy Durant	Dead	Red River
2						
3						
4						
5						
6						
7						
8						
9						
10						
11						
12						
13						
14						
15						
16				Date of Application for Enrollment	April 26/99	
17						

Choctaw By Blood Enrollment Cards 1898-1914

RESIDENCE: Red River   COUNTY.   **Choctaw Nation**   Choctaw Roll   CARD NO.
POST OFFICE: Janis, I.T.   *(Not Including Freedmen)*   FIELD NO.   939

Dawes' Roll No.	NAME	Relationship to Person	AGE	SEX	BLOOD	TRIBAL ENROLLMENT		
						Year	County	No.
2524	1 Tushka, Silvie ⁵⁹	First Named	56	F	Full	1896	Red River	12324
	2							
	3							
	4							
	5							
	6							
	7							
	8							
	9							
	10							
	11	ENROLLMENT						
	12	OF NOS. 1 HEREON APPROVED BY THE SECRETARY						
	13	OF INTERIOR DEC 12 1902						
	14							
	15							
	16							
	17							

TRIBAL ENROLLMENT OF PARENTS

	Name of Father	Year	County	Name of Mother	Year	County
1	Na-no-montubbee	Dead	Red River		Dead	Red River
2						
3						
4						
5						
6						
7						
8						
9						
10						
11						
12						
13						
14						
15						
16					Date of Application for Enrollment	April 26/99
17						

Choctaw By Blood Enrollment Cards 1898-1914

RESIDENCE: Red River COUNTY. **Choctaw Nation** Choctaw Roll CARD NO.
POST OFFICE: Janis *(Not Including Freedmen)* FIELD NO. 940

Dawes' Roll No.	NAME	Relationship to Person First Named	AGE	SEX	BLOOD	TRIBAL ENROLLMENT		
						Year	County	No.
2525	1 Tushka, James ~~DIED PRIOR TO SEPTEMBER 25, 190~~		~~18~~	~~M~~	~~Full~~	~~1896~~	~~Red River~~	~~12325~~
2526	2 " Eliza ²⁷	Wife	24	F	"	1896	" "	7044
2527	3 Wilson, Willie ⁵	S.Son	1	M	"			
2528	4 Tushka, Ida ²	Dau	1mo	F	"			
	5							
	6							
	7							
	8							
	9							
	10							
	11	ENROLLMENT						
	12	OF NOS. 1 2 3 and 4 HEREON APPROVED BY THE SECRETARY						
	13	OF INTERIOR DEC 12 1902						
	14							
	15							
	16							
	17							

TRIBAL ENROLLMENT OF PARENTS

Name of Father	Year	County	Name of Mother	Year	County
1 ~~Felin Tushka~~	~~Dead~~	~~Red River~~	~~Silway Tushka~~	~~1896~~	~~Red River~~
2 Arlin Jefferson	"	" "	Rhoda Jefferson	Dead	" "
3 Hohnan Wilson	"	" "	No 2		
4	No. 1		No. 2		
5					
6		No2 on 1896 roll as Eliza Jefferson			
7		No2 is now wife of Henry Alexander on Choctaw Card #1162			
8		No.4 Enrolled June 23d, 1900			
		~~No1 Died March 8,1900; proof of death filed Dec 3, 1902~~			
9	~~No1 died March 8,1900: Enrollment cancelled by Department July 8. 1904~~				
10		For child of No2 see NB (Apr 26-06) Card #387			
11		" " " " " (Mar 3-05) " #959			
12					
13					
14					
15				#1to3 inc	
16				Date of Application for Enrollment	April 26/99
17	P.O. Lukfata, I.T. 4/18/05				

40

Choctaw By Blood Enrollment Cards 1898-1914

Choctaw Nation

Choctaw Roll *(Not Including Freedmen)*

CARD NO. FIELD NO. **941**

Dawes' Roll No.	NAME		Relationship to Person First Named	AGE	SEX	BLOOD	TRIBAL ENROLLMENT Year	County	No.
2529	1 Thomas Russell W.	32	First Named	29	M	Full	1896	Bok Tuklo	12193
2530	2 " Lucy	23	Wife	20	F	"	1896	Towson	5481
2531	3 " Hampton	10	Son	7	M	"	1896	Bok Tuklo	12195
	4								
	5								
	6								
	7								
	8								
	9								
	10								
	11								
	12								
	13								
	14								
	15								
	16								
	17								

ENROLLMENT
OF NOS. 1 2 and 3 HEREON
APPROVED BY THE SECRETARY
OF INTERIOR Dec 12 1902

TRIBAL ENROLLMENT OF PARENTS

	Name of Father	Year	County	Name of Mother	Year	County
1	Wash Thomas	Dead	Bok Tuklo	Phoebe Thomas	1896	Bok Tuklo
2	Konich-tubbee	"	" "	Ta-le-na	Dead	" "
3	No.1			Nicey Ward	1896	" "
4						
5						
6			No.1 enrolled as R. W. Thomas			
7			No.2 " " Lucy Howard			
8			No.3 " " Hamilton Thomas			
9			No.2 on 1896 roll as Nocie Thomas, Page 1317			
			No.12194, Bok Tuklo			
10						
11						
12						
13						
14						
15					Date of Application for Enrollment.	
16					April 27/99	
17						

Choctaw By Blood Enrollment Cards 1898-1914

RESIDENCE: Bok Tuklo   COUNTY.   **Choctaw Nation**   **Choctaw Roll**   CARD NO.

POST OFFICE: Lukfata, I.T.   *(Not Including Freedmen)*   FIELD NO.   942

Dawes' Roll No.	NAME		Relationship to Person First Named	AGE	SEX	BLOOD	TRIBAL ENROLLMENT		
							Year	County	No.
2532	1 Willis, Edmond P.	43	First Named	40	M	Full	1896	Bok Tuklo	13415
2533	2 " Liza	31	Wife	28	F	"	1896	" "	13416
2534	3 " Harriet	7	Dau	4	"	"	1896	" "	13417
2535	4 " Nelson	18	Ward	15	M	"	1896	" "	13418"
	5								
	6								
	7								
	8								
	9								
	10								
	11	ENROLLMENT OF NOS. 1 2 3 and 4 HEREON APPROVED BY THE SECRETARY OF INTERIOR DEC 12 1902							
	12								
	13								
	14								
	15								
	16								
	17								

TRIBAL ENROLLMENT OF PARENTS

	Name of Father	Year	County	Name of Mother	Year	County
1	Pah-hu-tubbee	Dead	Bok Tuklo	Juisey Parker	Dead	Bok Tuklo
2	Okla-me-aby	"	" " "	I-ya-na	"	" " "
3	No 1			No 2		
4	Cornelius Parker	Dead	Bok Tuklo	I-e-nen-tema	Dead	Bok Tuklo
5						
6	No1 on 1896 roll as Ed. P. Willis					
7	No3 " 1896 " " Hiad "					
8						
9						
10						
11						
12						
13						
14				Date of Application for Enrollment.		
15						
16				April 27/99		
17						

Choctaw By Blood Enrollment Cards 1898-1914

RESIDENCE: Nashoba   COUNTY.
POST OFFICE: Alikchi, I.T.

Choctaw Nation

Choctaw Roll
(Not Including Freedmen)

CARD NO.
FIELD NO. 943

Dawes' Roll No.	NAME		Relationship to Person First Named	AGE	SEX	BLOOD	TRIBAL ENROLLMENT Year	County	No.
2536	1 Wood, Levi	38	First Named	35	M	1/2	1896	Nashoba	13356
2537	2 " Sean	29	Wife	26	F	Full	1896	"	13357
2538	3 " Stella	12	Dau	9	"	3/4	1896	"	13358
Dead	4 " ~~Jiney~~ DEAD.		"	7	"	3/4	1896	"	13359
2539	5 " Sampson	9	Son	6	M	3/4	1896	"	13360
2540	6 " Salom	2	Son	5mo	M	3/4			
	7								
	8								
	9								
	10								
	11								
	12								
	13								
	14								
	15								
	16								
	17								

ENROLLMENT
OF NOS. 1 2 3 5 and 6 HEREON
APPROVED BY THE SECRETARY
OF INTERIOR DEC 12 1902

No. 4 HEREON DISMISSED UNDER
ORDER OF THE COMMISSION TO THE FIVE
CIVILIZED TRIBES OF MARCH 31, 1905.

TRIBAL ENROLLMENT OF PARENTS

	Name of Father	Year	County	Name of Mother	Year	County
1	James Wood	1896	Non Citz	Ka-non-tema	Dead	Nashoba
2	Phila-man	Dead	Wade	Nok-tul-la	"	Wade
3	No1			No2		
4	No1			No2		
5	No1			No2		
6	No1			No2		
7			No4 died April 27, 1899. Proof of death filed Aug 27, 1901			
8			No6 Enrolled Aug 27, 1901			
9						
10			For child of Nos 1&2 see NB (Apr 26-06) Card #664			
11						
12						
13						
14					#1 to 5	
15					Date of Application for Enrollment.	
16					Apr.27/99	
17						

RESIDENCE: Red River	COUNTY:	**Choctaw Nation**	Choctaw Roll	CARD NO.
POST OFFICE: Garvin, I.T.			(Not Including Freedmen)	FIELD NO. 944

Dawes' Roll No.	NAME		Relationship to Person First Named	AGE	SEX	BLOOD	TRIBAL ENROLLMENT		
							Year	County	No.
254	1 Austin, Adam DIED PRIOR TO SEPTEMBER 25, 1902		First Named	40	M	Full	1896	Red River	322
2542	2 " Mary DIED PRIOR TO SEPTEMBER 25, 1902		Wife	36	F	"	1896	" "	323
2543	3 " Susan	15	Dau	12	"	"	1896	" "	325
2544	4 " George	4	Son	1	M	"			
	5								
	6								
	7								
	8								
	9								
	10								
	11	ENROLLMENT							
	12	OF NOS. 1 2 3 and 4 HEREON APPROVED BY THE SECRETARY							
	13	OF INTERIOR DEC 12 1902							
	14								
	15								
	16								
	17								

TRIBAL ENROLLMENT OF PARENTS

	Name of Father	Year	County	Name of Mother	Year	County
1	William Austin	Dead	Red River	E la ta ha no	Dead	Bok Tukla
2	Na ha la	"	" "	Fannie	"	Red River
3	No1			No2		
4	No1			No2		
5						
6	Nos 3 and 4 are now wards of Ellis Taylor on Choctaw card #749: Letters of					
7	guardianship filed December 3, 1902					
8	No1 died June 18,1899: proof of death filed Dec 4, 1902					
	No2 " January22,1900: " " " " " " "					
9	No1 died June18,1899:No2 died Jan 22,1900: Enrollment cancelled by Department July 8 1904					
10	For child of No.3 see NB (March3,1905) #1037					
11						
12						
13						
14						
15					Date of Application for Enrollment.	
16					April 27/99	
17						

44

Choctaw By Blood Enrollment Cards 1898-1914

RESIDENCE: Eagle COUNTY.
POST OFFICE: Eagletown, I.T.

Choctaw Nation

Choctaw Roll
(Not Including Freedmen)

CARD NO.
FIELD NO. **945**

Dawes' Roll No.	NAME	Relationship to Person First Named	AGE	SEX	BLOOD	TRIBAL ENROLLMENT		
						Year	County	No.
2545	1 Ebafokka, Simeon 20	First Named	17	M	Full	1896	Eagle	3754
2546	2 Winnie DIED PRIOR TO SEPTEMBER 25, 1902	Sister	18	F	"	1896	"	3755
2547	3 Emma DIED PRIOR TO SEPTEMBER 25, 1902	"	14	"	"	1896	"	3762
15392	4 McKinney, Milen 4	Son of No.2	3	M	"			
	5							
	6	ENROLLMENT						
	7	OF NOS. 1 2 and 3 HEREON APPROVED BY THE SECRETARY						
	8	OF INTERIOR Dec 12 1902						
	9							
	10	ENROLLMENT						
	11	OF NOS. ~~ 4 ~~ HEREON APPROVED BY THE SECRETARY						
	12	OF INTERIOR May 9 1904						
	13							
	14							
	15							
	16							
	17							

TRIBAL ENROLLMENT OF PARENTS

	Name of Father	Year	County	Name of Mother	Year	County
1	Ebafokka	Dead	Eagle	Jennie Ebafokka	dead	Eagle
2	"	"	"	" "	"	"
3	"	"	"	" "	"	"
4	Jackson McKinney	1896	"	No. 2		
5						
6						
7		No.1 On 1896 roll as Simmon Ebafokka.				
8						
9		No2 died Dec.16.1900: proof of death filed Dec. 16, 1902.				
10		No3 " June 17.1900: " " " " " "				
11	No.4 application first received Oct 23, 1902. No.4 Born Sept.3,1898. Enrolled March 24, 1904.					
12	Father of No.4 on Choctaw card #907					
13	No.2 died Dec.16,1900: No.3 died June17,1900: Enrollment cancelled by Department July 8,1904					
14						
15						
16					Date of Application for Enrollment	April 27/99
17						Nos. 2&3 Apr. 28/99

45

Choctaw By Blood Enrollment Cards 1898-1914

RESIDENCE: Eagle   COUNTY.   **Choctaw Nation**   **Choctaw Roll** *(Not Including Freedmen)*   CARD No. FIELD No. **946**

POST OFFICE: Eagletown, I.T.

Dawes' Roll No.	NAME	Relationship to Person First Named	AGE	SEX	BLOOD	TRIBAL ENROLLMENT		
						Year	County	No.
2548	1 Tonihka, Calvin ²³		20	M	Full	1896	Eagle	12210
2549	2 Wisey DIED PRIOR TO SEPTEMBER 25, 1902	Wife	18	F	"	1896	"	2640
	3							
	4							
	5							
	6							
	7							
	8							
	9							
	10							
	11	ENROLLMENT OF NOS. 1 and 2 HEREON APPROVED BY THE SECRETARY OF INTERIOR DEC 12 1902						
	12							
	13							
	14							
	15							
	16							
	17							

TRIBAL ENROLLMENT OF PARENTS

Name of Father	Year	County	Name of Mother	Year	County
1 To-nih-ka	Dead	Eagle	E-la-pin-tema	Dead	Eagle
2 Billis Colbert	1896	"	Susie Colbert	"	Nashoba
3					
4					
5					
6	No1 on 1896 roll as Cabel Tonihka				
7	No2 " 1896 " " Wisey Colbert				
8					
9	No2 died Jan – 1902 Enrollment cancelled by Department Dec. 24 1904				
10					
11					
12					
13					
14					
15			Date of Application for Enrollment.	April 27/99	
16					
17					

Choctaw By Blood Enrollment Cards 1898-1914

RESIDENCE: Red River   COUNTY. **Choctaw Nation**   **Choctaw Roll** (Not Including Freedmen)   CARD NO. FIELD NO. **947**
POST OFFICE: Harris, I.T.

Dawes' Roll No.	NAME		Relationship to Person First Named	AGE	SEX	BLOOD	TRIBAL ENROLLMENT		
							Year	County	No.
2550	1 Harris, Mary	22	First Named	19	F	1/2	1896	Towson	9267
2551	2 " Mary Lottie	2	Dau	6wks	F	9/32			
15025	3 " Bert Starr	25	Hus	25	M	1/16	1896	Red River	5702
	4								
	5								
	6								
	7	ENROLLMENT OF NOS. 1 and 2 HEREON APPROVED BY THE SECRETARY OF INTERIOR Dec 12, 1902							
	8								
	9								
	10								
	11	ENROLLMENT OF NOS. 3 HEREON APPROVED BY THE SECRETARY OF INTERIOR Oct 15 1903							
	12								
	13								
	14								
	15								
	16								
	17								

TRIBAL ENROLLMENT OF PARENTS

	Name of Father	Year	County	Name of Mother	Year	County
1	McKevers	Dead	Non Citz	Silvey McKevers	Dead	Kiamitia
2	B.S. Harris	1896	Red River	No.1		
3	H.C. Harris	1896	"	Maggie Harris	1896	Intermarriage
4						
5						
6						
7	No.1	On 1896 roll as May McEvers.				
8						
9		Wife of Bert Harris, Card No. D 122				
10		No.2 Enrolled Dec 6th 1900				
11		No.3 Transferred from Choctaw Card D 122 Aug 15 1903				
12		For children of Nos 1&3 see NB (Mar 3-1905)				
13						
14						
15					Date of Application for Enrollment.	
16					April	27/99
17					#3	8/15/03

47

Choctaw By Blood Enrollment Cards 1898-1914

RESIDENCE: Wheelock Seminary COUNTY. **Choctaw Nation** Choctaw Roll CARD No.
POST OFFICE: Garvin, I.T. (Not Including Freedmen) FIELD No. **948**

Dawes' Roll No.	NAME	Relationship to Person First Named	AGE	SEX	BLOOD	TRIBAL ENROLLMENT		
						Year	County	No.
2552	₁ Williams, Emma ¹⁷	First Named	14	F	Full	1896	Towson	13188
2553	₂ " Nora ¹⁵	Sister	12	"	"	1896	"	13189
	₃							
	₄							
	₅							
	₆							
	₇							
	₈							
	₉	ENROLLMENT						
	₁₀	OF NOS. 1 and 2 HEREON APPROVED BY THE SECRETARY						
	₁₁	OF INTERIOR Dec 12 1902						
	₁₂							
	₁₃							
	₁₄							
	₁₅							
	₁₆							
	₁₇							

TRIBAL ENROLLMENT OF PARENTS

	Name of Father	Year	County	Name of Mother	Year	County
₁	Ellis Williams	Dead	Towson	Sallie Williams	Dead	Towson
₂	" "	"	"	" "	"	"
₃						
₄						
₅						
₆						
₇		No2 on 1896 roll as Nora Williams				
₈						
₉		No.1 lives with H.L. Fowler on Choctaw Card #D127				
₁₀		No.2 is wife of G.W. Crawford, a non citizen.				
₁₁		For child of No.1 see N.B. (Apr.26,1906) Card No. 75.				
₁₂		" " " No.2 " (March3,1905) " " 1185				
₁₃						
₁₄					Date of Application for Enrollment.	
₁₅					April 27/99	
₁₆						
₁₇	#2 P.O. Wade, I.T. 12/5 '02					

No 2 P.O. Bennington, I.T. 9/17/07

Choctaw By Blood Enrollment Cards 1898-1914

RESIDENCE: Wheelock Seminary ~~COUNTY~~. **Choctaw Nation** Choctaw Roll CARD NO.
POST OFFICE: Garvin, I.T. *(Not Including Freedmen)* FIELD NO. 949

Dawes' Roll No.	NAME	Relationship to Person First Named	AGE	SEX	BLOOD	TRIBAL ENROLLMENT		
						Year	County	No.
2554	1 Ward, Maggie 17	First Named	14	F	Full	1896	Towson	13192
	2							
	3							
	4							
	5							
	6							
	7							
	8							
	9							
	10							
	11	ENROLLMENT						
	12	OF NOS. 1 HEREON APPROVED BY THE SECRETARY						
	13	OF INTERIOR DEC 12 1902						
	14							
	15							
	16							
	17							

TRIBAL ENROLLMENT OF PARENTS

	Name of Father	Year	County	Name of Mother	Year	County
1	Willie Ward	Dead	Towson	Sissie Ward	Dead	Towson
2						
3						
4						
5						
6						
7	Nº1 was married to Hall Greenwood on Choctaw card #1636, Jany 1,1903.					
8						
9	For child of No1 see NB (Apr 26-06) Card #844					
10	" " " " " (Mar 3-05) " #1202					
11						
12						
13						
14						
15						
16				Date of Application ~~for Enrollment.~~		April 27/99
17	P.O. Leukon I.T. 4/20/05					

49

Choctaw By Blood Enrollment Cards 1898-1914

RESIDENCE: Wheelock Seminary ~~COUNTY.~~ **Choctaw Nation** Choctaw Roll *(Not Including Freedmen)* CARD NO.

POST OFFICE: Garvin, I.T. FIELD NO. 950

NAME	Relationship to Person	AGE	SEX	BLOOD	TRIBAL ENROLLMENT		
					Year	County	No.
1 Pickens, Louisa 20	First Named	17	F	Full	1896	Towson	10339
2 Campbell, Charley 1	Son	8mo	M	"			
3							
4							
5							
6							
7							
8							
9							
10							
11							
12							
13							
14							
15							
16							
17							

ENROLLMENT OF NOS. 1 HEREON APPROVED BY THE SECRETARY OF INTERIOR DEC 12 1902

ENROLLMENT OF NOS. 2 HEREON APPROVED BY THE SECRETARY OF INTERIOR MAY 21 1903

TRIBAL ENROLLMENT OF PARENTS

Name of Father	Year	County	Name of Mother	Year	County
1	Dead	Gaines		Dead	Gaines
2 Reason Campbell	1896	Cedar	N̠o 1		
3					
4					
5					
6					
7 No.1 was wife of Reason Campbell, Choctaw Card #1069, 12/1 ,02					
8 Proof of birth of No.2 to be supplied. 12/1/02					
9 N̠o2 Born July14,1902, application first received Sept 30,1902, proof of birth filed March23,1902					
	For child of No.1 see NB (March3,1905) #1400					
10					
11					
12					
13					
14				Date of Application for Enrollment.	
15					
16				Apr 27/99	
17					

Choctaw By Blood Enrollment Cards 1898-1914

RESIDENCE: Nashoba COUNTY. **Choctaw Nation** Choctaw Roll CARD No.
POST OFFICE: Smithville I.T. *(Not Including Freedmen)* FIELD No. **951**

Dawes' Roll No.	NAME		Relationship to Person	AGE	SEX	BLOOD	TRIBAL ENROLLMENT		
							Year	County	No.
2556	1 Wilson, Witkin	27	First Named	24	M	Full	1896	Nashoba	13264
2557	2 " Susanna	25	Wife	22	F	"	1896	"	12146
	3								
	4								
	5								
	6								
	7								
	8								
	9								
	10								
	11	ENROLLMENT							
	12	OF NOS. 1 and 2 HEREON APPROVED BY THE SECRETARY							
	13	OF INTERIOR Dec 12 1902							
	14								
	15								
	16								
	17								

TRIBAL ENROLLMENT OF PARENTS

	Name of Father	Year	County	Name of Mother	Year	County
1	Aleck Wilson	1896	Nashoba	Liza Wilson	1896	Nashoba
2	John Taylor	1896	"	Sela Taylor	1896	"
3						
4						
5						
6						
7	No1 enrolled as Wilkin Wilson					
8	No2 " " Susana Taylor					
9	Nos1 and 2 have separated 12/1 '02					
10						
11						
12						
13						
14				Date of Application for Enrollment.		
15						
16				Apr 27/99		
17						

Choctaw By Blood Enrollment Cards 1898-1914

RESIDENCE: Cedar COUNTY. **Choctaw Nation** **Choctaw Roll** CARD NO.
POST OFFICE: Doaksville I.T. *(Not Including Freedmen)* FIELD NO. **952**

Dawes' Roll No.	NAME		Relationship to Person First Named	AGE	SEX	BLOOD	TRIBAL ENROLLMENT		
							Year	County	No.
2558	1 Holman Alfred	28	First Named	25	M	Full	1896	Cedar	5460
2559	2 " Eliza	25	Wife	22	F	"	1896	"	5461
2560	3 " Nelly	6	Dau	2	F	"			
2561	4 " Gillum	18	Bro.	15	M	"	1896	"	5463
2562	5 " Martain	3	Son	4mo	"	"			
2563	6 " Simon	1	Son	7mo	M	"			
	7								
	8								
	9								
	10								
	11	ENROLLMENT OF NOS. 1 2 3 4 5 and 6 HEREON							
	12	APPROVED BY THE SECRETARY OF INTERIOR Dec 12 1902							
	13								
	14								
	15								
	16								
	17								

TRIBAL ENROLLMENT OF PARENTS

	Name of Father	Year	County	Name of Mother	Year	County
1	Richmond Holman	Dead	Cedar	Jensy Lowman	Dead	Cedar
2	Charliss	"	Bok Tuklo	Silwy Hopson	"	"
3	No 1			No. 2		
4	Richmond Holman	Dead	Cedar	Jensy Lowman	Dead	Cedar
5	No 1			No 2		
6	No 1			No 2		
7			No.4 brother of No.1			
8						
9			No5 enrolled Dec 19/99. Affidavit			
10			irregular and returned for correction.			
11			Returned corrected and filed Feby.20,1900			
12			N°6 Born Oct.21,1901. enrolled May 19, 1902			
			For child of Nos 1&2 see NB (March 3,1905) #796			
13						
14				#1 to 4 inc		
15				Date of Application for Enrollment		
16				Apr. 27/99		
17	P.O. Corinne IT 4/4/05					

Choctaw By Blood Enrollment Cards 1898-1914

RESIDENCE: Wheelock Seminary COUNTY. **Choctaw Nation** Choctaw Roll CARD NO.

POST OFFICE: Garvin I.T.   (Not Including Freedmen) FIELD NO. 953

Dawes' Roll No.	NAME		Relationship to Person	AGE	SEX	BLOOD	TRIBAL ENROLLMENT		
							Year	County	No.
2564	₁ John Agnes	15	First Named	12	F	Full	1896	Towson	6773
	2								
	3								
	4								
	5								
	6								
	7								
	8								
	9								
	10								
	11	ENROLLMENT OF NOS. 1 HEREON							
	12	APPROVED BY THE SECRETARY							
	13	OF INTERIOR DEC 12 1902							
	14								
	15								
	16								
	17								

TRIBAL ENROLLMENT OF PARENTS

	Name of Father	Year	County	Name of Mother	Year	County
1						
2						
3						
4						
5						
6						
7	For child of No 1 see NB (March 3 1905) #973					
8						
9						
10						
11						
12						
13						
14						
15						
16				DATE OF APPLICATION FOR ENROLLMENT.	Apr. 27/99	
17	P.O. Lukfata IT 9/15/05					

53

Choctaw By Blood Enrollment Cards 1898-1914

RESIDENCE: Wheelock Seminary COUNTY. **Choctaw Nation** **Choctaw Roll** CARD NO.
POST OFFICE: Garvin I.T.   (Not Including Freedmen)   FIELD NO. 954

Dawes' Roll No.	NAME	Relationship to Person First Named	AGE	SEX	BLOOD	TRIBAL ENROLLMENT		
						Year	County	No.
1	Williams Ella		16	F	Full	1896	Towson	13190
2								
3								
4								
5								
6								
7								
8								
9								
10								
11								
12								
13								
14								
15								
16								
17								

TRIBAL ENROLLMENT OF PARENTS

	Name of Father	Year	County	Name of Mother	Year	County
1	Tom Williams	Dead	Kiamiatia[sic]	Lottie Williams	1896	Kiamatia[sic]
2						
3						
4						
5						
6						
7			Enrolled as Emma Williams			
8						
9						
10						
11						
12						
13						
14						
15						
16			Date of Application for Enrollment.	Apr. 27/99		
17						

CANCELLED

No. 1 is a duplicate of No. 3 on Choctaw 4587 Sept. 1902

54

Choctaw By Blood Enrollment Cards 1898-1914

RESIDENCE: Wheelock Seminary COUNTY.
POST OFFICE: Garvin, I.T.

Choctaw Nation

Choctaw Roll
(Not Including Freedmen)

CARD No.
FIELD No. 955

Dawes' Roll No.	NAME	Relationship to Person First Named	AGE	SEX	BLOOD	TRIBAL ENROLLMENT Year	County	No.
1	Williston Elizabeth		16	F	Full	1896	Towson	13193
2								
3								
4								
5								
6								
7								
8								
9								
10								
11								
12								
13								
14								
15								
16								
17								

TRIBAL ENROLLMENT OF PARENTS

	Name of Father	Year	County	Name of Mother	Year	County
1	Pryson Williston	De'd	Red River	Sarah Williston	De'd	Red River
2						
3						
4						
5						
6						
7						
8						
9						
10			No.1 on Choctaw roll as Elizabeth Wiliston			
11						
12						
13						
14						
15						
16				Date of Application for Enrollment	Apr. 27/99	
17						

CANCELLED

No. 1 is a duplicate of No. 1 on Choctaw, illegible, Sept 1902

Choctaw By Blood Enrollment Cards 1898-1914

RESIDENCE: Wheelock Seminary COUNTY.　**Choctaw Nation**　　Choctaw Roll　CARD NO.
POST OFFICE:　Garvin I.T.　　　　　　　　　　(Not Including Freedmen)　FIELD NO. **956**

Dawes' Roll No.	NAME	Relationship to Person First Named	AGE	SEX	BLOOD	TRIBAL ENROLLMENT		
						Year	County	No.
2565	1 Byington Frances 21	First Named	18	F	Full	1896	Towson	1097
	2							
	3							
	4							
	5							
	6							
	7							
	8							
	9							
	10							
	11	ENROLLMENT						
	12	OF NOS. 1 HEREON APPROVED BY THE SECRETARY						
	13	OF INTERIOR Dec 12 1902						
	14							
	15							
	16							
	17							

TRIBAL ENROLLMENT OF PARENTS

	Name of Father	Year	County	Name of Mother	Year	County
1	Jimmy Byington	De'd	Towson	Mary Byington	De'd	Kiamatia[sic]
2						
3						
4						
5	No1 On 1896 Roll as Francis Byington – Is wife of Edward Pisachubbe Choc. #1580					
6	wife of No.4 on Choctaw Card #1580					
7						
8						
9						
10						
11						
12						
13						
14					Date of Application for Enrollment.	
15						
16					Apr. 27/99	
17						

Choctaw By Blood Enrollment Cards 1898-1914

RESIDENCE: Wheelock Siminary COUNTY.
POST OFFICE: Garvin I.T.

Choctaw Nation

Choctaw Roll
(Not Including Freedmen)

CARD NO.
FIELD NO. **957**

Dawes' Roll No.	NAME		Relationship to Person	AGE	SEX	BLOOD	TRIBAL ENROLLMENT		
							Year	County	No.
2566	1 Jones Lottie	21	First Named	18	F	Full	1896	Towson	6776
	2								
	3								
	4								
	5								
	6								
	7								
	8								
	9								
	10								
	11	ENROLLMENT OF NOS. 1 HEREON APPROVED BY THE SECRETARY OF INTERIOR DEC 12 1902							
	12								
	13								
	14								
	15								
	16								
	17								

TRIBAL ENROLLMENT OF PARENTS

	Name of Father	Year	County	Name of Mother	Year	County
1				Rhoda Polk		Skullyville
2						
3						
4						
5	No.1 also on 1896 Choctaw roll as Lily Jones: page 158: #6463					
6	For child of No.1 see NB (March3,1905) #1257				Sept. 27th 1900	
7						
8	11/23/20 See Choctaw Card #2336					
9						
10						
11						
12						
13						
14						Date of Application for Enrollment.
15						
16					Apr. 27/99	
17	P.O. Howe IT 4/1/05					

Choctaw By Blood Enrollment Cards 1898-1914

RESIDENCE: Wheelock Seminary COUNTY.
POST OFFICE: Garvin I.T.

Choctaw Nation

Choctaw Roll
(Not Including Freedmen)

CARD NO.
FIELD NO. **958**

Dawes' Roll No.	NAME		Relationship to Person	AGE	SEX	BLOOD	TRIBAL ENROLLMENT		
							Year	County	No.
2567	₁ Fobb Vicey	17	First Named	14	F	Full	1896	Eagle	4186
14615	₂ James, Cinci	1	Dau	1	M	"			
	₃								
	₄								
	₅	ENROLLMENT							
	₆	OF NOS. 1 HEREON APPROVED BY THE SECRETARY							
	₇	OF INTERIOR Dec 12 1902							
	₈								
	₉								
	10	ENROLLMENT							
	11	OF NOS. 2 HEREON APPROVED BY THE SECRETARY							
	12	OF INTERIOR May 20 1903							
	13								
	14								
	15								
	16								
	17								

TRIBAL ENROLLMENT OF PARENTS

	Name of Father	Year	County	Name of Mother	Year	County
₁	Willie Fobb	Ded	Wolf	Mutsy Fobb	dead	Nashoba
₂	Allen James	1896	Nashoba	Nº 1		
₃						
₄						
₅						
₆	No.1 also on 1896 Choctaw roll Nashoba County, #4145 as Liney Forbb.					
₇	Nº1 is now the wife of Allen James on Choctaw card #873 See Affidavit signed					
₈	by E.C. Ward and Artin White with application for enrollment of Nº 2.					
	Nº2 Born Sept. 10, 1901, enrolled Oct. 11, 1902.					
₉	Above notation as to Nº1 being wife of Allen James on Choctaw card #873 is an error.					
10	She is the wife of Allen W. James Choctaw card #2069. See sworn statement of					
11	William H McKinney Dec. 11, 1902					
	Nº1 also on 1896 Choctaw census roll page 330 #12604 as Vicey Verb.					
12	For child of No 1 see NB (March 3, 1905) #1327					
13						
14					Date of Application for Enrollment.	
15						
16					Apr. 27/99	
17						

Choctaw By Blood Enrollment Cards 1898-1914

RESIDENCE: Wheelock Seminary COUNTY. **Choctaw Nation**   Choctaw Roll   CARD No.
POST OFFICE: Garvin, I.T.   *(Not Including Freedmen)*   FIELD No. **959**

Dawes' Roll No.	NAME	Relationship to Person First Named	AGE	SEX	BLOOD	TRIBAL ENROLLMENT Year	County	No.
2568	1 James Lottie 21	First Named	18	F	Full	1896	Atoka	6776
15827	2 Lucy, Harry J.	Son	1	M	1/2			
	3							
	4							
	5							
	6							
	7	ENROLLMENT OF NOS. 1 HEREON APPROVED BY THE SECRETARY OF INTERIOR Dec 12 1902						
	8							
	9							
	10							
	11							
	12							
	13	ENROLLMENT OF NOS. 2 HEREON APPROVED BY THE SECRETARY OF INTERIOR Jun 12 1905						
	14							
	15							
	16							
	17							

TRIBAL ENROLLMENT OF PARENTS

	Name of Father	Year	County	Name of Mother	Year	County
1						
2	J. W. Lucy		non citizen	No. 1		
3						
4						
5						
6						
7						
8			On roll as Lettie James			
9			No.2 born Sept 21, 1902: application received and No.2 placed			
10			on this card April 13, 1905, under Act of Congress approved March 3, 1905.			
11						
12						
13						
14						
15					#1	
16				Date of Application for Enrollment.	Apr. 27/99	
17	P.O. Ardmore, I.T. 4/3/05					

59

Choctaw By Blood Enrollment Cards 1898-1914

RESIDENCE: Wheelock Seminary COUNTY. **Choctaw Nation** **Choctaw Roll** CARD NO.
POST OFFICE: Garvin I.T. (Not Including Freedmen) FIELD NO. 960

Dawes' Roll No.	NAME	Relationship to Person First Named	AGE	SEX	BLOOD	TRIBAL ENROLLMENT		
						Year	County	No.
2569	1 Durant Nancy 15	First Named	12	F	Full	1896	Atoka	3372
	2							
	3							
	4							
	5							
	6							
	7							
	8							
	9							
	10							
	11	ENROLLMENT						
	12	OF NOS. 1 HEREON APPROVED BY THE SECRETARY						
	13	OF INTERIOR DEC 12 1902						
	14							
	15							
	16							
	17							

TRIBAL ENROLLMENT OF PARENTS

	Name of Father	Year	County	Name of Mother	Year	County
1	Alex Durant	Ded	Atoka	Jane Wilson		
2						
3						
4						
5						
6						
7	No.1 is duplicate of Nancy Durant No.3 on Choctaw card #4093					
8	Enrollment cancelled under Departmental instructions					
9	of September 27, 1905 I.T.B. 12442 – 1905 D.C. #45442-1905					
10						
11						
12						
13						
14						
15						
16				Date of Application for Enrollment Apr. 27/99		
17						

Choctaw By Blood Enrollment Cards 1898-1914

Choctaw Nation

Choctaw Roll
(Not Including Freedmen)

CARD No.
FIELD NO. **961**

Dawes' Roll No.	NAME	Relationship to Person	AGE	SEX	BLOOD	TRIBAL ENROLLMENT Year	County	No.
2570	1 Jackson Isabel 17	First Named	14	F	Full	1896	Bok Tuklo	6928
	2							
	3							
	4							
	5							
	6							
	7							
	8							
	9							
	10							
	11	ENROLLMENT OF NOS. 1 HEREON						
	12	APPROVED BY THE SECRETARY						
	13	OF INTERIOR DEC 12 1902						
	14							
	15							
	16							
	17							

TRIBAL ENROLLMENT OF PARENTS

	Name of Father	Year	County	Name of Mother	Year	County
1	Amos Jackson	Ded	Bok Tuklo	Nancy Jackson	De'd	Bok Tuk-lo
2						
3						
4			No1 on 1896 Roll as Isabell Jackson			
5						
6						
7						
8						
9						
10						
11						
12						
13						
14					Date of Application for Enrollment.	
15						
16					Apr. 27/99	
17						

61

Choctaw By Blood Enrollment Cards 1898-1914

RESIDENCE: Wheelock Seminary COUNTY. **Choctaw Nation** **Choctaw Roll** CARD No.
POST OFFICE: Garvin I.T. (Not Including Freedmen) FIELD NO. 962

Dawes' Roll No.	NAME	Relationship to Person First Named	AGE	SEX	BLOOD	TRIBAL ENROLLMENT		
						Year	County	No.
2571	1 Ward Cornelia 11	First Named	8	F	Full	1896	Eagle	13479
	2							
	3							
	4							
	5							
	6							
	7							
	8							
	9							
	10							
	11	ENROLLMENT OF NOS. 1 HEREON						
	12	APPROVED BY THE SECRETARY						
	13	OF INTERIOR DEC 12 1902						
	14							
	15							
	16							
	17							

TRIBAL ENROLLMENT OF PARENTS

	Name of Father	Year	County	Name of Mother	Year	County
1				Sylva Ward	Ded	Eagle
2						
3						
4						
5						
6						
7						
8						
9						
10						
11						
12						
13						
14						
15						
16					Date of Application for Enrollment Apr. 27/99	
17						

Choctaw By Blood Enrollment Cards 1898-1914

RESIDENCE: Weelock[sic]Seminary COUNTY. **Choctaw Nation** Choctaw Roll CARD NO.
POST OFFICE: Garvin I.T. *(Not Including Freedmen)* FIELD NO. 963

Dawes' Roll No.	NAME	Relationship to Person First Named	AGE	SEX	BLOOD	TRIBAL ENROLLMENT Year	County	No.
2572	1 Wright Annie *DIED PRIOR TO SEPTEMBER 25, 1914*		11	F	Full	1896	Red River	13587
	2							
	3							
	4							
	5							
	6							
	7							
	8							
	9							
	10							
	11							
	12							
	13							
	14							
	15							
	16							
	17							

ENROLLMENT
OF NOS. 1 HEREON
APPROVED BY THE SECRETARY
OF INTERIOR DEC 12 1902

TRIBAL ENROLLMENT OF PARENTS

	Name of Father	Year	County	Name of Mother	Year	County
1	Hampton Wright	Ded		Sissy Wright	De'd	
2						
3						
4						
5						
6						
7	No 1 Died August 29, 1902: proof of death filed Dec 3, 1902					
8						
9						
10						
11						
12						
13						
14						
15						
16				Date of Application for Enrollment	Apr 27/99	
17						

Choctaw By Blood Enrollment Cards 1898-1914

RESIDENCE: Wheelock Seminary COUNTY.
POST OFFICE: Garvin I.T.

Choctaw Nation

Choctaw Roll
(Not Including Freedmen)

CARD NO.
FIELD NO. **964**

Dawes' Roll No.	NAME	Relationship to Person First Named	AGE	SEX	BLOOD	TRIBAL ENROLLMENT		
						Year	County	No.
2573	1 Loman, Mary Jane 13	First Named	10	F	Full	1896	Jack's Fork	8368
	2							
	3							
	4							
	5							
	6							
	7							
	8							
	9							
	10							
	11	ENROLLMENT						
	12	OF NOS. 1 HEREON APPROVED BY THE SECRETARY						
	13	OF INTERIOR Dec 12 1902						
	14							
	15							
	16							
	17							

TRIBAL ENROLLMENT OF PARENTS

Name of Father	Year	County	Name of Mother	Year	County
1 John Loman	Dead	Jacks Fork	Mary Lucy Lowman	De'd	Jack's Fork
2					
3					
4					
5					
6					
7					
8					
9					
10					
11					
12					
13					
14					
15					
16			Date of Application for Enrollment Apr. 27/99		
17					

Choctaw By Blood Enrollment Cards 1898-1914

RESIDENCE: Red River   COUNTY.   **Choctaw Nation**   Choctaw Roll   CARD NO.
POST OFFICE: Kullituklo, I.T.   (Not Including Freedmen)   FIELD NO.   965

Dawes' Roll No.	NAME		Relationship to Person First Named	AGE	SEX	BLOOD	TRIBAL ENROLLMENT		
							Year	County	No.
2574	1 Juzan, Emma	79	First Named	76	F	Full	1896	Red River	7004
2575	2 " Philliston	23	G.Son	20	M	"	1896	" "	7005
2576	3 " Tennessee	21	G.Dau	18	F	"	1896	" "	7006
2577	4 " Jacoway	16	G.Son	13	M	"	1896	" "	7007
2578	5 " Hannah	13	G.Dau	10	F	"	1896	" "	7008
2579	6 Sillis		"	7	"	"	1896	" "	7009
	7								
	8								
	9								
	10								
	11								
	12								
	13								
	14								
	15								
	16								
	17								

DIED PRIOR TO SEPTEMBER 25, 1902 *(struck through, row 6)*

ENROLLMENT
OF NOS. 1 2 3 4 5 and 6 HEREON
APPROVED BY THE SECRETARY
OF INTERIOR DEC 12 1902

No3 is now wife of Pitman Peter on
Choctaw card #503: evidence of marriage
filed Dec.3 1902
For child of No2 see NB (Mar 3 1905) #905

TRIBAL ENROLLMENT OF PARENTS

	Name of Father	Year	County	Name of Mother	Year	County
1	Andy Kincaide	Dead	Bok Tuklo	Pollie Kincaide	Dead	Bok Tuklo
2	Isom Juzan	"	Red River	Betsey Juzan	"	Red River
3	" "	"	" "	" "	"	" "
4	" "	"	" "	" "	"	" "
5	" "	"	" "	" "	"	" "
6	" "	"	" "	" "	"	" "
7	No1 on 1896 roll as Emmie Josund					
8	No2 " 1896 " " Philliston "					
9	No3 " 1896 " " Tennessee " also on 1896 roll No 6775 as Tennessee Jusant					
10	No4 " 1896 " " Jackway "					
11	No5 " 1896 " " Hannah "					
	No6 " 1896 " " Sillis "					
12	No3 was first enrolled April 27/99 as an orphan at Wheelock Seminary					
13	N⁰2 is now the husband of Sallie McClure on Choctaw card #1339 Sept. 18,1902					
	No6 died Jan 22, 1902. Enrollment cancelled by Department July 8 1904.					
14	No6 died January 22, 1902: proof of death filed Dec 4, 1902					
15						Date of Application for Enrollment.
16						Apr 29/99
17						

65

Choctaw By Blood Enrollment Cards 1898-1914

RESIDENCE: Wheelock Seminary COUNTY. **Choctaw Nation** Choctaw Roll CARD No.
POST OFFICE: Garvin, I.T. (Not Including Freedmen) FIELD No. **966**

Dawes' Roll No.	NAME	Relationship to Person	AGE	SEX	BLOOD	TRIBAL ENROLLMENT		
						Year	County	No.
2580	1 Durant, Lizzie 16	First Named	13	F	Full	1896	Towson	3371
14616	2 Gibbs, Isaam 1	Son	3mo	M	1/2			
	3							
	4							
	5							
	6							
	7	ENROLLMENT OF NOS. 1 HEREON APPROVED BY THE SECRETARY OF INTERIOR Dec 12 1902			No			
	8							
	9							
	10							
	11	ENROLLMENT OF NOS. 2 HEREON APPROVED BY THE SECRETARY OF INTERIOR May 20 1903						
	12							
	13							
	14							
	15							
	16							
	17							

TRIBAL ENROLLMENT OF PARENTS

	Name of Father	Year	County	Name of Mother	Year	County
1	Thomas Durant	Dead	Bok Tuklo		Dead	Nashoba
2	Fred Gibbs			No 1		
3						
4						
5						
6	No2 born Aug. 30, 1902; enrolled Dec 8, 1902					
7	No.1 is wife of Fred Gibbs, a non citizen, and has one child					
8	For child of #1 see N.B. (Apr.26 '06) Card #269					
9	" " " #1 " (Mar 3 '05) " #896					
10						
11						
12						
13						
14						
15						#1
16					Date of Application for Enrollment	Apr. 27/99
17	P.O. Glover, I.T. 12/8 '02					

Choctaw By Blood Enrollment Cards 1898-1914

RESIDENCE: Wheelock Seminary COUNTY.
POST OFFICE: Garvin, I.T.

Choctaw Nation

Choctaw Roll
(Not Including Freedmen)

CARD NO.
FIELD NO. 967

Dawes' Roll No.	NAME	Relationship to Person First Named	AGE	SEX	BLOOD	TRIBAL ENROLLMENT Year	TRIBAL ENROLLMENT County	TRIBAL ENROLLMENT No.
14617	1 Hickman, Lizzie ⁱ⁶		13	F	Full	1896	Towson	5477
14618	2 Stephen, Juilious ¹	Son	1	M	1/2			
	3							
	4	ENROLLMENT						
	5	OF NOS. 1 and 2 HEREON APPROVED BY THE SECRETARY						
	6	OF INTERIOR MAY 20 1903						
	7							
	8							
	9							
	10							
	11							
	12							
	13							
	14							
	15							
	16							
	17							

TRIBAL ENROLLMENT OF PARENTS

	Name of Father	Year	County	Name of Mother	Year	County
1		Dead		Susan Hickman	Dead	Bok Tuklo
2	Lewis Stephen			No 1		
3						
4						
5						
6						
7	No 2 Enrolled Dec 9 1902					
8	For child of No.1 see NB (March 3, 1905) #1496					
9						
10						
11						
12						
13						
14						
15						
16					Date of Application for Enrollment	Apr. 27/99
17						

Choctaw By Blood Enrollment Cards 1898-1914

RESIDENCE: Wheelock Seminary COUNTY.
POST OFFICE: Garvin, I.T.

Choctaw Nation

Choctaw Roll
(Not Including Freedmen)

CARD NO.
FIELD NO. 968

Dawes' Roll No.	NAME	Relationship to Person First Named	AGE	SEX	BLOOD	TRIBAL ENROLLMENT		
						Year	County	No.
2581	1 Kincade, Sissie 17	First Named	14	F	Full	1896	Sugar Loaf	7470
	2							
	3							
	4							
	5							
	6							
	7	ENROLLMENT						
	8	OF NOS. 1 HEREON APPROVED BY THE SECRETARY						
	9	OF INTERIOR DEC 12 1902						
	10							
	11							
	12							
	13							
	14							
	15							
	16							
	17							

TRIBAL ENROLLMENT OF PARENTS

	Name of Father	Year	County	Name of Mother	Year	County
1		Dead	Sugar Loaf		Dead	Sugar Loaf
2						
3						
4						
5						
6						
7						
8						
9						
10						
11						
12						
13						
14						
15						
16				Date of Application for Enrollment	Apr. 27/99	
17						

Choctaw By Blood Enrollment Cards 1898-1914

RESIDENCE: Wheelock Seminary COUNTY. **Choctaw Nation**   Choctaw Roll   CARD NO.
POST OFFICE: Garvin, I.T.   *(Not Including Freedmen)*   FIELD NO.   969

Dawes' Roll No.	NAME	Relationship to Person First Named	AGE	SEX	BLOOD	TRIBAL ENROLLMENT Year	County	No.
2582	1 Phillips, Selena ¹⁵	First Named	12	F	Full	1896	Sugar Loaf	10115
	2							
	3							
	4							
	5							
	6							
	7							
	8							
	9							
	10							
	11	ENROLLMENT						
	12	OF NOS. 1 HEREON APPROVED BY THE SECRETARY						
	13	OF INTERIOR DEC 12 1902						
	14							
	15							
	16							
	17							

TRIBAL ENROLLMENT OF PARENTS

	Name of Father	Year	County	Name of Mother	Year	County
1		Dead	Sugar Loaf	Martha Phillips	Dead	Sugar Loaf
2						
3						
4						
5						
6						
7	On 1896 roll as Selina Phillip					
8	Mary LeFlore Choctaw card #3045 is guardian of N°1. See copy					
9	of papers filed in Choctaw case #3045, Feby 3,1903					
10						
11	For twin children of No1 see NB (Apr 26-06) Card #653					
12						
13						
14						
15						
16				Date of Application for Enrollment.	Apr. 27/99	
17						

Choctaw By Blood Enrollment Cards 1898-1914

RESIDENCE: Wheelock Seminary COUNTY.　**Choctaw Nation**　Choctaw Roll　CARD NO.
POST OFFICE:　Garvin, I.T.　*(Not Including Freedmen)*　FIELD NO.　**970**

Dawes' Roll No.	NAME	Relationship to Person First Named	AGE	SEX	BLOOD	TRIBAL ENROLLMENT		
						Year	County	No.
2583	1 Harlin, Bency 18	First Named	15	F	Full	1896	Towson	5476
	2							
	3							
	4							
	5							
	6							
	7							
	8							
	9							
	10							
	11	ENROLLMENT						
	12	OF NOS. 1 HEREON APPROVED BY THE SECRETARY						
	13	OF INTERIOR DEC 12 1902						
	14							
	15							
	16							
	17							

TRIBAL ENROLLMENT OF PARENTS

	Name of Father	Year	County	Name of Mother	Year	County
1		Dead	Nashoba		Dead	Nashoba
2						
3						
4						
5						
6						
7		On 1896 roll as Bency Harland				
8	5/23/06	No1 now wife of Sampson Wright, Choctaw Card No.3039.				
9						
10		For child of No.1 see N.B. (Apr. 26,1906) Card No. 109				
11		" " " " " " " (March 3,1905) " " 810				
12						
13						
14						
15						
16				Date of Application for Enrollment.	Apr. 27/99	
17						

70

Choctaw By Blood Enrollment Cards 1898-1914

RESIDENCE: Wheelock Seminary COUNTY. **Choctaw Nation**   Choctaw Roll   CARD NO.
POST OFFICE: Garvin, I.T.   (Not Including Freedmen)   FIELD NO. 971

Dawes' Roll No.	NAME	Relationship to Person First Named	AGE	SEX	BLOOD	TRIBAL ENROLLMENT Year	County	No.
2584	1 Frazier, Cordelia 20	First Named	17	F	Full	1896	Towson	4131
	2							
	3							
	4							
	5							
	6							
	7							
	8	ENROLLMENT OF NOS. 1 HEREON APPROVED BY THE SECRETARY OF INTERIOR DEC 12 1902						
	9							
	10							
	11							
	12							
	13							
	14							
	15							
	16							
	17							

TRIBAL ENROLLMENT OF PARENTS

	Name of Father	Year	County	Name of Mother	Year	County
1	Benjamin Frazier	Dead	Blue	Emily Frazier	Dead	Blue
2						
3						
4						
5						
6						
7	On 1896 roll as Cordie Frazier					
8						
9						
10						
11						
12						
13						
14						
15						
16				Date of Application for Enrollment	Apr. 27/99	
17						

Choctaw By Blood Enrollment Cards 1898-1914

RESIDENCE: Wheelock Seminary COUNTY. **Choctaw Nation** **Choctaw Roll** CARD No.
POST OFFICE: Garvin, I.T. *(Not Including Freedmen)* FIELD No. 972

Dawes' Roll No.	NAME	Relationship to Person First Named	AGE	SEX	BLOOD	TRIBAL ENROLLMENT		
						Year	County	No.
2585	1 Thomas, Sina ~~DIED PRIOR TO SEPTEMBER 25, 1902~~		12	F	Full	1896	Red River	12298
	2							
	3							
	4							
	5							
	6							
	7							
	8							
	9							
	10							
	11	ENROLLMENT OF NOS. 1 HEREON						
	12	APPROVED BY THE SECRETARY						
	13	OF INTERIOR DEC 12 1902						
	14							
	15							
	16							
	17							

TRIBAL ENROLLMENT OF PARENTS

	Name of Father	Year	County	Name of Mother	Year	County
1		Dead			Dead	
2						
3						
4						
5						
6						
7	No 1 died in December 1898 or 1899· Enrollment cancelled by Department May 2 1906					
8						
9						
10						
11						
12						
13						
14						
15						
16				Date of Application for Enrollment Apr. 27/99		
17						

Choctaw By Blood Enrollment Cards 1898-1914

RESIDENCE: Wheelock Seminary COUNTY.   **Choctaw Nation**   **Choctaw Roll**   CARD NO.
POST OFFICE: Garvin, I.T.   (Not Including Freedmen)   FIELD NO.   973

Dawes' Roll No.	NAME	Relationship to Person First Named	AGE	SEX	BLOOD	TRIBAL ENROLLMENT		
						Year	County	No.
2586	1 Hutcherson, Estella ^17	First Named	14	F	1/2	1896	Jackson	5789
14619	2 Shoemake, Alma ^1	Dau	1mo	F	1/4			
	3							
	4							
	5	ENROLLMENT						
	6	OF NOS. 1 HEREON						
	7	APPROVED BY THE SECRETARY OF INTERIOR DEC 12 1902						
	8							
	9	ENROLLMENT						
	10	OF NOS. 2 HEREON						
	11	APPROVED BY THE SECRETARY OF INTERIOR MAY 20 1903						
	12							
	13							
	14							
	15							
	16							
	17							

TRIBAL ENROLLMENT OF PARENTS

	Name of Father	Year	County	Name of Mother	Year	County
1	Jim Hutcherson	Dead	Blue	Clara Gardner	Dead	Blue
2	J F Shumake[sic]		non-citizen	No 1		
3						
4						
5	No 1 is now the wife of J.F. Shumake – non-citizen. Evidence					
6	of marriage filed Oct. 13, 1902.					
7	No 2 Born Sept. 10, 1902 enrolled Oct. 13, 1902.					
8						
9	For child of No 1 see NB (Apr 26-06) Card #441					
10	" " " " " (Mar 3-05) " #588					
11						
12						
13						
14						
15						
16				Date of Application for Enrollment.		Apr. 27/99
17						

73

Choctaw By Blood Enrollment Cards 1898-1914

RESIDENCE: Wheelock Seminary COUNTY.
POST OFFICE: Garvin, I.T.

Choctaw Nation

Choctaw Roll
(Not Including Freedmen)

CARD NO.
FIELD NO. **974**

Dawes' Roll No.	NAME	Relationship to Person First Named	AGE	SEX	BLOOD	TRIBAL ENROLLMENT Year	County	No.
2587	1 Gardner, Carrie 15	First Named	12	F	Full	1896	Towson	4732
	2							
	3							
	4							
	5							
	6							
	7							
	8							
	9							
	10							
	11	ENROLLMENT OF NOS. 1 HEREON						
	12	APPROVED BY THE SECRETARY						
	13	OF INTERIOR Dec 12 1902						
	14							
	15							
	16							
	17							

TRIBAL ENROLLMENT OF PARENTS

	Name of Father	Year	County	Name of Mother	Year	County
1	Jerry Gardner	Dead	Towson	Jennie Gardner	Dead	Towson
2						
3						
4						
5						
6						
7						
8						
9						
10						
11	Guardian of No.1 is on Choctaw #1144 11/28 ,02					
12						
13	For child of No1 see N.B. (Apr.26-06) Card #782					
14	" " " " " (March3-1905) " #811				Date of Application for Enrollment.	
15						
16					April 27/99	
17	P.O. Parsons, I.T. 4/8/05					

74

Choctaw By Blood Enrollment Cards 1898-1914

RESIDENCE: Wheelock Seminary ~~COUNTY.~~ **Choctaw Nation** **Choctaw Roll** CARD NO.
POST OFFICE: Garvin, I.T. *(Not Including Freedmen)* FIELD NO. **975**

Dawes' Roll No.	NAME		Relationship to Person	AGE	SEX	BLOOD	TRIBAL ENROLLMENT		
							Year	County	No.
2588	1 Jones, Cora	15	First Named	12	F	Full	1896	Jackson	7099
	2								
	3								
	4								
	5								
	6								
	7								
	8								
	9								
	10								
	11	ENROLLMENT OF NOS. 1 HEREON APPROVED BY THE SECRETARY OF INTERIOR Dec 12 1902							
	12								
	13								
	14								
	15								
	16								
	17								

TRIBAL ENROLLMENT OF PARENTS

	Name of Father	Year	County	Name of Mother	Year	County
1	William Jones	Dead	Jackson	Nannie Jones	Dead	Jackson
2						
3						
4						
5		On 1896 roll as Corie Jones				
6						
7						
8		No.1 lives with Billy Jones, Choc. Card #3356 – 12/1 '02				
9						
10		For child of No 1 see NB (Apr 26 '06) Card #375				
11						
12						
13						
14						
15						
16				Date of Application for Enrollment Apr. 27/99		
17						

RESIDENCE: Wheelock Seminary COUNTY. **Choctaw Nation** **Choctaw Roll** CARD No.
POST OFFICE: Garvin I.T. *(Not Including Freedmen)* FIELD No. 976

Dawes' Roll No.	NAME	Relationship to Person First Named	AGE	SEX	BLOOD	TRIBAL ENROLLMENT		
						Year	County	No.
1	Fisher Alice		14	F	Full	1896	Towson	4133
2								
3								
4								
5								
6								
7								
8								
9								
10								
11								
12								
13								
14								
15								
16								
17								

TRIBAL ENROLLMENT OF PARENTS

	Name of Father	Year	County	Name of Mother	Year	County
1	Charley Fisher	Dead				
2						
3						
4						
5						
6						
7						
8						
9						
10						
11						
12						
13						
14					Date of Application for Enrollment.	
15					Apr 27/99	
16						
17						

No1 duplicate of No5 on Choctaw Card #2357

No. 1 Duplicate of No5 on Choctaw #2357 Sept. 1900

Choctaw By Blood Enrollment Cards 1898-1914

RESIDENCE: Wheelock Seminary COUNTY.   **Choctaw Nation**   **Choctaw Roll**   CARD NO.
POST OFFICE: Garvin I.T.   *(Not Including Freedmen)*   FIELD NO.   977

Dawes' Roll No.	NAME		Relationship to Person	AGE	SEX	BLOOD	TRIBAL ENROLLMENT		
							Year	County	No.
2589	1 Homer Mary	17	First Named	14	F	Full	1896	Jackson	5806
2590	2 " Eden	14	Bro	11	M	"	1896	"	5807
	3								
	4								
	5								
	6								
	7								
	8								
	9								
	10								
	11	ENROLLMENT							
	12	OF NOS. 1 and 2 HEREON APPROVED BY THE SECRETARY							
	13	OF INTERIOR DEC 12 1902							
	14								
	15								
	16								
	17								

TRIBAL ENROLLMENT OF PARENTS

	Name of Father	Year	County	Name of Mother	Year	County
1	Jesse Homer	Dead	Blue	Polly Homer	Dead	Jackson
2	" "	"	"	" "	"	"
3						
4						
5						
6						
7		No.1 also on 1896 roll, Page 133, No 5480,				
8		Towson Co., as Mary Homa.				
9						
10						
11						
12						
13						
14						
15				Date of Application for Enrollment.	Apr. 27/99	
16				No2 enrolled Aug 22/99		
17						

Choctaw By Blood Enrollment Cards 1898-1914

RESIDENCE: Wheelock Seminary COUNTY. **Choctaw Nation** Choctaw Roll *(Not Including Freedmen)* CARD NO.
POST OFFICE: Garvin, I.T. FIELD NO. 978

Dawes' Roll No.	NAME	Relationship to Person First Named	AGE	SEX	BLOOD	TRIBAL ENROLLMENT Year	County	No.
2591	1 Cobb, Sophia ¹⁶	First Named	13	F	Full	1896	Jacks Fork	3003
	2							
	3							
	4							
	5							
	6							
	7							
	8							
	9							
	10							
	11	ENROLLMENT						
	12	OF NOS. 1 HEREON APPROVED BY THE SECRETARY						
	13	OF INTERIOR DEC 12 1902						
	14							
	15							
	16							
	17							

TRIBAL ENROLLMENT OF PARENTS

	Name of Father	Year	County	Name of Mother	Year	County
1	Noel Harrison	Dead	Jacks Fork	Susan Harrison	Dead	Jacks Fork
2						
3						
4						
5						
6						
7						
8						
9						
10						
11						
12						
13						
14					Date of Application for Enrollment.	
15						
16					Apr.	27/99
17						

Choctaw By Blood Enrollment Cards 1898-1914

RESIDENCE: Wheelock Seminary COUNTY. **Choctaw Nation** **Choctaw Roll** CARD No.
POST OFFICE: Garvin, I.T. (Not Including Freedmen) FIELD NO. 979

Dawes' Roll No.	NAME	Relationship to Person First Named	AGE	SEX	BLOOD	TRIBAL ENROLLMENT		
						Year	County	No.
DEAD.	1 Thompson, Frances DEAD.		14	F	Full	1896	Cedar	12079
2592	2 Ghoing, Martha 1	Dau	1mo	F	"			
	3							
	4							
	5							
	6 ENROLLMENT							
	7 OF NOS. 2 HEREON APPROVED BY THE SECRETARY							
	8 OF INTERIOR DEC 12 1902							
	9							
	10							
	11							
	12 No. 1 HEREON DISMISSED UNDER ORDER OF THE COMMISSION TO THE FIVE							
	13 CIVILIZED TRIBES OF MARCH 31, 1905.							
	14							
	15							
	16							
	17							

TRIBAL ENROLLMENT OF PARENTS

Name of Father	Year	County	Name of Mother	Year	County
1 Simon Thompson	Dead	Cedar	Lucy Thompson	Dead	Cedar
2 Ben Going	1896	Red River	Nº 1		
3					
4					
5					
6					
7 Nº1 was the wife of Ben Going on Choctaw card #1120 at time of her death					
8 Nº2 Born July 7, 1902: enrolled Aug. 12, 1902.					
9 Nº1 Died July 13, 1902: proof of death filed Aug. 12, 1902.					
10					
11					
12					
13					
14					
15					
16			Date of Application for Enrollment	Apr. 27/99	
17					

Choctaw By Blood Enrollment Cards 1898-1914

RESIDENCE: Wheelock Seminary COUNTY. **Choctaw Nation** Choctaw Roll CARD NO.
POST OFFICE: Garvin, I.T. (Not Including Freedmen) FIELD NO. **980**

Dawes' Roll No.	NAME	Relationship to Person First Named	AGE	SEX	BLOOD	TRIBAL ENROLLMENT		
						Year	County	No.
2593	1 James, Mary Ann 18	First Named	15	F	Full	1893	Towson	P.R. 415
	2							
	3							
	4							
	5							
	6							
	7							
	8							
	9							
	10							
	11	ENROLLMENT OF NOS. 1 HEREON						
	12	APPROVED BY THE SECRETARY						
	13	OF INTERIOR Dec 12 1902						
	14							
	15							
	16							
	17							

TRIBAL ENROLLMENT OF PARENTS

	Name of Father	Year	County	Name of Mother	Year	County
1	Patterson James	Dead	Towson	Anna James	Dead	Towson
2						
3						
4						
5						
6						
7	On 1893 Pay roll as Mary Ann Washington					
8						
9	Also on 1896 roll Page 166 No. 6774 as					
10	Mary Jamison					
11						
12						
13						
14						
15				Date of Application for Enrollment.		
16				Apr. 27/99		
17						

Choctaw By Blood Enrollment Cards 1898-1914

RESIDENCE: Wheelock Seminary ~~COUNTY.~~ **Choctaw Nation** Choctaw Roll *(Not Including Freedmen)* CARD NO. FIELD NO. **981**
POST OFFICE: Garvin, I.T.

Dawes' Roll No.	NAME	Relationship to Person First Named	AGE	SEX	BLOOD	TRIBAL ENROLLMENT		
						Year	County	No.
1	Parker, Lizzie		13	F	Full	1896	Red River	10417
2								
3								
4								
5								
6								
7								
8								
9								
10								
11								
12								
13								
14								
15								
16								
17								

TRIBAL ENROLLMENT OF PARENTS

	Name of Father	Year	County		Name of Mother	Year	County
1	Farlis Parker	Dead	Red River		Cissie Parker	Dead	Red River
2							
3							
4							
5							
6							
7							
8							
9							
10							
11							
12							
13							
14							
15							
16					Date of Application for Enrollment	Apr. 27/99	
17							

No. 1 Duplicate of No. 4 on Choctaw # [illegible]

CANCELLED

Choctaw By Blood Enrollment Cards 1898-1914

RESIDENCE: Wheelock Seminary COUNTY. **Choctaw Nation** **Choctaw Roll** CARD NO.
POST OFFICE: Garvin, I.T. (Not Including Freedmen) FIELD NO. 982

Dawes' Roll No.	NAME	Relationship to Person First Named	AGE	SEX	BLOOD	TRIBAL ENROLLMENT		
						Year	County	No.
2594	1 Barnes, Hattie ~~19~~	First Named	16	F	1/2	1896	Towson	1099
	2							
	3							
	4							
	5							
	6							
	7							
	8							
	9							
	10							
	11	ENROLLMENT OF NOS. 1 HEREON APPROVED BY THE SECRETARY OF INTERIOR DEC 12 1902						
	12							
	13							
	14							
	15							
	16							
	17							

TRIBAL ENROLLMENT OF PARENTS

	Name of Father	Year	County	Name of Mother	Year	County
1	Sol Barnes	Dead	Skullyville	Rosa Barnes	Dead	Sugar Loaf
2						
3						
4			No1 is duplicate of No2 Harriet C. Gollihare Choctaw card #2569			
5			Roll No. 7458. Enrollment hereon cancelled under Departmental			
6			instructions of July 15, 1904 (D.C. #25571 – 1904)			
7						
8						
9			On 1896 roll as Hattie Barns			
10						
11						
12						
13						
14						
15						
16				Date of Application for Enrollment. Apr. 27/99		
17						

Choctaw By Blood Enrollment Cards 1898-1914

RESIDENCE: Towson COUNTY.
POST OFFICE: Fowlerville, I.T.

Choctaw Nation

Choctaw Roll CARD NO.
(Not Including Freedmen) FIELD NO. 983

Dawes' Roll No.	NAME		Relationship to Person	AGE	SEX	BLOOD	TRIBAL ENROLLMENT		
							Year	County	No.
I.W. 510	1 Byram, Miles	30	First Named	26	M	I W	1896	Towson	14312
2595	2 " Susie W	29	Wife	26	F	3/4	1896	"	1085
	3								
	4								
	5								
	6	ENROLLMENT OF NOS. 2 HEREON APPROVED BY THE SECRETARY OF INTERIOR DEC 12 1902							
	7								
	8								
	9								
	10	ENROLLMENT OF NOS. ~~~ 1 ~~~ HEREON APPROVED BY THE SECRETARY OF INTERIOR DEC 24 1903							
	11								
	12								
	13								
	14								
	15								
	16								
	17								

TRIBAL ENROLLMENT OF PARENTS

	Name of Father	Year	County	Name of Mother	Year	County
1	Sam Byram	1896	Non Citz	Frances Byram	Dead	Non Citz
2		Dead	Jacks Fork		"	Jacks Fork
3						
4						
5						
6						
7		No2 was an inmate of Wheelock Seminary, Garvin, I.T. when she				
8		married Miles Byram. Claims she never knew or heard the				
9		names of her parents.				
10						
11						
12						
13						
14					DATE OF APPLICATION FOR ENROLLMENT.	
15						
16					Apr. 27/99	
17	P.O. Swink I.T.					

Choctaw By Blood Enrollment Cards 1898-1914

RESIDENCE: Eagle   COUNTY.
POST OFFICE: Eagletown, I.T.

Choctaw Nation

Choctaw Roll
(Not Including Freedmen)

CARD NO.
FIELD NO. 984

Dawes' Roll No.	NAME		Relationship to Person First Named	AGE	SEX	BLOOD	TRIBAL ENROLLMENT		
							Year	County	No.
2596	1	Hudson, Davis ~~DIED PRIOR TO SEPTEMBER 25, 1902~~	First Named	24	M	Full	1896	Eagle	5579
2597	2	" Inis 23	Wife	20	F	"	1896	"	13550
2598	3	" Evelina 2	Dau	8mo	F	"			
	4								
	5								
	6								
	7								
	8								
	9								
	10								
	11	ENROLLMENT OF NOS. 1 2 and 3 HEREON							
	12	APPROVED BY THE SECRETARY							
	13	OF INTERIOR DEC 12 1902							
	14								
	15								
	16								
	17								

TRIBAL ENROLLMENT OF PARENTS

	Name of Father	Year	County	Name of Mother	Year	County
1	Daniel Hudson	1896	Eagle	Ellen Mambi	1896	Eagle
2	Me-ha-taka	Dead	"	Fillis Byington	Dead	"
3	No. 1			No. 2		
4						
5						
6						
7	No.1 died April 20, 1902; Proof of death requested Nov. 24, 1902					
8	No2 on 1896 roll as Ainis Wilson					
9	No3 Enrolled March 5th 1901					
10	As to correct spelling of name of No.2 See letter of David[sic] Hudson Filed March 22,1901					
11	No1 died Dec, 1901: proof of death filed Dec 12, 1902					
12	No1 died Dec, 1901: Enrollment cancelled by Department July 8, 1904					
13						
14						
15				Date of Application for Enrollment.	Apr.	27/99
16						
17						

Choctaw By Blood Enrollment Cards 1898-1914

RESIDENCE: Wheelock Seminary COUNTY. **Choctaw Nation** Choctaw Roll CARD NO.
POST OFFICE: Garvin I.T. (Not Including Freedmen) FIELD NO. **985**

Dawes' Roll No.	NAME	Relationship to Person First Named	AGE	SEX	BLOOD	TRIBAL ENROLLMENT		
						Year	County	No.
2599	1 Martin Lizzie 11	First Named	8	F	Full	1896	Kiamatia[sic]	8700
	2							
	3							
	4							
	5							
	6							
	7							
	8							
	9							
	10							
	11	ENROLLMENT						
	12	OF NOS. 1 HEREON APPROVED BY THE SECRETARY						
	13	OF INTERIOR Dec 12 1902						
	14							
	15							
	16							
	17							

TRIBAL ENROLLMENT OF PARENTS

	Name of Father	Year	County	Name of Mother	Year	County
1						
2						
3						
4						
5						
6			No1 died Sept. 25, 1902; Evidence of death filed Dec 5, 1902.			
7		Oct. 4, 1911				
8			Reported to have died prior go Sept. 25, 1902			
9						
10						
11						
12						
13						
14						
15						
16				Date of Application for Enrollment Apr. 27/99		
17						

Choctaw By Blood Enrollment Cards 1898-1914

RESIDENCE: Wheelock Seminary COUNTY.
POST OFFICE: Garvin I.T.

Choctaw Nation

Choctaw Roll
(Not Including Freedmen)

CARD NO.
FIELD NO. 986

Dawes' Roll No.	NAME	Relationship to Person First Named	AGE	SEX	BLOOD	TRIBAL ENROLLMENT		
						Year	County	No.
2600	1 Anderson Rachel 15	First Named	12	F	Full	1896	Towson	
	2							
	3							
	4							
	5							
	6							
	7							
	8							
	9							
	10							
	11	ENROLLMENT OF NOS. 1 HEREON APPROVED BY THE SECRETARY OF INTERIOR DEC 12 1902						
	12							
	13							
	14							
	15							
	16							
	17							

TRIBAL ENROLLMENT OF PARENTS

	Name of Father	Year	County	Name of Mother	Year	County
1						
2						
3						
4						
5						
6						
7			Also on 1896 roll Richol Anderson			
8			Page 6, No 244, Bok Tuklo Cd.			
9						
10						
11						
12						
13						
14						
15						
16					Date of Application for Enrollment	Apr. 27/99
17						

Choctaw By Blood Enrollment Cards 1898-1914

RESIDENCE: Wheelock Seminary COUNTY.
POST OFFICE: Garvin I.T.

Choctaw Nation

Choctaw Roll *(Not Including Freedmen)*

CARD No.
FIELD No. 987

Dawes' Roll No.	NAME	Relationship to Person First Named	AGE	SEX	BLOOD	TRIBAL ENROLLMENT Year	County	No.
dead	1 Harkins Emeline		15	F	Full	1896	Towson	5478
	2							
	3							
	4							
	5							
	6							
	7							
	8							
	9							
	10							
	11							
	12							
	13							
	14							
	15							
	16							
	17							

ENROLLMENT
OF NOS. HEREON
APPROVED BY THE SECRETARY
OF INTERIOR

CANCELLED

No. 1 Duplicate of No. 6 on Choctaw #2444 Sept. 10/02

TRIBAL ENROLLMENT OF PARENTS

	Name of Father	Year	County		Name of Mother	Year	County
1	Sha bi	De'd	San-Bois		Mih-yo-te-ma	De'd	San Bois
2							
3							
4							
5							
6							
7							
8							
9							
10							
11	No.1 is a duplicate enrollment of No.6 on Choctaw card #2444.						
12							
13							
14							
15					Date of Application for Enrollment		Apr. 27/99
16							
17							

Choctaw By Blood Enrollment Cards 1898-1914

NAME		Relationship to Person First Named	AGE	SEX	BLOOD	TRIBAL ENROLLMENT		
						Year	County	No.
1 Hudson, Jackson	63	First Named	61	M	Full	1896	Eagle	5581
2 " Ishtema	68	Wife	65	F	"	1893	"	P.R. 357
3 McCoy, Alice	25	Ward	22	"	"	1896	"	9312
4								
5								
6								
7								
8								
9								
10								
11								
12								
13								
14								
15								
16								
17								

E: Eagle COUNTY. **Choctaw Nation** **Choctaw Roll** (Not Including Freedmen) CARD NO. FIELD NO. 988
ICE: Eagletown, I.T.

ENROLLMENT
OF NOS. 1 2 and 3 HEREON
APPROVED BY THE SECRETARY
OF INTERIOR DEC 12 1902

TRIBAL ENROLLMENT OF PARENTS

Name of Father	Year	County	Name of Mother	Year	County
1 James Hudson	Dead	Eagle		Dead	Eagle
2 Ah-te-he	"	"	Ish-te-ma-he-ma	"	"
3 Filliston McCoy	"	"	Alona McCoy	"	"
4					
5					
6					
7	No2 on 1893 roll as Ishteoma Hudson				
8	No2 also on 1896 roll, Eagle Co., Page				
9	154 No 6290 as Ishtemahoke				
	For children of No.3 see NB (March 3, 1905) #1069				
10					
11					
12					
13					
14				Date of Application for Enrollment.	
15					
16				Apr. 27/99	
17					

Choctaw By Blood Enrollment Cards 1898-1914

RESIDENCE: Cedar   COUNTY.   **Choctaw Nation**   **Choctaw Roll**   CARD No.

POST OFFICE: Doaksville, I.T.   *(Not Including Freedmen)*   FIELD No.   **989**

Dawes' Roll No.	NAME	Relationship to Person First Named	AGE	SEX	BLOOD	TRIBAL ENROLLMENT Year	TRIBAL ENROLLMENT County	TRIBAL ENROLLMENT No.
2604	1 Loyd, Sarah 21	First Named	18	F	Full	1896	Cedar	4079
	2							
	3							
	4							
	5							
	6							
	7							
	8							
	9							
	10							
	11	ENROLLMENT						
	12	OF NOS. 1 HEREON APPROVED BY THE SECRETARY						
	13	OF INTERIOR Dec. 12, 1902						
	14							
	15							
	16							
	17							

TRIBAL ENROLLMENT OF PARENTS

	Name of Father	Year	County	Name of Mother	Year	County
1	Edward Frazier	1896	Cedar	Wicey Frazier	1896	Cedar
2						
3						
4						
5						
6	On 1896 roll as Sarah Frazier					
7						
8	Wife of J.L. Loyd on Card No. D 131 = Divorced and now wife					
9	of No.1 on Choctaw Card #927: Evidence of Marriage requested 12/10 '02					
10						
11	For child of No1 see NB (Mar 3rd 1905) Card #97.					
12						
13						
14					Date of Application for Enrollment.	
15						
16					April 27/99	
17						

Choctaw By Blood Enrollment Cards 1898-1914

RESIDENCE: Red River COUNTY.	Choctaw Nation	Choctaw Roll (Not Including Freedmen)	CARD NO.
POST OFFICE: Garvin, I.T.			FIELD NO. 990

Dawes' Roll No.	NAME	Relationship to Person First Named	AGE	SEX	BLOOD	TRIBAL ENROLLMENT		
						Year	County	No.
I.W. 1399	1 Kirk, J.W. 48		45	M	I.W.	1896	Towson	4722
15393	2 " , Sarah 38	Wife	35	F	1/2	1896	"	7525
15394	3 " , Gabriella 19	Dau	16	"	1/4	1896	"	7526
	4							
	5							
	6							
	7	ENROLLMENT OF NOS. 2—3— HEREON APPROVED BY THE SECRETARY OF INTERIOR May 9, 1904						
	8							
	9							
	10							
	11	ENROLLMENT OF NOS. ---1--- HEREON APPROVED BY THE SECRETARY OF INTERIOR Jun 12-1905						
	12							
	13							
	14							
	15							
	16							
	17							

TRIBAL ENROLLMENT OF PARENTS

	Name of Father	Year	County	Name of Mother	Year	County
1	James Kirk	Dead	Non Citz	Gabriella Kirk	1896	Non Citz
2	Isaac McClure	"	Blue	Laura McClure	Dead	" "
3	No. 1			No. 2		
4						
5						
6						
7	Nos1,2 and3 restored to roll by Departmental authority of January19, 1909 (File 5-51)					
8	Enrollment of Nos 1,2&3 cancelled by order of Department March 4, 1907					
9						
10	No3 on 1896 Roll as Gabriella[sic] Kirk					
11	As to marriage of parents of No.2 see					
12	testimony of S.E. Lewis, attached to Card No. 3345.					
13	Dec 6/99 No1 See Dawes Commission					
14	record 1896, Case No. 948.					
15	Nos 1 2&3 denied in 1896 by Dawes Commission					
16	Choctaw case #948. appealed and appeal dissmised[sic] by attorney for appellant			Date of Application for Enrollment		Apr. 27/99
17						

Choctaw By Blood Enrollment Cards 1898-1914

...wson   COUNTY.   **Choctaw ...**
Doaksville, I.T.

NAME		Relationship to Person First Named	AGE	SEX	BLOOD	TRIBAL ENROLLMENT		
						Year	County	No.
1	Thomas, Mahlone ³⁶	First Named	33	F	Full	1896	Towson	12131
2	" Emma ¹⁹	Dau	16	"	"	1896	"	12133
3	" Moses ¹⁴	Son	11	M	"	1896	"	12134
6								
7								
8								
9								
10								
11	ENROLLMENT OF NOS. 1 2 and 3 HEREON							
12	APPROVED BY THE SECRETARY							
13	OF INTERIOR DEC 12 1902							
14								
15								
16								
17								

TRIBAL ENROLLMENT OF PARENTS

	Name of Father	Year	County	Name of Mother	Year	County
1	Peter	Dead	Eagle	Lo-na-hoh-ke	Dead	Towson
2	Billy Thomas	"	Towson	No1		
3	" "	"	"	No1		
4						
5						
6						
7	No1 on 1896 roll as Timaye Thomas					
8	No2 " 1896 " " Emma Timaye					
9	No3 " 1896 " " Moses "					
10	For child of No.2 see N.B. (Apr.26,1906) Card #256					
	" children " " " " (March3,1905) " #1303					
11						
12						
13						
14					Date of Application for Enrollment.	
15						
16					Apr. 27/99	
17						

Choctaw By Blood Enrollment Cards 1898-1914

RESIDENCE: Towson COUNTY.
POST OFFICE: Clear Creek, I.T.

Choctaw Nation

Choctaw Roll
(Not Including Freedmen)

CARD NO.
FIELD NO. **992**

Dawes' Roll No.	NAME	Relationship to Person First Named	AGE	SEX	BLOOD	TRIBAL ENROLLMENT		
						Year	County	No.
2608	₁ Wilson, Emma J ²⁵	First Named	22	F	1/4	1896	Towson	13220
2609	₂ Bohanan, Brazil ¹⁷	Bro	14	M	1/4	1896	Kiamitia	1462
2610	₃ Wilson, Tom ³	Dau	4mo	F	1/8			
2611	₄ " , Raphael L ¹	Son	2mo	M	1/8			
	5							
	6							
	7							
	8							
	9							
	10							
	11	ENROLLMENT OF NOS. 1 2 3 and 4 HEREON						
	12	APPROVED BY THE SECRETARY						
	13	OF INTERIOR Dec 12, 1902						
	14							
	15							
	16							
	17							

TRIBAL ENROLLMENT OF PARENTS

	Name of Father	Year	County	Name of Mother	Year	County
1	Joshua Bohanan	Dead	Kiamitia	Serena Bohanan	Dead	Kiamitia
2	" "	"	"	" "	"	"
3	R.F. Wilson		Chickasaw	No. 1		
4	" " "		" "	No. 1		
5						
6	For child of No.2 see N.B.(Apr.26,1906) Card No. 117					
7	" " " " " 1 " " (March3,1905) " " 701					
8						
9	No3 is named "Torn" Wilson 12/4/02					
10						
11	No3 Enrolled May 24, 1900					
12	No4 born Nov. 17, 1901: Enrolled Jan. 7, 1902					
13					#1&2 inc	
14					Date of Application	
15					for Enrollment.	
16					Apr. 27/99	
17	P.O. Valliant I.T. 3/27/05					

92

Choctaw By Blood Enrollment Cards 1898-1914

RESIDENCE: Eagle COUNTY.
POST OFFICE: Eagletown, I.T.

Choctaw Nation

Choctaw Roll (Not Including Freedmen)

CARD No.
FIELD No. **993**

Dawes' Roll No.	NAME		Relationship to Person First Named	AGE	SEX	BLOOD	TRIBAL ENROLLMENT		
							Year	County	No.
2612	1 On chili, Sim			29	M	Full	1893	Eagle	P.R. 554
2613	2 " Bicey	31	Wife	28	F	"	1896	"	12217
2614	3 Tonihka, George	15	S.Son	12	M	"	1896	"	12223
2615	4 " Jowicks	12	"	9	"	"	1896	"	12219
2616	5 " Gissel	11	"	8	"	"	1896	"	12215
2617	6 " Willie	7	"	4	"	"	1896	"	12229
15828	7 James, Imy		Dau	3	F	"			
	8								
	9	ENROLLMENT							
	10	OF NOS. 1 2 3 4 5 and 6 HEREON APPROVED BY THE SECRETARY							
	11	OF INTERIOR Dec 12 1902							
	12								
	13								
	14	ENROLLMENT							
	15	OF NOS. ~~~ 7 ~~~ HEREON APPROVED BY THE SECRETARY							
	16	OF INTERIOR Jun 12 1905							
	17								

TRIBAL ENROLLMENT OF PARENTS

	Name of Father	Year	County	Name of Mother	Year	County
1	James Onchili	Dead	Eagle	Maley Onchili	Dead	Eagle
2	Thle-o-tom-be	1896	"	Betsey		
3	Simpson Tonihka	Dead	"	No.2		
4	" "	"	"	No.2		
5	" "	"	"	No.2		
6	" "	"	"	No.2		
7	No. 1			No.2		
8						
9			No.2 on 1896 roll as Bicey Tonihka			
10			No.6 1896 " " William "			
11			No.3 1896 " " Georgiana "			
			No.1 also on 1896 Choctaw Roll, page 171, #6975 as Sim James			
12			No.1 Died Nov. 1900: proof of death filed Dec 3, 1902			
13			No.1 died Nov 1900: Enrollment cancelled by Department July 8, 1904.			
14			No.7 born in December, 1899: application received and No7 placed			
15			on this card April 12, 1905, under Act of Congress approved March		#1 to 6 Date of Application for Enrollment.	
16			For child of No.2 see NB (March3,1905) #967			
17	P.O. Lukfata, Ok.				Apr. 27/99	

Choctaw By Blood Enrollment Cards 1898-1914

RESIDENCE: Eagle   COUNTY.   **Choctaw Nation**   **Choctaw Roll** (Not Including Freedmen)   CARD No.

POST OFFICE: Eagletown, I T   FIELD No. 994

Dawes' Roll No.	NAME	Relationship to Person First Named	AGE	SEX	BLOOD	TRIBAL ENROLLMENT Year	County	No.
2618	DIED PRIOR TO SEPTEMBER 25, 1902 1 Nowahima	Named	65	F	Full	1896	Eagle	9721
	2							
	3							
	4							
	5							
	6							
	7							
	8							
	9							
	10							
	11	ENROLLMENT OF NOS. 1 HEREON APPROVED BY THE SECRETARY OF INTERIOR DEC 12 1902						
	12							
	13							
	14							
	15							
	16							
	17							

TRIBAL ENROLLMENT OF PARENTS

	Name of Father	Year	County	Name of Mother	Year	County
1	Ah-te-he	Dead	Eagle	Sha-te-ma	Dead	Eagle
2						
3						
4	No. 1 died before Sept. 25, 1902; Enrollment cancelled by Department May 2, 1906					
5						
6						
7						
8						
9						
10						
11						
12						
13						
14					Date of Application for Enrollment.	
15						
16					Apr. 27/99	
17						

Choctaw By Blood Enrollment Cards 1898-1914

RESIDENCE: Eagle COUNTY.
POST OFFICE: Eagletown, I.T.

Choctaw Nation

Choctaw Roll
(Not Including Freedmen)

CARD No.
FIELD No. 995

Dawes' Roll No.	NAME	Relationship to Person First Named	AGE	SEX	BLOOD	TRIBAL ENROLLMENT Year	TRIBAL ENROLLMENT County	TRIBAL ENROLLMENT No.
2619	1 Nowahima, Esean 30	First Named	27	F	Full	1896	Eagle	9722
2620	2 " Hitty 13	Dau	10	"	"	1896	"	9723
2621	3 Tonihka, Silas 12	Son	9	M	"	1896	"	9724
14683	4 Tushka, Sophy 3	Dau	3	F	"			
	5							
	6							
	7							
	8 ENROLLMENT OF NOS. 1 2 and 3 HEREON APPROVED BY THE SECRETARY							
	9 OF INTERIOR DEC 12 1902							
	10							
	11							
	12 ENROLLMENT OF NOS. 4 HEREON							
	13 APPROVED BY THE SECRETARY							
	14 OF INTERIOR MAY 20 1903							
	15							
	16							
	17							

TRIBAL ENROLLMENT OF PARENTS

	Name of Father	Year	County	Name of Mother	Year	County
1	Ta-ma-hel-aby	Dead	Eagle	No-wa-hi-ma	1896	Eagle
2	Albert Tonihka	"	"	No 1		
3	" "	"	"	No 1		
4	Levi Tushka	1896	"	Nº 1		
5						
6						
7			No1 on 1896 roll as Lucy Ann Nowahima			
8			No3 " 1896 " " Silas "			
9			Nº4 Born Sept. 2, 1899, enrolled Sept. 3, 1902.			
10						
11						
12						
13						
14						
15					#1 to 3	
16				Date of Application for Enrollment	Apr. 27/99	
17						

Choctaw By Blood Enrollment Cards 1898-1914

RESIDENCE: Cedar	COUNTY.	Choctaw Nation	Choctaw Roll	CARD No.
POST OFFICE: Alikchi, I.T.			(Not Including Freedmen)	FIELD No. 996

Dawes' Roll No.	NAME	Relationship to Person First Named	AGE	SEX	BLOOD	TRIBAL ENROLLMENT		
						Year	County	No.
2622	1 Wesley, Johnson 21		18	M	Full	1896	Cedar	13152
	2							
	3							
	4							
	5							
	6							
	7							
	8							
	9							
	10							
	11	ENROLLMENT						
	12	OF NOS. 1 HEREON APPROVED BY THE SECRETARY						
	13	OF INTERIOR DEC 12 1902						
	14							
	15							
	16							
	17							

TRIBAL ENROLLMENT OF PARENTS

	Name of Father	Year	County	Name of Mother	Year	County
1	James Mullin	Dead	Cedar	Ugle-mah	Dead	Cedar
2						
3						
4	For child of No1 see NB (Apr 26-06) Card #863					
5						
6	Wife of No1 on Choctaw Card #873 – Roll #2292 as Lucy James					
7						
8						
9						
10						
11						
12						
13						
14						
15						
16				Date of Application for Enrollment	Apr. 27/99	
17	P.O. Kullituklo 12/26/06					

Choctaw By Blood Enrollment Cards 1898-1914

RESIDENCE: Towson COUNTY.
POST OFFICE: Fowlerville, I.T.

Choctaw Nation

Choctaw Roll
(Not Including Freedmen)

CARD NO.
FIELD NO. 997

Dawes' Roll No.	NAME	Relationship to Person First Named	AGE	SEX	BLOOD	TRIBAL ENROLLMENT Year	County	No.
2623	1 Chinka, Annie ⁶⁶	First Named	63	F	Full	1896	Towson	2459
2624	2 Daniel, Esias ²⁶	Son	23	M	"	1896	"	3370
	3							
	4	ENROLLMENT						
	5	OF NOS. 1 and 2 HEREON APPROVED BY THE SECRETARY						
	6	OF INTERIOR DEC 12 1902						
	7							
	8							
	9							
	10							
	11							
	12							
	13							
	14							
	15							
	16							
	17							

TRIBAL ENROLLMENT OF PARENTS

	Name of Father	Year	County	Name of Mother	Year	County
1	Na-ne-man-teby	Dead	Towson	Tah-hu-na	Dead	Blue
2	Chinka	"	"	No1		
3						
4						
5						
6						
7	No.1 on Choctaw roll as Annie Chika					
8						
9						
10						
11						
12						
13						
14						
15						
16				Date of Application for Enrollment	Apr. 27/99	
17						

Choctaw By Blood Enrollment Cards 1898-1914

RESIDENCE: Towson COUNTY.
POST OFFICE: Garvin, I.T.

Choctaw Nation

Choctaw Roll
(Not Including Freedmen)

CARD NO.
FIELD NO. 998

Dawes' Roll No.	NAME	Relationship to Person	AGE	SEX	BLOOD	TRIBAL ENROLLMENT		
						Year	County	No.
2625	1 Ward, Lucinda 63	First Named	60	F	Full	1896	Towson	13216
	2							
	3							
	4							
	5							
	6							
	7							
	8							
	9							
	10							
	11							
	12							
	13							
	14							
	15							
	16							
	17							

ENROLLMENT
OF NOS. 1 HEREON
APPROVED BY THE SECRETARY
OF INTERIOR DEC 12 1902

TRIBAL ENROLLMENT OF PARENTS

	Name of Father	Year	County	Name of Mother	Year	County
1	Battiest Parrish	Dead	Towson	Pollie Parrish	Dead	Towson
2						
3						
4						
5						
6						
7						
8						
9						
10						
11						
12						
13						
14				Date of Application		
15				for Enrollment.		
16				Apr 27/99		
17						

98

Choctaw By Blood Enrollment Cards 1898-1914

RESIDENCE: Nashoba COUNTY.	POST OFFICE: Alikchi, I.T.	**Choctaw Nation**	Choctaw Roll (Not Including Freedmen)	CARD NO. FIELD NO. 999

Dawes' Roll No.	NAME	Relationship to Person First Named	AGE	SEX	BLOOD	TRIBAL ENROLLMENT Year	County	No.
2626	1 Hayes, Jesse 28	First Named	25	M	Full	1896	Nashoba	5541
2627	2 " Rhoda 38	Wife	35	F	"	1896	"	5542
2628	3 " Mary 8	Dau	5	"	"	1896	"	5543
14684	4 " Josephine 3	Dau	2	"	"			
	5							
	6	ENROLLMENT OF NOS. 1, 2 and 3 HEREON APPROVED BY THE SECRETARY OF INTERIOR Dec 12, 1902						
	7							
	8							
	9							
	10							
	11	ENROLLMENT OF NOS. 1 HEREON APPROVED BY THE SECRETARY OF INTERIOR May 20 1903						
	12							
	13							
	14							
	15							
	16							
	17							

TRIBAL ENROLLMENT OF PARENTS

Name of Father	Year	County	Name of Mother	Year	County
1 Wicklis Hayes	Dead	Nashoba	Hoteya Hayes	Dead	Nashoba
2 Jack Thompson	"	Eagle	Lujoka Thompson	"	Eagle
3 No. 1			No. 2		
4 No. 1			No. 2		
5					
6					
7 No 4 born December 13, 1900 enrolled December 17 1902					
8					
9					
10					
11					
12					
13					
14					
15				#1 to 3 inc	
16				Date of Application for Enrollment Apr. 27/99	
17 P.O. Garvin, I.T. 11/29/02					

Choctaw By Blood Enrollment Cards 1898-1914

RESIDENCE: Nashoba   COUNTY.

POST OFFICE: Alikchi, I.T.

Choctaw Nation

Choctaw Roll (Not Including Freedmen)

CARD NO.

FIELD NO. **1000**

Dawes' Roll No.	NAME		Relationship to Person	AGE	SEX	BLOOD	TRIBAL ENROLLMENT		
							Year	County	No.
2629	1 Jefferson, Ellis	33	First Named	30	M	Full	1896	Nashoba	6836
2630	2 " Davis	12	Son	9	"	"	1896	"	6838
2631	3 " Jacob	10	"	7	"	"	1896	"	6839
2632	4 ~~Ephraim~~ DIED PRIOR TO SEPTEMBER 25, 1902		"	3	"	"	1896	"	6840
	5								
	6								
	7								
	8								
	9								
	10								
	11								
	12								
	13								
	14								
	15								
	16								
	17								

ENROLLMENT OF NOS. 1 2 3 and 4 HEREON APPROVED BY THE SECRETARY OF INTERIOR Dec. 12, 1902

TRIBAL ENROLLMENT OF PARENTS

	Name of Father	Year	County	Name of Mother	Year	County
1	Filiston Jefferson	Dead	Nashoba	Elizabeth Jefferson	1896	Wade
2	No 1			Litsie Jefferson	Dead	Nashoba
3	No 1			" "	"	"
4	~~No 1~~			" "	"	"
5						
6						
7						
8	No 2 on 1896 roll as Lewis Jefferson					
9						
10						
11	No 1 is now husband of Lizzie Morrison on Choctaw Card #699					
12	No 4 died October 12, 1900: Proof of death filed Dec. 4, 1902					
13	No 4 died Oct. 12, 1900: Enrollment cancelled by Department July 8, 1904					
14	For child of No 1 see NB (March3,1905) #934.					
15	" " " " " (April26,1906) #483			Date of Application for Enrollment.		
16	Date of application for enrollment			April 27/99		
17	P.O. Garvin, I.T. 11/5/06					

100

Choctaw By Blood Enrollment Cards 1898-1914

RESIDENCE: Bok Tuklo   COUNTY.
POST OFFICE: Lukfata, I T.

Choctaw Nation

CARD NO.

Choctaw Roll
(Not Including Freedmen)   FIELD NO. **1001**

Dawes' Roll No.	NAME		Relationship to Person First Named	AGE	SEX	BLOOD	TRIBAL ENROLLMENT		
							Year	County	No.
2633	1 Willis, Sampson	36	First Named	33	M	Full	1896	Bok Tuklo	13422
2634	2 " , Emma	46	Wife	43	F	"	1896	" "	13423
	3								
	4								
	5	ENROLLMENT							
	6	OF NOS. 1 and 2 HEREON APPROVED BY THE SECRETARY							
	7	OF INTERIOR Dec 12, 1902							
	8								
	9								
	10								
	11								
	12								
	13								
	14								
	15								
	16								
	17								

TRIBAL ENROLLMENT OF PARENTS

	Name of Father	Year	County	Name of Mother	Year	County
1	Willis	Dead	Bok Tuklo	Ah-yo-uah	Dead	Bok Tuklo
2	Parker	"	" "	Susan Parker	"	" "
3						
4						
5						
6						
7	No.1 and 2 are seperated[sic]					
8	No2 on 1896 roll as Emmie Willis					
9	No1 said to be dead. Proof of death requested, Dec 5, 1902					
10						
11						
12						
13						
14						
15				Date of Application for Enrollment.		Apr. 27/99
16						
17						

Choctaw By Blood Enrollment Cards 1898-1914

RESIDENCE: Bok Tuklo   COUNTY.   **Choctaw Nation**   **Choctaw Roll**   CARD NO.
POST OFFICE: Lukfata, I.T.   *(Not Including Freedmen)*   FIELD NO. **1002**

Dawes' Roll No.	NAME		Relationship to Person	AGE	SEX	BLOOD	TRIBAL ENROLLMENT		
							Year	County	No.
2635	1 John, Albert	30	First Named	27	M	Full	1896	Bok Tuklo	6902
2636	2 " , Elizabeth	36	Wife	33	F	"	1896	" "	6903
2637	3 " , Watson	7	Son	4	M	"	1896	" "	6904
2638	4 " , Silmon ~~DIED PRIOR TO SEPTEMBER 25, 1902~~		"	2	"	"			
2639	5 " , Quintus	10	"	7	"	"	1896	" "	6905
2640	6 " , Isaac	2	Son	7mo	M	"			
	7								
	8								
	9								
	10								
	11	ENROLLMENT OF NOS. 1 2 3 4 5 and 6 HEREON APPROVED BY THE SECRETARY OF INTERIOR Dec. 12, 1902							
	12								
	13								
	14								
	15								
	16								
	17								

TRIBAL ENROLLMENT OF PARENTS

	Name of Father	Year	County	Name of Mother	Year	County
1	John Ishtiah	Dead	Bok Tuklo	Siney John	Dead	Bok Tuklo
2	Jackson Shota	"	Towson	Iney Shota	"	Towson
3	No. 1			No. 2		
4	~~No. 1~~			~~No. 2~~		
5	Johnson Mahatambe	Dead	Bok Tuklo	No. 2		
6	No. 1			No. 2		
7						
8	No2 on 1896 roll as Lizbet John					
9	No6 Enrolled May 8, 1901					
10	No4 died Oct. 7, 1899: Proof of death filed Dec. 3, 1902					
11	No4 died Oct. 7, 1899: Enrollment cancelled by Department July 8, 1904					
12	For child of Nos 1and2 see NB (April 26, 1906) Card No 815					
13	" " " " " " " " (March3,1905) " " 1026					
14						#1 to 5 ~~Date of Application for Enrollment.~~
15						
16			Date of application for Enrollment	Apr. 27/99		
17						

Choctaw By Blood Enrollment Cards 1898-1914

RESIDENCE: Bok Tuklo COUNTY. **Choctaw Nation** **Choctaw Roll** *(Not Including Freedmen)* CARD NO.
POST OFFICE: Lukfata, I.T. FIELD NO. **1003**

Dawes' Roll No.	NAME		Relationship to Person First Named	AGE	SEX	BLOOD	TRIBAL ENROLLMENT		
							Year	County	No.
2641	1 Parker, Stephen	33	First Named	30	M	Full	1896	Bok Tuklo	10384
2642	2 " Lena	9	Dau	6	F	"	1896	" "	10386
2643	3 " Edwin	7	Son	4	M	"	1896	" "	10387
2644	4 " Emerson	6	"	3	"	"	1896	" "	10388
	5								
	6								
	7	ENROLLMENT OF NOS. 1 2 3 and 4 HEREON APPROVED BY THE SECRETARY OF INTERIOR Dec 12 1902							
	8								
	9								
	10								
	11								
	12								
	13								
	14								
	15								
	16								
	17								

TRIBAL ENROLLMENT OF PARENTS

	Name of Father	Year	County	Name of Mother	Year	County
1	James Parker	Dead	Bok Tuklo	Susie Parker	Dead	Bok Tuklo
2	No. 1			Cealey Parker	"	" " "
3	No. 1		" "		"	" " "
4	No. 1		" "		"	" " "
5						
6						
7	No.2 on 1896 roll as Lemies Parker					
8	No.1 is now husband of Susan Wade on Choc. #1033			11-28-02		
9						
10						
11						
12						
13					Date of Application for Enrollment.	
14						
15					Apr 27/99	
16						
17						

Choctaw By Blood Enrollment Cards 1898-1914

RESIDENCE: Bok Tuklo   COUNTY.   **Choctaw Nation**   Choctaw Roll   CARD NO.

POST OFFICE: Lukfata, I.T.   *(Not Including Freedmen)*   FIELD NO. **1004**

Dawes' Roll No.	NAME	Relationship to Person First Named	AGE	SEX	BLOOD	TRIBAL ENROLLMENT		
						Year	County	No.
2645	1 Hickman, Coleman F. ~~DIED PRIOR TO SEPTEMBER 25, 1902~~	First Named	46	M	Full	1896	Bok Tuklo	5565
2646	2 " , Littie ³⁰	Wife	27	F	"	1896	" "	4160
2647	3 " , Wilson ¹⁸	Son	15	M	"	1896	" "	5568
2548	4 " , Thompson ¹⁹	Bro.	16	"	"	1896	" "	5569
	5							
	6							
	7							
	8							
	9							
	10							
	11							
	12							
	13							
	14							
	15							
	16							
	17							

ENROLLMENT OF NOS. 1 2 3 and 4 HEREON APPROVED BY THE SECRETARY OF INTERIOR Dec. 12, 1902

TRIBAL ENROLLMENT OF PARENTS

Name of Father	Year	County	Name of Mother	Year	County
1 ~~Fillo-min-tubbee~~	~~Dead~~	~~Bok Tuklo~~	~~Elsic~~	~~Dead~~	~~Bok Tuklo~~
2 Franklin	"	" "	Liza A. Simpson	1896	" "
3 No 1			Kinsie Hickman	Dead	" "
4 Fillo-min-tubbee	Dead	Bok Tuklo	Susan	"	" "
5					
6					
7					
8	No2 on 1896 roll as Littie Franklin				
9	No1 " 1896 " " C.F. Hickman				
10					
11	No1 died June 30,1900: Proof of death filed Dec. 3, 1902				
12	No4 is now husband of Sina Hinson on Choc Card #1011 Dec. 4/1902				
13	No1 died June 30, 1900: Enrollment cancelled by Department by July 8, 1904				
14					
15	For child of No4 see NB (Mar 3-1905) #18		Date of Application for Enrollment.	Apr. 27/99	
16					
17					

104

Choctaw By Blood Enrollment Cards 1898-1914

RESIDENCE: Eagle COUNTY.   **Choctaw Nation**   Choctaw Roll   CARD No.

POST OFFICE: Lukfata, I.T.   *(Not Including Freedmen)*   FIELD No. **1005**

Dawes' Roll No.	NAME		Relationship to Person	AGE	SEX	BLOOD	TRIBAL ENROLLMENT		
							Year	County	No.
2649	1 Tashka, Levi	22	First Named	19	M	Full	1896	Eagle	12239
	2								
	3								
	4	ENROLLMENT							
	5	OF NOS. 1 HEREON APPROVED BY THE SECRETARY							
	6	OF INTERIOR Dec 12, 1902							
	7								
	8								
	9								
	10								
	11								
	12								
	13								
	14								
	15								
	16								
	17								

TRIBAL ENROLLMENT OF PARENTS

	Name of Father	Year	County	Name of Mother	Year	County
1	Wallace Tashka	1896	Eagle	Isbie Tashka	Dead	Eagle
2						
3						
4						
5						
6						
7	Is No1 husband of Louisa Hayakonubbi on Choc. #620 6/4/01					
8	For child of No1 see NB (March 3, 1905) #1146.					
9						
10						
11						
12						
13						
14						
15					Date of Application for Enrollment.	Apr. 27/99
16						
17						

Choctaw By Blood Enrollment Cards 1898-1914

RESIDENCE: Eagle	COUNTY.	**Choctaw Nation**		**Choctaw Roll** (Not Including Freedmen)	CARD NO.	
POST OFFICE: Lukfata, I.T.					FIELD NO.	**1006**

Dawes' Roll No.	NAME	Relationship to Person First Named	AGE	SEX	BLOOD	TRIBAL ENROLLMENT		
						Year	County	No.
2650	1 Wilson, Cooper ~~DIED PRIOR TO SEPTEMBER 25, 1902~~	First Named	46	M	Full	1896	Eagle	13488
2651	2 ", Chisney ~~DIED PRIOR TO SEPTEMBER 25, 1902~~	Wife	45	F	"	1896	"	13489
2652	3 ", Mimie 18	Dau	15	F	"	1896	"	13497
2653	4 ", Bob 16	Son	13	M	"	1896	"	13557
2654	5 ", Stevison 10	"	7	"	"	1896	"	13542
	6							
	7							
	8							
	9							
	10							
	11							
	12							
	13							
	14							
	15 For child of No.3 see NB (March 3, 1905) #1530.							
	16							
	17							

ENROLLMENT OF NOS. 1234and5 HEREON APPROVED BY THE SECRETARY OF INTERIOR Dec 12, 1902

TRIBAL ENROLLMENT OF PARENTS

	Name of Father	Year	County	Name of Mother	Year	County
1	Tu-chen-a-by	Dead	Eagle	Betsey Wilson	1896	Eagle
2	Ma-he-etuby	"	"	Ish-te-mo-hohke	Dead	"
3	No 1			No 2		
4	No 1			No 2		
5	No 1			No 2		
6						
7						
8		No1 on 1896 roll as Cooper Wilson				
9		No2 " 1896 " " Chisney "				
10		No3 " 1896 " " Maimie Wilson				
		No5 " 1896 " " Stephen "				
11		No1 died Feby 1, 1900. Proof of death filed Dec. 24, 1902				
12		No2 Died Feby 24, 1900. Proof of death filed Dec 24, 1902				
13		No1 died Feb.1,1900. No2 died Feb24,1900. Enrollment cancelled by Department July 8, 1904 No3 Name changed from "Wilson" to "Mimie" and sex changed				
14		from "Male" to "Female" under Departmental authority of				Date of Application for Enrollment.
15		July 17, 1906 (I.T.D. 12528-1906) D.C. 30519-1906.				
16					Apr.	27/99
17						

RESIDENCE: Red River	COUNTY.								

RESIDENCE: Red River   **COUNTY.**   **Choctaw Nation**   **Choctaw Roll** *(Not Including Freedmen)*   **CARD No.**
POST OFFICE: Shawneetown, I.T.   **FIELD No. 1007**

Dawes' Roll No.	NAME	Relationship to Person First Named	AGE	SEX	BLOOD	TRIBAL ENROLLMENT		
						Year	County	No.
I.W. 221	1 Denison, John W 33	First Named	30	M	I.W.	1896	Red River	14471
2655	2 " Mary 24	Wife	21	F	Full	1893	Towson	P.R. 9
2656	3 " Henry C. 6	Son	3	M	1/2			
2657	4 " Sanford 4	"	8mo	"	1/2			
2658	5 " Lewie 1	"	3mo	"	1/2			
	6							
	7							
	8	ENROLLMENT OF NOS. 2 3 4 and 5 HEREON APPROVED BY THE SECRETARY OF INTERIOR Dec 12 1902						
	9							
	10							
	11	ENROLLMENT OF NOS. 1 HEREON APPROVED BY THE SECRETARY OF INTERIOR Sep 12 1903						
	12							
	13							
	14							
	15							
	16	For children of Nos. 1 & 2 see NB (Mar 3-1905) Card #17						
	17							

TRIBAL ENROLLMENT OF PARENTS

	Name of Father	Year	County	Name of Mother	Year	County
1	Sanford Denison	1896	Non Citz	Liza Denison	Dead	Non Citz
2	Hinta Hinson	Dead	Bok Tuklo	Sallie Hinson	"	Bok Tuklo
3	No.1			No.2		
4	No.1			No.2		
5	No.1			No.2		
6						
7						
8						
9	No.1 on 1896 roll as J.W. Denison He was also admitted					
10	by Dawes Commission Case No. 306, Dec.1,1896. No appeal					
11	No.2 on 1893 Pay Roll as Mary Hinson, Page 53, Towson Co No.3 Affidavit of birth to be supplied. Rec'd May 9/99					
12	No.4 " " " " " " " 9/99					
13	No.2 also on 1896 roll, Page 178, No. 7581, as Mamie Kinson, Red River Co.					
14	No.3 was admitted as a citizen by blood by Dawes Commission			#1 to 4		
15	in 1896 Choctaw Case #306: no appeal					
16	No.5 Enrolled Aug 9, 1901			Date of Application for Enrollment Apr. 27/99		
17						

Choctaw By Blood Enrollment Cards 1898-1914

RESIDENCE: Eagle   COUNTY.   **Choctaw Nation**   **Choctaw Roll**   CARD NO.
POST OFFICE: Lukfata, I.T.   *(Not Including Freedmen)*   FIELD NO. **1008**

Dawes' Roll No.	NAME	Relationship to Person	AGE	SEX	BLOOD	TRIBAL ENROLLMENT Year	TRIBAL ENROLLMENT County	TRIBAL ENROLLMENT No.
2659	1 Wilson, Bolin 51	First Named	48	M	Full	1896	Eagle	13555
2660	2 " , Lucy Ann 39	Wife	36	F	"	1896	"	13499
2661	3 " , Angeline 23	Dau	20	"	"	1896	"	13495
2662	4 " , Marcus 21	Son	18	M	"	1896	"	13496
2663	5 " , Raymond 19	"	16	"	"	1896	"	13552
2664	6 " , Ailin 17	Dau	14	F	"	1896	"	13558
	7							
	8 ENROLLMENT							
	9 OF NOS. 12345and6 HEREON APPROVED BY THE SECRETARY							
	10 OF INTERIOR Dec. 12, 1902							
	11							
	12							
	13							
	14							
	15							
	16							
	17							

TRIBAL ENROLLMENT OF PARENTS

Name of Father	Year	County	Name of Mother	Year	County
1 Ah-to-chin-ubbee	Dead	Eagle	Betsey	1896	Eagle
2 Tick-ba-tubbee	"	Bok Tuklo	Isin	1896	"
3 No 1			No 2		
4 No 1			No 2		
5 No 1			No 2		
6 No 1			No 2		
7					
8		No.4 on 1896 roll as Markis Wilson			
9		No.5 " 1896 " " Raymon "			
10		No.6 " 1896 " " Ailen "			
11					
12					
13					
14				Date of Application for Enrollment.	
15					
16				Apr. 27/99	
17					

Choctaw By Blood Enrollment Cards 1898-1914

RESIDENCE: Eagle   COUNTY.   **Choctaw Nation**   Choctaw Roll *(Not Including Freedmen)*   CARD NO.

POST OFFICE: Lukfata, I.T.   FIELD NO. 1009

Dawes' Roll No.	NAME	Relationship to Person First Named	AGE	SEX	BLOOD	TRIBAL ENROLLMENT		
						Year	County	No.
2665	1 Tikebatubbi, Isin 56	First Named	53	F	Full	1896	Eagle	12233
	2							
	3							
	4							
	5							
	6							
	7							
	8							
	9							
	10							
	11							
	12							
	13							
	14							
	15							
	16							
	17							

ENROLLMENT
OF NOS. 1 HEREON
APPROVED BY THE SECRETARY
OF INTERIOR DEC 12 1902

TRIBAL ENROLLMENT OF PARENTS

	Name of Father	Year	County	Name of Mother	Year	County
1	Billy Frye	Dead		Pisa-hok-te	Dead	Bok Tuklo
2						
3						
4						
5						
6						
7	On 1896 roll as Aisin Tikbatubbi					
8						
9						
10						
11						
12						
13						
14						
15						
16				Date of Application for Enrollment	Apr. 27/99	
17						

Choctaw By Blood Enrollment Cards 1898-1914

RESIDENCE: Eagle   COUNTY.
POST OFFICE: Eagletown, I.T.

Choctaw Nation

Choctaw Roll
(Not Including Freedmen)

CARD NO.
FIELD NO. **1010**

Dawes' Roll No.	NAME	Relationship to Person First Named	AGE	SEX	BLOOD	TRIBAL ENROLLMENT Year	County	No.
2666	1 Billy, Wilmon 43	First Named	40	M	Full	1896	Eagle	1333
2667	2 " Lisiana 41	Wife	38	F	"	1896	"	1260
2668	3 " Simon 23	Son	20	M	"	1896	"	1318
2669	4 " Naswis 21	Dau	18	F	"	1896	"	1304
2670	5 " Nelis 19	"	16	"	"	1896	"	1305
2671	6 " Salisa 15	"	12	"	"	1896	"	1319
2672	7 DIED PRIOR TO SEPTEMBER 25, 1902 Sissy	"	7	"	"	1896	"	1320
2673	8 " Easton 8	Son	5	M	"	1896	"	1273
14631	9 " Winnissie 6	Dau	3	F	"			
2674	10 " Watson 17	S.Son	14	M	"	1896	Eagle	1330
2675	11 " Linda 15	"	12	F	"	1896	"	1295
	12 No.10 on 1896 roll as Watson							
	13 Larsin, Page 199, No.8024							
	14 Eagles Co. No.3 is now husband of Jincey Jefferson Choc card #1185							
	14 No.11 on 1896 roll as Lindley							
	15 Larsin, Page 199, No 8025 No.9 Proof of birth received filed Dec 8, 1902							
	16 Eagle Co.							
	17 No.7 died March 25, 1902 proof of death filed Dec 3, 1902							

TRIBAL ENROLLMENT OF PARENTS

	Name of Father	Year	County	Name of Mother	Year	County
1	Billy	Dead	Eagle	Amas-hu-na	Dead	Eagle
2	Benjamin	"	"	Sha-wa-na	1896	Nashoba
3	No.1	ENROLLMENT		Eunice Billy	Dead	Eagle
4	No.1	OF NOS. 1 2 3 4 5 6 7 8 9 10 and 11 HEREON APPROVED BY THE SECRETARY		" "	" "	" "
5	No.1	OF INTERIOR Dec 12 1902		" "	" "	" "
6	No.1			" "	" "	" "
7	No.1			No.2		
8	No.1			No.2	ENROLLMENT	
9	No.1			No.2	OF NOS. ~9~ HEREON APPROVED BY THE SECRETARY
10	Larsen Arteubbee	Dead	Eagle	No.2	OF INTERIOR May 20, 1903
11	" "	"	"	No.2		
12	No.2 on 1896 roll as Alisana Billy					
13	No.7 " 1896 " " Sisey	"				
14	No.8 " 1896 " " Eston	"				
15	No.11 " 1896 " " Lena				Date of Application for Enrollment.
15	For child of No4 see N.B. (Apr 26/06) Card #490				
16	" " " 5 " "	"	" " "		Apr 27/99
16	" " " 6 " "	"	" "586		
17	" " " 1&2 " "	"	" "915		

110

Choctaw By Blood Enrollment Cards 1898-1914

RESIDENCE: Bok Tuklo   COUNTY. **Choctaw Nation**   Choctaw Roll   CARD NO.
POST OFFICE: Lukfata, I.T.   *(Not Including Freedmen)*   FIELD NO. **1011**

Dawes' Roll No.	NAME	Relationship to Person First Named	AGE	SEX	BLOOD	TRIBAL ENROLLMENT Year	County	No.
2676	1 Hinson, David 31	First Named	28	M	Full	1896	Bok Tuklo	5556
2677	2 " Sina 21	Sister	18	F	"	1896	" "	5479
2678	3 Jefferson, Mollie 20	Ward	17	"	"	1896	" "	6920
	4							
	5							
	6							
	7							
	8							
	9							
	10							
	11	ENROLLMENT						
	12	OF NOS. 1 2 and 3 HEREON APPROVED BY THE SECRETARY						
	13	OF INTERIOR DEC 12 1902						
	14							
	15							
	16							
	17							

TRIBAL ENROLLMENT OF PARENTS

	Name of Father	Year	County	Name of Mother	Year	County
1	Hin-da-bay	Dead	Bok Tuklo	Le-tus	Dead	Bok Tuklo
2	"	"	" "	Sallie	"	" "
3	Mullis Jefferson	"	" "	Wisey Jefferson	"	" "
4						
5						
6						
7						
8						

9   No1 on 1896 roll as David Henderson
10   No3 " 1896 " " Marley Jefferson
   No2 also on 1896 roll as Sany Henderson
11   Page 135 No 5538, Bok Tuklo
12   No. 1 is the husband of Elian Ward on Choc. card #664
13   No2 is now wife of Thompson Hickman on Choc card #1004
   Evidence of marriage recd Dec 4, 1902.
14

15   Date of Application for Enrollment.
16   For child of No2 see NB (Mar 3-1905) Card No 18.   Apr. 27/99
17   Glover I.T. 12/10/02

111

Choctaw By Blood Enrollment Cards 1898-1914

RESIDENCE: Eagle   COUNTY.   **Choctaw Nation**   Choctaw Roll   CARD NO.

POST OFFICE: Eagletown, I.T.   *(Not Including Freedmen)*   FIELD NO. **1012**

Dawes' Roll No.	NAME	Relationship to Person	AGE	SEX	BLOOD	TRIBAL ENROLLMENT		
						Year	County	No.
2679	1 Going, Isham ~~DIED PRIOR TO SEPTEMBER 25, 1902~~	First Named	71	M	Full	1896	Eagle	4789
2680	2 Konatima ~~DIED PRIOR TO SEPTEMBER 25, 1902~~	Wife	56	F	"	1896	"	4794
	3							
	4							
	5							
	6							
	7							
	8							
	9							
	10							
	11							
	12							
	13							
	14							
	15							
	16							
	17							

ENROLLMENT OF NOS. 1 and 2 HEREON APPROVED BY THE SECRETARY OF INTERIOR Dec 12 1902

TRIBAL ENROLLMENT OF PARENTS

Name of Father	Year	County	Name of Mother	Year	County
1 Jim Going	Dead	Jackson	Ha-ka-tema	Dead	Eagle
2 Ka-non-tobbe	"	in Mississippi	Ko-ne-ah-ho-ma	"	"
3					
4					
5					
6					
7		No 2 on 1896 roll as Konitima Going			
8		No1 died May 26, 1901: proof of death filed Dec 3, 1902			
9	No2 " Sept 30, 1899: No.1 died May26,1901: No.2 died Sept30,1899: Enrollment cancelled by Department July8,1904				
10					
11					
12					
13					
14					
15				Date of Application for Enrollment.	
16				Apr. 27/99	
17					

Choctaw By Blood Enrollment Cards 1898-1914

RESIDENCE: Bok Tuklo COUNTY.
POST OFFICE: Lukfata, I.T.

Choctaw Nation

Choctaw Roll *(Not Including Freedmen)*

CARD NO.
FIELD NO. **1013**

Dawes' Roll No.	NAME			Relationship to Person First Named	AGE	SEX	BLOOD	TRIBAL ENROLLMENT		
								Year	County	No.
2681	1 Henderson, Abel	42		First Named	39	M	Full	1896	Bok Tuklo	5559
2682	2 " , Mary	57		Wife	54	F	"	1896	" "	5560
2683	3 Hickman, Winie	20		Dau	17	"	"	1896	" "	5561
2684	4 ~~Henderson, Hettie~~ DIED PRIOR TO SEPTEMBER 25, 1902			"	14	"	"	1896	" "	5562
2685	5 Jackson, Jesse	20		Ward	17	M	"	1896	" "	6927
2686	6 Hickman, Joseph	2		Grandson	1	M	"			
	7									
	8									
	9									
	10									
	11									
	12									
	13									
	14									
	15									
	16									
	17									

ENROLLMENT
OF NOS. 1 2 3 4 5 and 6 HEREON
APPROVED BY THE SECRETARY
OF INTERIOR Dec 12 1902

TRIBAL ENROLLMENT OF PARENTS

	Name of Father	Year	County	Name of Mother	Year	County
1	Me-hin-tubbee	Dead	Bok Tuklo	Se-win	Dead	Bok Tuklo
2	Ta-na-pun-abee	"	" "	A-me-hutcho	"	" " "
3	No.1			No.2		
4	~~No.1~~			~~No.2~~		
5	Amos Jackson	Dead	Bok Tuklo	Naise Jackson	Dead	Bok Tuklo
6	James Hickman	1896	Bok Tuklo1	No.3		
7						
8			No5 on 1896 roll as Jessie Jackson			
9			No3 is the wife of James Hickman on Choctaw card #1192, Nov 15, 1901			
10			No.6 born Dec. 25, 1900: Enrolled Nov 15, 1901.			
11						
12			No4 died May 16, 1902: proof of death filed Dec 6, 1902.			
13			No.4 died May 16, 1902: Enrollment cancelled by Department July 8, 1904			
14					Date of Application for Enrollment.	#1 to 5 inc
15						
16					Apr 27/99	
17						

113

Choctaw By Blood Enrollment Cards 1898-1914

RESIDENCE: Bok Tuklo   COUNTY. **Choctaw Nation**   **Choctaw Roll**   CARD No.
POST OFFICE: Lukfata, I.T.   *(Not Including Freedmen)*   FIELD No. **1014**

Dawes' Roll No.	NAME	Relationship to Person First Named	AGE	SEX	BLOOD	TRIBAL ENROLLMENT Year	County	No.
Dead	1 Mintihaya, Ayahona		60	F	Full	1893	Bok Tuklo	P.R. 195
2687	2 Mintihaya, Silmy ³¹	Dau	28	"	"	1893	" "	196
	3							
	4							
	5							
	6	ENROLLMENT						
	7	OF NOS. 2 HEREON APPROVED BY THE SECRETARY OF INTERIOR Dec 12 1902						
	8							
	9							
	10	No. 1 HEREON DISMISSED UNDER ORDER OF THE COMMISSION TO THE FIVE						
	11	CIVILIZED TRIBES OF MARCH 31, 1905.						
	12							
	13							
	14							
	15							
	16							
	17							

TRIBAL ENROLLMENT OF PARENTS

	Name of Father	Year	County	Name of Mother	Year	County
1	Died in Mississippi			Died in Mississippi		
2	Mintihaya	Dead	Bok Tuklo	No 1		
3						
4						
5	No2 on 1893 Pay roll as Salmy Mintihaya					
6						
7	No1 Died October 20, 1900. Evidence of death filed April 12, 1901					
8						
9	No2 said to be duplicate of No1 on Choctaw card #4903 who died in					
10	Spring of 1900					
11						
12						
13						
14						
15						
16				Date of Application for Enrollment	Apr. 27/99	
17						

114

Choctaw By Blood Enrollment Cards 1898-1914

RESIDENCE: Bok Tuklo   COUNTY. **Choctaw Nation**   **Choctaw Roll** CARD NO.
POST OFFICE: Lukfata, I.T.   *(Not Including Freedmen)* FIELD NO. 1015

Dawes' Roll No.	NAME	Relationship to Person First Named	AGE	SEX	BLOOD	TRIBAL ENROLLMENT		
						Year	County	No.
2688	1 Jackson, Susan 53	First Named	50	F	Full	1896	Bok Tuklo	6901
	2							
	3							
	4	ENROLLMENT OF NOS. 1 HEREON APPROVED BY THE SECRETARY OF INTERIOR DEC 12 1902						
	5							
	6							
	7							
	8							
	9							
	10							
	11							
	12							
	13							
	14							
	15							
	16							
	17							

TRIBAL ENROLLMENT OF PARENTS

	Name of Father	Year	County	Name of Mother	Year	County
1	Charley Cullin	Dead	Bok Tuklo		Dead	Eagle
2						
3						
4						
5						
6						
7						
8						
9						
10						
11						
12						
13						
14						
15						
16					Date of Application for Enrollment	Apr. 27/99
17						

Choctaw By Blood Enrollment Cards 1898-1914

RESIDENCE: Bok Tuklo   COUNTY: **Choctaw Nation**   **Choctaw Roll**   CARD NO.

POST OFFICE: Lukfata, O.T.   *(Not Including Freedmen)*   FIELD NO. **1016**

Dawes' Roll No.		NAME	Relationship to Person First Named	AGE	SEX	BLOOD	TRIBAL ENROLLMENT		
							Year	County	No.
2689	1	DIED PRIOR TO SEPTEMBER 25, 1902 Louis, Simon 48	First Named	45	M	Full	1896	Bok Tuklo	8008
2690	2	" Liza 51	Wife	48	F	"	1896	" "	8009
	3								
	4								
	5	ENROLLMENT							
	6	OF NOS. 1 and 2 HEREON APPROVED BY THE SECRETARY							
	7	OF INTERIOR DEC 12 1902							
	8								
	9								
	10								
	11								
	12								
	13								
	14								
	15								
	16								
	17								

TRIBAL ENROLLMENT OF PARENTS

	Name of Father	Year	County	Name of Mother	Year	County
1	Louis Mahah	Dead	Bok Tuklo	Noah-e-ma	Dead	Bok Tuklo
2	A-ka-nan-tubbee	"	" "	Ka-ne-a-hona	"	" "
3						
4						
5						
6						
7		No1 on 1896 roll as Silborn Louis				
8		No2 " 1896 " " Lissie "				
9						
10		No1 died Oct 10/99; proof of death filed Dec 3, 1902				
11	No1 died Oct 10 1899: Enrollment cancelled by Department July 8, 1904					
12						
13						
14						
15						
16					Date of Application for Enrollment	Apr. 27/99
17						

Choctaw By Blood Enrollment Cards 1898-1914

RESIDENCE: Bok Tuklo COUNTY. **Choctaw Nation** Choctaw Roll CARD NO.
POST OFFICE: Lukfata, I.T. *(Not Including Freedmen)* FIELD NO. 1017

Dawes' Roll No.	NAME		Relationship to Person First Named	AGE	SEX	BLOOD	TRIBAL ENROLLMENT		
							Year	County	No.
2691	1 Thomas, Ben W.	34	First Named	31	M	Full	1896	Bok Tuklo	12180
2692	2 " Edna	36	Wife	33	F	"	1896	" "	12181
2693	3 " Lena	11	Dau	8	"	"	1896	" "	12182
2694	4 " Webster	9	Son	6	M	"	1896	" "	12183
	5								
	6								
	7	ENROLLMENT OF NOS. 1 2 3 and 4 HEREON APPROVED BY THE SECRETARY OF INTERIOR DEC 12 1902							
	8								
	9								
	10								
	11								
	12								
	13								
	14								
	15								
	16								
	17								

TRIBAL ENROLLMENT OF PARENTS

	Name of Father	Year	County	Name of Mother	Year	County
1	Washington Thomas	Dead	Bok Tuklo	Phoebe Thomas	1896	Bok Tuklo
2	Ah-po-wan-toby	"	" "	Nora	Dead	" "
3	No1			No2		
4	No1			No2		
5						
6						
7			No1 on 1896 roll as B. W. Thomas			
8						
9			For child of No2 see N.B. (Apr 26-06) Card #325			
10						
11						
12						
13						
14						
15					Date of Application for Enrollment.	
16					Apr. 27/99	
17						

Choctaw By Blood Enrollment Cards 1898-1914

	NAME	Relationship to Person First Named	AGE	SEX	BLOOD	TRIBAL ENROLLMENT		
						Year	County	No.
2695	1 Peter, Simon J 55	First Named	52	M	Full	1896	Bok Tuklo	10390
2696	2 Sophie	Wife	40	F	"	1896	" "	10391
2697	3 " Sibbie 8	Dau	5	"	"	1896	" "	10393
2698	4 " Lyda 6	"	2	"	"			
2699	5 Tikbombe, Henry 13	Ward	10	M	"	1896	Bok Tuklo	P.R. 216
	6							
	7							
	8							
	9							
	10							
	11							
	12							
	13							
	14							
	15							
	16							
	17							

DIED PRIOR TO SEPTEMBER 25, 1902

ita, I.T. COUNTY. **Choctaw Nation** Choctaw Roll (Not Including Freedmen) CARD No. FIELD No. **1018**

ENROLLMENT OF NOS. 1 2 3 4 and 5 HEREON APPROVED BY THE SECRETARY OF INTERIOR DEC 12 1902

TRIBAL ENROLLMENT OF PARENTS

	Name of Father	Year	County	Name of Mother	Year	County
1	Pish-tash-a-bee	Dead	Bok Tuklo	Na-ne-ma	Dead	Bok Tuklo
2	Ah-took-lan-tubbee	"	" "	Sukey	"	" "
3	No 1			No 2		
4	No 1			No 2		
5	Alfred Tikbombe	Dead	Bok Tuklo	Ellen Tikbombe	Dead	Bok Tuklo
6						
7						
8		No1 on 1896 roll as S.J. Peter				
9		No3 " 1896 " " Sibbey "				
10		No5 " 1893 Pay roll as Henry Tikbambe				
		No5 is now living with Sallie Durant Choc #1701				
11		No 2 died Jan. 8, 1901; Enrollment cancelled by Department July 8, 1904				
12						
13						
14					Date of Application for Enrollment.	
15						
16					Apr. 27/99	
17						

Choctaw By Blood Enrollment Cards 1898-1914

RESIDENCE: Eagle   COUNTY. **Choctaw Nation**   **Choctaw Roll** *(Not Including Freedmen)*   CARD NO.

POST OFFICE: Lukfata, I.T.   FIELD NO. 1019

Dawes' Roll No.	NAME		Relationship to Person First Named	AGE	SEX	BLOOD	TRIBAL ENROLLMENT		
							Year	County	No.
2700	1 Anderson, Louis	49	First Named	46	M	Full	1896	Eagle	287
2701	2 " Louisa	44	Wife	41	F	"	1896	"	288
2702	3 " Roberson	18	Son	15	M	"	1896	"	298
2703	4 " Jimmie	12	"	9	"	"	1893	"	P.R. 28
2704	5 " Sillian	8	Dau	5	F	"	1896	"	274
	6								
	7	ENROLLMENT OF NOS. 1 2 3 4 and 5 HEREON APPROVED BY THE SECRETARY OF INTERIOR DEC 12 1902							
	8								
	9								
	10								
	11								
	12								
	13								
	14								
	15								
	16								
	17								

TRIBAL ENROLLMENT OF PARENTS

	Name of Father	Year	County	Name of Mother	Year	County
1	E-le-nin-me	Dead	Eagle	E-chop-e-huna	Dead	Eagle
2	Ya-hok-a-tubbee	"	"	Ka-na-e-ma	1896	"
3	No1			No2		
4	No1			No2		
5	No1			No2		
6						
7			No5 on 1896 roll as Eleah Anderson			
8						
9			No4 on 1896 roll, Eagle Co, Page [sic], No7 No282			
10						
11						
12						
13						
14					Date of Application for Enrollment.	
15						
16					Apr. 27/99	
17						

Choctaw By Blood Enrollment Cards 1898-1914

RESIDENCE: Eagle   COUNTY.   **Choctaw Nation**   **Choctaw Roll**   CARD NO.

POST OFFICE: Lukfata, I.T.   *(Not Including Freedmen)*   FIELD NO. **1020**

Dawes' Roll No.	NAME	Relationship to Person	AGE	SEX	BLOOD	TRIBAL ENROLLMENT		
						Year	County	No.
2705	1 Anderson, Eliza ²⁵	First Named	22	F	Full	1896	Eagle	270
2706	2 " Wicey ¹⁰	Dau	7	"	"	1896	"	304
	3							
	4							
	5	ENROLLMENT						
	6	OF NOS. 1 and 2 HEREON APPROVED BY THE SECRETARY						
	7	OF INTERIOR Dec 2 1902						
	8							
	9							
	10							
	11							
	12							
	13							
	14							
	15							
	16							
	17							

TRIBAL ENROLLMENT OF PARENTS

Name of Father	Year	County	Name of Mother	Year	County
1 Louis Anderson	1896	Eagle	Louisa Anderson	1896	Eagle
2 John McKinney	1896	"	No.1		
3					
4					
5					
6					
7		For child of no.1 see NB (March 3, 1905) #1147			
8					
9					
10					
11					
12					
13					
14				Date of Application for Enrollment.	
15					
16				Apr. 27/99	
17					

Choctaw By Blood Enrollment Cards 1898-1914

RESIDENCE: Cedar COUNTY.				
POST OFFICE: Doaksville, I.T.				

Choctaw Nation
Choctaw Roll *(Not Including Freedmen)*
CARD NO. FIELD NO. **1021**

Dawes' Roll No.	NAME	Relationship to Person First Named	AGE	SEX	BLOOD	TRIBAL ENROLLMENT Year	TRIBAL ENROLLMENT County	No.
2707	1 Taylor, John ⁵⁵	First Named	52	M	Full	1896	Cedar	12090
2708	2 " Margaret ⁵⁷	Wife	54	F	"	1896	"	12091
2709	3 " Selin ²⁹	Son	26	M	"	1893	"	P.R. 438
2710	4 Cobb, Selena ¹³	Ward	10	F	"	1896	"	2445
	5							
	6							
	7	ENROLLMENT OF NOS. 1 2 3 and 4 HEREON						
	8	APPROVED BY THE SECRETARY OF INTERIOR Dec 12 1902						
	9							
	10							
	11							
	12							
	13							
	14							
	15							
	16							
	17							

TRIBAL ENROLLMENT OF PARENTS

Name of Father	Year	County	Name of Mother	Year	County
1 Fih-na-bbee	Dead	Cedar	Ikla-ho-na	Dead	Cedar
2 Ish-te-mabee	"	Towson	E-to-na-hona	"	Towson
3 No.1			No.2		
4 Ellis Cobb	Dead	Nashoba	Nicey Cobb	Dead	Cedar
5					
6					
7					
8	No4 on 1896 Celena Cobb				
9	No.3 " 1893 Pay roll as Celum Taylor also on 1896				
10	roll Page 314 No. 12092, Solomon Taylor, Cedar Co.				
11					
12	Nº3 was married in Jany. or Feby. 1900 to Sophia Choate				
13	Choctaw card #806. See his testimony and that of Reason				
14	See 7-806 and 1826 Hopson of May 22, 1903				
15					
16		Date of Application for Enrollment Apr. 27/99			
17	For child of No.3 see NB (Mar 3-1905) #20				

" " " " " " " " " #627

121

Choctaw By Blood Enrollment Cards 1898-1914

RESIDENCE: Bok Tuklo COUNTY. **Choctaw Nation** Choctaw Roll CARD NO.

POST OFFICE: Lukfata, I.T. *(Not Including Freedmen)* FIELD NO. 1022

Dawes' Roll No.	NAME	Relationship to Person First Named	AGE	SEX	BLOOD	TRIBAL ENROLLMENT		
						Year	County	No.
DEAD	1 Sampson, Laymus B		39	M	Full	1896	Bok Tuklo	11425
2711	2 " Lisean 46	Wife	43	F	"	1896	" "	11426
2712	3 Franklin, Harkins 23	S.Son	20	M	"	1896	" "	4161
	4							
	5 ENROLLMENT							
	6 OF NOS. 2 and 3 HEREON APPROVED BY THE SECRETARY							
	7 OF INTERIOR DEC 12 1902							
	8							
	9							
	10 No. 1 HEREON DISMISSED UNDER							
	11 ORDER OF THE COMMISSION TO THE FIVE CIVILIZED TRIBES OF MARCH 31, 1905							
	12							
	13							
	14							
	15							
	16							
	17							

TRIBAL ENROLLMENT OF PARENTS

	Name of Father	Year	County	Name of Mother	Year	County
1	Billy Sampson	Dead	Bok Tuklo	Eve Sampson	Dead	Bok Tuklo
2	Geo. Tikbombe	"	" "	Ah-no-le-huna	"	" "
3	Franklin Campbell	"	" "	No 2		
4						
5						
6						
7	No2 on 1896 roll as Lasian Sampson					
8	No1 " 1896 " " L.B. "					
9	No1 Died Dec. 15, 1900, proof of death filed Nov. 10, 1902. For child of No.3 see N.B. (Apr. 26, 1906) Card No. 33					
10						
11						
12						
13						
14				Date of Application for Enrollment.		
15						
16				Apr. 27/99		
17						

122

Choctaw By Blood Enrollment Cards 1898-1914

RESIDENCE: Red River   COUNTY.   **Choctaw Nation**   **Choctaw Roll** *(Not Including Freedmen)*   CARD NO.

POST OFFICE: Kullituklo, I.T.   FIELD NO.   1023

Dawes' Roll No.	NAME	Relationship to Person First Named	AGE	SEX	BLOOD	Year	County	No.
Dead	1 Harley, Thomas		72	M	Full	1896	Red River	5663
2713	2 Maytobe, Annie ¹⁸	Ward	15	F	"	1896	" "	12297
2714	3 " Lazin ¹	Dau of № 2	5mo	F	"			
	4							
	5	ENROLLMENT OF NOS. 2 and 3 HEREON APPROVED BY THE SECRETARY OF INTERIOR DEC 12 1902						
	6							
	7							
	8							
	9 No. 1 HEREON DISMISSED UNDER ORDER OF THE COMMISSION TO THE FIVE CIVILIZED TRIBES OF MARCH 31, 1905.							
	10							
	11							
	12							
	13							
	14							
	15							
	16							
	17							

TRIBAL ENROLLMENT OF PARENTS

	Name of Father	Year	County	Name of Mother	Year	County
1	Pish-ban-ubbee	Dead	Red River	Pisa-ho-na	Dead	Red River
2	Kan-e-mon-abee	"	" "	Nancy	"	" "
3	Benson Maytobe	1896	Red River	No.2		
4						
5						
6						
7	No1 Died August 5, 1900. Evidence of death filed April 9, 1901.					
8	No.2 is now the wife of Benson Maytobe on Choc. card 601 Feby 17, 1902.					
9	No.3 born Sept. 10, 1901. Enrolled Feb. 17, 1902.					
10						
11						
12						
13						
14						
15				#1&2		
16				Date of Application for Enrollment	Apr. 27/99	
17						

123

Choctaw By Blood Enrollment Cards 1898-1914

RESIDENCE: Red River COUNTY.
POST OFFICE: Kullituklo, I.T.

Choctaw Nation

Choctaw Roll
(Not Including Freedmen)

CARD NO.
FIELD NO. 1024

Dawes' Roll No.	NAME	Relationship to Person First Named	AGE	SEX	BLOOD	TRIBAL ENROLLMENT Year	County	No.
2715	1 Watkins, Ben 44	First Named	41	M	Full	1896	Red River	13687
2716	2 " Silva 43	Wife	40	F	"	1896	" "	13688
2717	3 Fisher, Sibbel 12	S.Dau	9	"	"	1896	" "	4221
	4							
	5							
	6							
	7	ENROLLMENT OF NOS. 1 2 and 3 HEREON						
	8	APPROVED BY THE SECRETARY						
	9	OF INTERIOR DEC 12 1902						
	10							
	11							
	12							
	13							
	14							
	15							
	16							
	17							

TRIBAL ENROLLMENT OF PARENTS

Name of Father	Year	County	Name of Mother	Year	County
1 Isaac Watkins	Dead	Red River	Okla-ho-tema	Dead	Eagle
2 Ka-lo-cha-ta-he	"	" "	Ah-tob-bee	"	Red River
3 Stephen Peter	"	" "	No 2		
4					
5					
6					
7	No1 on 1896 roll as Ben Watkin				
8	No2 " 1896 " " Silve "				
9					
10					
11					
12					
13					
14					
15					
16			Date of Application for Enrollment Apr. 27/99		
17					

Choctaw By Blood Enrollment Cards 1898-1914

RESIDENCE: Red River   COUNTY. **Choctaw Nation**   **Choctaw Roll**   CARD NO.
POST OFFICE: Kullituklo, I.T.   *(Not Including Freedmen)*   FIELD NO. **1025**

Dawes' Roll No.	NAME	Relationship to Person First Named	AGE	SEX	BLOOD	TRIBAL ENROLLMENT Year	County	No.
2718	1 Kincade, George ⁵⁸		55	M	Full	1896	Red River	7561
DEAD	2 " Lyman DEAD	Son	22	"	"	1896	" "	7562
	3							
	4							
	5	ENROLLMENT OF NOS. ~ 1 ~ HEREON						
	6	APPROVED BY THE SECRETARY OF INTERIOR Dec 2 1902						
	7							
	8	No. 2 hereon dismissed under order						
	9	of the Commission to the Five Civilized						
	10	Tribes of March 31, 1905.						
	11							
	12							
	13							
	14							
	15							
	16							
	17							

TRIBAL ENROLLMENT OF PARENTS

	Name of Father	Year	County	Name of Mother	Year	County
1	Andy Kincade	Dead	Bok Tuklo	Polly Kincade	Dead	Bok Tuklo
2	No. 1			Salina Kincade	"	" " "
3						
4						
5						
6						
7	No. 1 on 1896 roll as George Kincaide					
8	No.2 " 1896 " " Lemon "					
9						
10	No. 2 died April 24, 1899; proof of death filed Dec 3, 1902					
11						
12						
13						
14				Date of Application for Enrollment.		
15				Apr 27/99		
16						
17						

Choctaw By Blood Enrollment Cards 1898-1914

RESIDENCE: Towson COUNTY.
POST OFFICE: Alikchi, I.T.

Choctaw Nation
Choctaw Roll *(Not Including Freedmen)*

CARD NO.
FIELD NO. 1026

NAME	Relationship to Person First Named	AGE	SEX	BLOOD	TRIBAL ENROLLMENT		
					Year	County	No.
1 Caldwell, Willie 29	First Named	26	M	1/2	1896	Towson	2473
2 " Mary Ann 24	Wife	21	F	Full	1896	"	2474
3 " Clarissa 6	Dau	3	"	3/4	1896	"	2475
4 " Nancy ~~DIED PRIOR TO SEPTEMBER 25~~ 1902 "	"	6m	"	3/4			
2723 5 " Mycie 2	Dau	2½mo	F	3/4			
2724 6 " Molcy 2	Dau	2½mo	F	3/4			
7							
8							
9							
10							
11							
12							
13							
14							
15							
16							
17							

ENROLLMENT
OF NOS. 12345and6 HEREON
APPROVED BY THE SECRETARY
OF INTERIOR DEC 12 1902

TRIBAL ENROLLMENT OF PARENTS

Name of Father	Year	County	Name of Mother	Year	County
1 Finnie Caldwell	1896	Non Citz	Liza Caldwell	Dead	Towson
2 Johnson Wallace	Dead	Nashoba	Hanie Wallace	"	Nashoba
3 No1			No2		
4 ~~No1~~			~~No2~~		
5 No1			No.2		
6 No. 1			No. 2		
7					
8		~~No5 Enrolled April 25, 1901.~~			
9		No6 Enrolled April 25, 1901.			
10		Nos 5 and 6 are twins			
11		No4 died Sept 17, 1902; proof of death filed Dec 3, 1902.			
12		~~No.4 died Sept. 17, 1902. Enrollment cancelled by Department July 8, 1904~~			
13		For child of Nos. 1 and 2 see NB (Mar 3 '05) #438			
14				#1to4 inc	
15				Date of Application for Enrollment. Apr 27/99	
16 P O Rufe I T 3/14/07					
17 Doaksville I.T 11/20/02					

Choctaw By Blood Enrollment Cards 1898-1914

RESIDENCE: Cedar COUNTY.
POST OFFICE: Doaksville, I.T.

Choctaw Nation

Choctaw Roll *(Not Including Freedmen)*

CARD No.
FIELD No. **1027**

Dawes' Roll No.		NAME		Relationship to Person First Named	AGE	SEX	BLOOD	TRIBAL ENROLLMENT		
								Year	County	No.
DEAD	1	Loman, Gillum DEAD		First Named	45	M	Full	1896	Cedar	7896
Dead	2	" Nancy		Wife	53	F	"	1896	"	7899
2725	3	Loman Willie	11	Ward	8	M	1/2	1896	Towson	7931
14632	4	" Gilliam	1	Son	2mo	M	1/2			
I.W. 632	5	" Nellie E.	18	Wife	18	F	I.W.			
	6	ENROLLMENT								
	7	OF NOS. 3 HEREON APPROVED BY THE SECRETARY					No. 2 hereon dismissed under order of the Commission to the Five Civilized Tribes of March 31, 1905.			
	8	OF INTERIOR Dec 12 1902								
	9									
	10	ENROLLMENT OF NOS. 4 HEREON								
	11	APPROVED BY THE SECRETARY								
	12	OF INTERIOR May 20 1903								
	13	ENROLLMENT								
	14	OF NOS. ~ 5 ~ HEREON APPROVED BY THE SECRETARY								
	15	OF INTERIOR Mar 26 1904								
	16			No1 died April 28, 1902: Proof of death filed May 28, 1902							
	17	No. 1 DisMissed Aug 22 1906									

TRIBAL ENROLLMENT OF PARENTS

	Name of Father	Year	County	Name of Mother	Year	County
1	Forbis Loman	Dead	Towson	Lucy Cravatte	Dead	Cedar
2	John Thompson	"	Cedar	Betsy Thompson	"	"
3			Non Citz	Alice Loman	"	Towson
4	Nº 1			Nellie Loman		intermarried
5	George Brandon		noncitizen	Josie Brandon		noncitizen
6						
7						
8						
9						
10	No3's father was a white man name unknown.					
11	No.2 died August 13, 1899. Evidence of death filed April 18, 1901.					
12	No.1 died April 28, 1902: see testimony of Nellie Loman: May 28, 1902					
13	No1 was the husband of Nellie Loman on Choctaw card #D729					
14	No 4 Born Aug 14, 1902 enrolled Oct 20, 1902					
15	No.5 transferred from Choctaw card D729 January 23, 1904:					
16	See decision of January 6 1904				#1 to 3 inc	
17	P.O. Hugo I.T. 7/3/04			Date of Application for Enrollment	Apr. 28/99	

For child of No.5 see NB. (Apr 26 '06) #1154

127

RESIDENCE: Cedar   COUNTY.
POST OFFICE: Doaksville, I.T.

Choctaw Nation

Choctaw Roll *(Not Including Freedmen)*

CARD NO.
FIELD NO. **1028**

Dawes' Roll No.	NAME		Relationship to Person First Named	AGE	SEX	BLOOD	TRIBAL ENROLLMENT Year	County	No.
2726	1 Taylor, John	34	First Named	31	M	Full	1896	Cedar	12094
2727	2 " Eliza	32	Wife	29	F	"	1896	"	12095
2728	3 " Levi	13	1896	"	M	"	1896	"	12096
2729	4 " Harriet	9	1896	"	F	"	1896	"	12097
2730	5 " Robinson	7	Son	4	M	"	1896	"	12098
2731	6 " Elizabeth	3	Dau	3½mo	F	"			
2732	7 " Susanna	1	Dau	5mo	F	"			
~~3/4/06~~	8 ~~" Newsom~~		~~Son~~	~~1~~	~~M~~	~~"~~			
	9								
	10 ENROLLMENT OF NOS. 123456and7 HEREON APPROVED BY THE SECRETARY								
	11 OF INTERIOR Dec 12 1902								
	12 No8 died Sept 25, 1904. Proof of death								
	13 filed April 26, 1906.								
	14								
	15 ~~No8~~								
	16 ~~DISMISSED~~								
	17 ~~May 21 1906~~								

TRIBAL ENROLLMENT OF PARENTS

	Name of Father	Year	County	Name of Mother	Year	County
1	John Taylor	1896	Cedar	Margaret Taylor	1896	Cedar
2	Michael Christy	Dead	Towson	Agnes Christy	Dead	Cedar
3	No 1			No 2		
4	No 1			No 2		
5	No 1			No 2		
6	No 1			No 2		
7	No 1			No 2		
8	~~No 1~~			~~No 2~~		
9						
10	No.1 on Choctaw roll as Joseph Taylor					
11	correct name of No 1 is " "					
12	~~No 6 enrolled Dec 19/99~~ Affidavit ~~irregular and returned for correction~~					
13	Returned corrected and filed Feby. 20, 1900.					
14	Nº7 Born March 2, 1902 enrolled Aug. 26, 1902					
15	~~No8 was born Sept 24, 1902, application received and No8 placed on this card March 28, 1905 under Act of Congress, approved~~					
16	March 3, 1905.			Date of Application for Enrollment Apr. 28/99		
17	P.O. Spencerville IT 3/27/05 Hold up until further testimony is taken			↘1 to 6 inc		

5/13/05

Choctaw By Blood Enrollment Cards 1898-1914

	NAME		Relationship to Person First Named	AGE	SEX	BLOOD	TRIBAL ENROLLMENT		
							Year	County	No.
1	Jefferson, Peter		First Named	50	M	Full	1896	Cedar	6749
2	" Pikey	51	Wife	48	F	"	1896	"	6750
3	" Sissy	21	Dau	18	"	"	1896	"	6751
4	" Emily	11	"	8	"	"	1896	"	6752
5									
6									
7									
8									
9									
10									
11									
12									
13									
14									
15									
16									
17									

CE: Cedar COUNTY. **Choctaw Nation** Choctaw Roll (Not Including Freedmen) CARD NO. FIELD NO. 1029
FICE: Doaksville, I.T.

DIED PRIOR TO SEPTEMBER 25, 1902

ENROLLMENT OF NOS. 1 2 3 and 4 HEREON APPROVED BY THE SECRETARY OF INTERIOR DEC 12 1902

TRIBAL ENROLLMENT OF PARENTS

	Name of Father	Year	County	Name of Mother	Year	County
1	Tih-nubbee	Dead	Cedar	Okla-hu-na	Dead	Cedar
2	Che-ko-pa-huma	"	"	Afa-he-na-to-na	"	"
3	No1			No2		
4	No1			No2		
5						
6						
7			No2 on 1896 roll as Pagie Jefferson.			
8						
9						
10			No1 died March 9, 1902: proof of death filed Dec 8, 1902.			
11			No.1 died March 9, 1902: Enrollment cancelled by Department July 8, 1904			
12						
13						
14					Date of Application for Enrollment.	
15					Apr. 28/99	
16						
17						

Choctaw By Blood Enrollment Cards 1898-1914

RESIDENCE: Cedar   COUNTY.   **Choctaw Nation**   **Choctaw Roll**   CARD NO.

POST OFFICE: Doaksville, I.T.   *(Not Including Freedmen)*   FIELD NO. 1030

Dawes' Roll No.	NAME	Relationship to Person First Named	AGE	SEX	BLOOD	TRIBAL ENROLLMENT		
						Year	County	No.
2737	1 Fletcher, Mary ²⁹	First Named	26	F	Full	1896	Cedar	4111
	2							
	3							
	4							
	5							
	6							
	7							
	8							
	9							
	10							
	11							
	12							
	13							
	14							
	15							
	16							
	17							

ENROLLMENT
OF NOS. 1 HEREON
APPROVED BY THE SECRETARY
OF INTERIOR DEC 12 1902

TRIBAL ENROLLMENT OF PARENTS

Name of Father	Year	County	Name of Mother	Year	County
1 Jerome Fletcher	Dead	Cedar	E-li-a-to-na	Dead	Cedar
2					
3					
4	On 1896 roll as Mary Flutcher				
5	No1 is now wife of Morris Tom Choc #904 11/25/02				
6					
7					
8					
9					
10					
11					
12					
13					
14					
15					
16				Date of Application for Enrollment	Apr 28/99
17					

Choctaw By Blood Enrollment Cards 1898-1914

RESIDENCE: Bok Tuklo   COUNTY.   **Choctaw Nation**   Choctaw Roll   CARD No.
POST OFFICE: Lukfata, I.T.   *(Not Including Freedmen)*   FIELD No. **1031**

Dawes' Roll No.	NAME		Relationship to Person First Named	AGE	SEX	BLOOD	TRIBAL ENROLLMENT		
							Year	County	No.
DEAD	1	Edward. Morrison		27	M	Full	1896	Bok Tuklo	3743
2738	2	" Lena 23	Wife	20	F	"	1896	Nashoba	2527
2739	3	" Jimpson 4	Son	7mo	M	"			
2740	4	" May Estell 1	Dau	9mo	F	"			
	5								
	6	ENROLLMENT							
	7	OF NOS. 2 3 and 4 HEREON APPROVED BY THE SECRETARY							
	8	OF INTERIOR Dec 12 1902							
	9								
	10	No. 1 hereon dismissed under order of							
	11	the Commission to the Five Civilized							
	12	Tribes of March 31, 1905.							
	13								
	14								
	15								
	16								
	17								

TRIBAL ENROLLMENT OF PARENTS

	Name of Father	Year	County	Name of Mother	Year	County
1	Thomas Edward	Dead	Bok Tuklo	E-lan-tema	Dead	Bok Tuklo
2	Wallace Carney	"	Nashoba	Phoebe Carney	"	Nashoba
3	No. 1			No. 2		
4	No. 1			No. 2		
5						
6						
7			No 2 on 1896 roll as Leany Carney			
8			No.4 born May 18, 1901: Enrolled Feby. 6th 1902			
9			No.1 died April 5, 1901, proof of death filed Nov. 1, 1902			
			For child of no.2 see NB (March 3,1905) #897			
10						
11						
12						
13						
14						
15					Date of Application for Enrollment.	
16				Date of application for enrollment Apr. 28/99		
17	P.O. Glover, I.T. 4/11/05					

131

RESIDENCE: Nashoba   COUNTY.   **Choctaw Nation**   **Choctaw Roll**   CARD NO.
POST OFFICE: Alikchi, I.T.   *(Not Including Freedmen)*   FIELD NO. **1032**

Dawes' Roll No.	NAME		Relationship to Person	AGE	SEX	BLOOD	TRIBAL ENROLLMENT		
							Year	County	No.
2741	1 Lowman, Ellis	43	First Named	40	M	Full	1896	Nashoba	7978
2742	2 " Lista	22	Wife	19	F	"	1896	"	4144
2743	3 " Sallie	14	Dau	11	F	"	1896	"	7980
2744	4 " Robert	12	Son	9	M	"	1896	"	7981
2745	5 " Davis	10	"	7	"	"	1896	"	7982
2746	6 " Keith	8	"	5	"	"	1896	"	7983
14633	7 " Leviah	1	"	10mo	M	"			
	8								
	9	ENROLLMENT							
	10	OF NOS. 1 2 3 4 5 and 6 HEREON APPROVED BY THE SECRETARY							
	11	OF INTERIOR Dec 12 1902							
	12								
	13	ENROLLMENT							
	14	OF NOS. ~ 7 ~ HEREON APPROVED BY THE SECRETARY							
	15	OF INTERIOR May 20 1903							
	16								
	17								

TRIBAL ENROLLMENT OF PARENTS

	Name of Father	Year	County	Name of Mother	Year	County
1	Loman Okchabob	Dead	Nashoba	Che-ma-ya	Dead	Nashoba
2	Loman Frazier	"	"	Artie Frazier	"	"
3	No.1			Lina Lowman	"	"
4	No.1			" "	"	"
5	No.1			" "	"	No.1
6	No.1			" "	"	No.1
7	No 1			No 2		
8						
9						
10						
11	No 1 on 1896 roll as Ilis Lowman					
12	No.2 " 1896 " " Listie Frazier					
13	No.3 " 1896 " " Saillie Lowman					
14	No.7 Born Dec 13, 1901 enrolled Oct 6 1902					
	For child of nos 1&2 see NB (Apr 26-06) Card #642				Date of Application for Enrollment.	#1 to 6
15	" " " No 3 " " " " #699					
16					Apr. 28/99	
17						

Choctaw By Blood Enrollment Cards 1898-1914

RESIDENCE: Bok Tuklo   COUNTY.   **Choctaw Nation**   **Choctaw Roll** CARD NO.

POST OFFICE: Lukfata, I.T.   *(Not Including Freedmen)* FIELD NO. 1033

Dawes' Roll No.	NAME	Relationship to Person First Named	AGE	SEX	BLOOD	TRIBAL ENROLLMENT		
						Year	County	No.
2747	1 Wade, Susan 38	First Named	35	F	Full	1893	Bok Tuklo	P.R. 198
	2							
	3	ENROLLMENT						
	4	OF NOS. 1 HEREON APPROVED BY THE SECRETARY						
	5	OF INTERIOR DEC 12 1902						
	6							
	7							
	8							
	9							
	10							
	11							
	12							
	13							
	14							
	15							
	16							
	17							

TRIBAL ENROLLMENT OF PARENTS

Name of Father	Year	County	Name of Mother	Year	County
1 Dolin Wade	Dead	Bok Tuklo	Hitey Wade	Dead	Bok Tuklo
2					
3					
4					
5					
6	On 1893 Pay roll as Susan Mihitambe. She was				
7	then the wife of John " , now deceased, also				
8	on 1896 roll as Susan Mihatabe, Page 216, No 8641, Bok Tuklo Co.				
9	No1 is now wife of Stephen Parks on Choc 1003 11-28-02				
10					
11					
12					
13					
14					
15					
16				Date of Application for Enrollment.	Apr. 28/99
17					

133

Choctaw By Blood Enrollment Cards 1898-1914

Choctaw Nation

Choctaw Roll
(Not Including Freedmen)

CARD NO.
FIELD NO. 1034

Dawes' Roll No.	NAME	Relationship to Person First Named	AGE	SEX	BLOOD	TRIBAL ENROLLMENT		
						Year	County	No.
2748	1 Nanomantube, Solomon 48	First Named	45	M	Full	1896	Towson	9659
2749	2 DIED PRIOR TO SEPTEMBER 25, 1902 Silvey	Wife	34	F	"	1896	"	9660
2750	3 " Louisa 19	Dau	16	"	"	1896	"	9661
2751	4 " Dennie 14	"	11	"	"	1896	"	9662
2752	5 " Jacob 7	Son	4	M	"	1896	"	9663
	6							
	7							
	8							
	9							
	10							
	11	ENROLLMENT						
	12	OF NOS. 1 2 3 4 and 5 HEREON APPROVED BY THE SECRETARY						
	13	OF INTERIOR DEC 12 1902						
	14							
	15							
	16							
	17							

TRIBAL ENROLLMENT OF PARENTS

	Name of Father	Year	County	Name of Mother	Year	County
1	Nanomontube[sic]	Dead	Towson	Mary Nanomantube	1896	Towson
2	Jimpson David	"	Cedar	Isabelle David	Dead	Cedar
3	No1			No2		
4	No1			No2		
5	No1			No2		
6						
7	No2 died August 13, 1902: proof of death filed Dec 3, 1902					
8	No2 died Aug. 13, 1902: Enrollment cancelled by Department July 8, 1904					
9	For child of No 3 see NB (Apr 26-06) Card #835					
10						
11						
12						
13						
14						
15						
16				Date of Application for Enrollment,	Apr 28/99	
17						

134

Choctaw By Blood Enrollment Cards 1898-1914

RESIDENCE: Red River COUNTY. **Choctaw Nation** Choctaw Roll CARD NO.
POST OFFICE: Kully Tuklo I.T. *(Not Including Freedmen)* FIELD NO. 1035

Dawes' Roll No.	NAME		Relationship to Person First Named	AGE	SEX	BLOOD	TRIBAL ENROLLMENT		
							Year	County	No.
2753	1 Walker, Isham	62		59	M	Full	1896	Red River	13603
Dead	2 " Sallie		Wife	42	F	"	1896	" "	1352
2754	3 Byington Zona	21	S Dau	18	"	"	1896	" "	1355
	4 " Simeon	19	S Son	16	M	"	1896	" "	1354
	5								
	6	ENROLLMENT OF NOS. 1 3 and 4 HEREON							
	7	APPROVED BY THE SECRETARY OF INTERIOR DEC 12 1902							
	8								
	9	No. 2 HEREON DISMISSED UNDER							
	10	ORDER OF THE COMMISSION TO THE FIVE CIVILIZED TRIBES OF MARCH 31, 1905							
	11								
	12								
	13								
	14								
	15								
	16								
	17								

TRIBAL ENROLLMENT OF PARENTS

	Name of Father	Year	County	Name of Mother	Year	County
1	Snake Walker	Ded	Blue		Ded	Blue
2	Thomas Hawley	1896	Red River		"	Red River
3	Thomas Byington	Ded	" "	No 2	1896	" "
4	" "	"	" "	No 2		
5						
6			No 2 enrolled as Sallie Byington			
7			No 2 died June 26 1899. Evidence of death filed May 2, 1901			
8			No 3 is now wife of Arlington King on Choc 1206 - 12-27-02			
			No 4 " " husband " Mary Louis " " 1196 12 27 02			
9			For child of No.3 see NB (March 3, 1905) #886			
10						
11						
12						
13						
14					Date of Application for Enrollment.	
15						
16					Apr 28/99	
17	Goodwater I.T. 11/27/02					

135

Choctaw By Blood Enrollment Cards 1898-1914

RESIDENCE: Red River COUNTY. **Choctaw Nation** **Choctaw Roll** CARD NO.
POST OFFICE: Shawnee Town I.T. *(Not Including Freedmen)* FIELD NO. 1036

Dawes' Roll No.	NAME	Relationship to Person First Named	AGE	SEX	BLOOD	TRIBAL ENROLLMENT		
						Year	County	No.
2756	1 Tuska [sic] Phoebe DIED PRIOR TO SEPTEMBER 25, 1902		57	F	Full	1896	Red River	12300
	2							
	3							
	4							
	5							
	6							
	7							
	8							
	9							
	10							
	11							
	12							
	13							
	14							
	15							
	16							
	17							

ENROLLMENT
OF NOS. 1 HEREON
APPROVED BY THE SECRETARY
OF INTERIOR DEC 12 1902

TRIBAL ENROLLMENT OF PARENTS

	Name of Father	Year	County	Name of Mother	Year	County
1	Tush-ka	Ded	Red River	Mary Tush-ka	Ded	Red River
2						
3						
4						
5						
6						
7				Enrolled as Feby Tushka		
8						
9		No.1 died August 18, 1902; proof of death filed Dec 3, 1902				
10	No.1 died Aug. 18, 1902		Enrollment cancelled by Department Sept 16, 1904			
11						
12						
13						
14						
15						
16				Date of Application for Enrollment	Apr 28/99	
17						

Choctaw By Blood Enrollment Cards 1898-1914

RESIDENCE: Nashoba	COUNTY.	**Choctaw Nation**				Choctaw Roll	CARD NO.	
POST OFFICE: Alikchi, I.T.						*(Not Including Freedmen)*	FIELD NO.	**1037**

Dawes' Roll No.	NAME		Relationship to Person First Named	AGE	SEX	BLOOD	TRIBAL ENROLLMENT		
							Year	County	No.
2757	1 Gipson, Stephen	30	First Named	27	M	Full	1896	Nashoba	4757
2758	2 " Jincey	27	Wife	24	F	"	1896	"	4758
~~Dead~~	3 ~~" Daniel~~		~~Son~~	~~4~~	~~M~~	~~"~~	~~1896~~	~~"~~	~~4759~~
2759	4 " Charley	2	Son	13mo	M	"			
	5								
	6	ENROLLMENT							
	7	OF NOS. 1 2 and 4 HEREON							
	8	APPROVED BY THE SECRETARY OF INTERIOR Dec 12 1902							
	9								
	10	No. 3 hereon dismissed under order of							
	11	the Commission to the Five Civilized Tribes of March 31, 1905.							
	12								
	13								
	14								
	15								
	16								
	17								

TRIBAL ENROLLMENT OF PARENTS						
Name of Father	Year	County	Name of Mother	Year	County	
1 James Gipson	1896	Nashoba	Elizabeth Gipson	1896	Nashoba	
2 Thompson Morrison	Ded	Nashoba	Alies Morrison	1896	"	
3 ~~No.1~~			~~No. 2~~			
4 No.1			No. 2			
5						
6						
7	No.4 Enrolled July 30, 1901					
8	No.3 Died Sept. 15, 1900, proof of death filed Feby 17, 1903					
9	For child of No.2 see NB (Mar 3 1905) #482					
10						
11						
12						
13						
14				#1 to 3		
15				~~Date of Application for Enrollment.~~		
16				Apr 28/99		
17	P.O. seems to be Bethel I.T. 7/30/01					

RESIDENCE:	Eagle	COUNTY.							

RESIDENCE: Eagle COUNTY. **Choctaw Nation** **Choctaw Roll** (Not Including Freedmen) CARD NO.
POST OFFICE: Eagle Town IT FIELD NO. 1038

Dawes' Roll No.	NAME	Relationship to Person	AGE	SEX	BLOOD	TRIBAL ENROLLMENT		
						Year	County	No.
2760	₁ Dyer, Joel ³⁵	First Named	32	M	Full	1896	Eagle	3418
2761	₂ " Mary ²⁸	Wife	25	F	"	1896	"	13371
2762	₃ Homa Anson ¹¹	S Son	8	M	"	1896	"	5599
2763	₄ Dyer Israel ⁴	Bro[sic]	1	"	"		"	
	5							
	6	ENROLLMENT						
	7	OF NOS. 1 2 3 and 4 HEREON APPROVED BY THE SECRETARY						
	8	OF INTERIOR DEC 12 1902						
	9							
	10	No2 also on 1896 roll, Page 82,						
	11	No 3423, Eagle Co.						
	12							
	13							
	14							
	15							
	16							
	17							

TRIBAL ENROLLMENT OF PARENTS

	Name of Father	Year	County	Name of Mother	Year	County
1	Moses Dyer	De'd	Eagle	Lottie Dyer	1896	Eagle
2	Stephen Watkins	1896	Nashoba	Ceon Watkins	Ded	Nashoba
3	Silas Homa	Ded	"	Fanny Homa	Ded	"
4	No.1			No 2		
5						
6						
7						
8						
9						
10			No2 on 1896 roll as Mary Watkins			
11			No3 " " " " Antsom Homa			
12			No3 new born			
			For child of Nos. 1 &2 see NB (March 3, 1905) #928			
13						
14						
15				Date of Application for Enrollment.		
16				Apr 28/99		
17						

Choctaw By Blood Enrollment Cards 1898-1914

Dawes' Roll No.	NAME		Relationship to Person	AGE	SEX	BLOOD	TRIBAL ENROLLMENT		
							Year	County	No.
2764	1 Billy Always	27	First Named	24	M	Full	1896	Eagle	1258
	2								
	3	ENROLLMENT							
	4	OF NOS. 1 HEREON APPROVED BY THE SECRETARY							
	5	OF INTERIOR DEC 12 1902							
	6								
	7								
	8								
	9								
	10								
	11								
	12								
	13								
	14								
	15								
	16								
	17								

TRIBAL ENROLLMENT OF PARENTS

	Name of Father	Year	County	Name of Mother	Year	County
1	Fisher Billy	Ded	Eagle	Sophia Billy	Ded	Eagle
2						
3						
4						
5	No1 now the Husband of Easter Hotubbion Choctaw Card #1051. Evidence of marriage filed July 14" 1902					
6	For child of No.1 see NB (March 3 1905) #975					
7						
8						
9						
10						
11						
12						
13						
14					Date of Application for Enrollment.	
15						
16					Apr. 28/99	
17						

Choctaw By Blood Enrollment Cards 1898-1914

RESIDENCE: Nashoba   COUNTY.   **Choctaw Nation**   Choctaw Roll   CARD NO.
POST OFFICE: Alikchi I.T.   (Not Including Freedmen)   FIELD NO. 1040

Dawes' Roll No.	NAME		Relationship to Person First Named	AGE	SEX	BLOOD	TRIBAL ENROLLMENT		
							Year	County	No.
2765	1 Willis Allen	27	First Named	24	M	Full	1896	Nashoba	13347
2766	2 " Sistie	22	Wife	19	F	"	1896	"	13348
2767	3 " Matsie	6	Dau	3	"	"	1896	"	13349
2768	4 Rosie	DIED PRIOR TO SEPTEMBER 25, 190	"	1	"	"			
	5								
	6								
	7								
	8								
	9								
	10								
	11	ENROLLMENT							
	12	OF NOS. 1 2 3 and 4 HEREON APPROVED BY THE SECRETARY							
	13	OF INTERIOR DEC 12 1902							
	14								
	15								
	16								
	17								

TRIBAL ENROLLMENT OF PARENTS

	Name of Father	Year	County	Name of Mother	Year	County
1	Rayson Willis	1896	Nashoba	Alisse Willis	1896	Cedar
2	Lake John	Ded	"	Ignia John	Ded	Nashoba
3	No 1			No 2		
4	No 1			No 2		
5						
6						
7	For child of Nos 1&2 see NB (Apr 26-06) Card #663					
8	" " " " " " (Mar 3-05) " #1412					
9						
10	No 4 died May 31 1900; Enrollment cancelled by Department Sept. 16, 1904					
11						
12						
13						
14						
15					Date of Application for Enrollment.	
16					Apr 28/99	
17						

140

Choctaw By Blood Enrollment Cards 1898-1914

RESIDENCE: Nashoba COUNTY. **Choctaw Nation** Choctaw Roll CARD NO.
POST OFFICE: Alikchi I.T. *(Not Including Freedmen)* FIELD NO. **1041**

Dawes' Roll No.	NAME		Relationship to Person First Named	AGE	SEX	BLOOD	TRIBAL ENROLLMENT		
							Year	County	No.
2769	1 Ischcomer Lincoln N [38]			35	M	Full	1896	Nashoba	6268
2770	2 " Meson [28]		Wife	25	F	"	1896	"	6269
2771	3 " Kensie [8]		Dau	5	"	"	1896	"	6271
2772	4 " Mary J. [6]		"	3	"	"	1896	"	6272
2773	5 " Kaler [3]		"	4m	F	"			
2774	6 " Jeulus [1]		Son	6wks	M	"			
	7								
	8	ENROLLMENT							
	9	OF NOS. 12345and6 HEREON APPROVED BY THE SECRETARY							
	10	OF INTERIOR DEC 12 1902							
	11								
	12								
	13								
	14								
	15								
	16								
	17								

TRIBAL ENROLLMENT OF PARENTS

	Name of Father	Year	County	Name of Mother	Year	County
1	Nelson Iscomer	Ded	Bok Tuklo	Ishtayoke	Ded	Bok Tuklo
2	Shaliahla	"	Nashoba	Mary King	1896	Nashoba
3	No 1			No 2		
4	No 1			No 2		
5	No 1			No 2		
6	№ 1			№ 2		
7						
8						
9		№ 6 Born March 29, 1902: enrolled May 10, 1902				
10						
11		For child of Nos 1&2 see NB (Apr 26-06) Card #487				
12		" " " " " " " " (March3-1905) " #1463				
13						
14						
15				No5 enrolled Nov 1/99		
16				Date of Application for Enrollment Apr 28/99		
17	Garvin I.T. 1/17/06)			1 to 4 inc		

Choctaw By Blood Enrollment Cards 1898-1914

RESIDENCE: Red River COUNTY.								

RESIDENCE: Red River **COUNTY.**
POST OFFICE: Garvin I.T.

Choctaw Nation

Choctaw Roll *(Not Including Freedmen)* **CARD No.**
FIELD No. 1042

Dawes' Roll No.	NAME	Relationship to Person First Named	AGE	SEX	BLOOD	TRIBAL ENROLLMENT		
						Year	County	No.
2775	1 Le-Flore James ³¹	First Named	28	M	Full	1896	Red River	8053
DEAD.	2 " " Creasy	Wife	23	F	"	1896	" "	8054
Dead	3 " " Michael DEAD.	Son	4	M	"	1896	" "	8055
DEAD.	4 " " Lena	Dau	9mo	F	"			
	5							
	6							
	7	ENROLLMENT						
	8	OF NOS. 1 HEREON APPROVED BY THE SECRETARY						
	9	OF INTERIOR DEC 12 1902						
	10							
	11	No. 2-3-&4 HEREON DISMISSED UNDER						
	12	ORDER OF THE COMMISSION TO THE FIVE CIVILIZED TRIBES OF MARCH 31, 1905.						
	13							
	14							
	15							
	16							
	17							

TRIBAL ENROLLMENT OF PARENTS

	Name of Father	Year	County	Name of Mother	Year	County
1	Phelan LeFlore	1896	Jackson	Miky LeFlore	1896	Red River
2	George Williams	De'd	Towson	Lucy McAfee	Ded	" "
3	No 1		No 2 [sic]			
4	No 1		No 2 [sic]			
5						
6						
7	For child of No.1 see NB (March 3 1905) #1037					
8			No 1 1896 toll as Jimmy Le-Flore			
9	No3 Dies June 11, 1899: Evidence of death filed March 23, 1901.					
10	No2 is dead. Died June 11, 1899. Proof of death filed Sept 16, 1901.					
11	No1 is now the husband of Narcissa Jacob on Choctaw Card #1065.					
12	No.4 died Sept-19, 1899. Proof of death filed Sept 16, 1901.					
13						
14				Date of Application for Enrollment.		
15						
16				Apr 28/99		
17						

Choctaw By Blood Enrollment Cards 1898-1914

RESIDENCE: Red River   COUNTY.   **Choctaw Nation**   Choctaw Roll   CARD No.
POST OFFICE: Garvin I.T.   (Not Including Freedmen)   FIELD NO. 1043

Dawes' Roll No.	NAME	Relationship to Person First Named	AGE	SEX	BLOOD	TRIBAL ENROLLMENT		
						Year	County	No.
2776	1 Le Flore Miky 68	First Named	65	F	Full	1896	Red River	8056
	2							
	3	ENROLLMENT						
	4	OF NOS. 1 HEREON APPROVED BY THE SECRETARY						
	5	OF INTERIOR DEC 12 1902						
	6							
	7							
	8							
	9							
	10							
	11							
	12							
	13							
	14							
	15							
	16							
	17							

TRIBAL ENROLLMENT OF PARENTS

	Name of Father	Year	County	Name of Mother	Year	County
1	Anosh-ko-na	Ded	Red River	Betsy Anosh-ko-na	De'd	Red River
2						
3						
4						
5						
6						
7						
8						
9						
10						
11						
12						
13						
14				Date of Application for Enrollment.		
15						
16				Apr 28/99		
17						

Choctaw By Blood Enrollment Cards 1898-1914

RESIDENCE: Towson COUNTY.
POST OFFICE: Doaksville, I.T.

Choctaw Nation

Choctaw Roll
(Not Including Freedmen)

CARD No.
FIELD No. 1044

Dawes' Roll No.	NAME	Relationship to Person First Named	AGE	SEX	BLOOD	TRIBAL ENROLLMENT		
						Year	County	No.
2777	1 Davis, Viney 25	First Named	22	F	Full	1896	Towson	3374
	2							
	3							
	4	ENROLLMENT						
	5	OF NOS. I HEREON APPROVED BY THE SECRETARY						
	6	OF INTERIOR DEC 12 1902						
	7							
	8							
	9							
	10							
	11							
	12							
	13							
	14							
	15							
	16							
	17							

TRIBAL ENROLLMENT OF PARENTS

	Name of Father	Year	County	Name of Mother	Year	County
1	Henry Davis	Dead	Non Citz	Betsey Davis	Dead	Towson
2						
3						
4						
5						
6						
7	For child of No 1, see N.B. (Apr. 26, 1906) Card No 31					
8						
9						
10						
11						
12						
13						
14						
15						
16					Date of Application for Enrollment	Apr 28/99
17						

144

Choctaw By Blood Enrollment Cards 1898-1914

| RESIDENCE: Eagle | COUNTY. | **Choctaw Nation** | Choctaw Roll | CARD NO. |
| POST OFFICE: Eagletown, I.T. | | | (Not Including Freedmen) | FIELD NO. 1045 |

Dawes' Roll No.	NAME	Relationship to Person First Named	AGE	SEX	BLOOD	TRIBAL ENROLLMENT Year	County	No.
2778	1 Wilson, Daniel	DIED PRIOR TO SEPTEMBER 25, 1902 Named	16	M	Full	1896	Eagle	13517
2779	2 " Douglas 18	Bro	15	"	"	1896	"	13546
2780	3 " Tom 14	"	11	"	"	1896	"	13519
	4							
	5 ENROLLMENT OF NOS. 1 2 and 3 HEREON							
	6 APPROVED BY THE SECRETARY OF INTERIOR DEC 12 1902							
	7							
	8							
	9							
	10							
	11							
	12							
	13							
	14							
	15							
	16							
	17							

TRIBAL ENROLLMENT OF PARENTS

	Name of Father	Year	County	Name of Mother	Year	County
1	David Wilson	Dead	Eagle	Ana Wilson	Dead	Eagle
2	" "	"	"	" "	"	"
3	" "	"	"	" "	"	"
4						
5						
6						
7	Nº1 also on Choctaw census roll 1896 page 365 #13914					
8						
9						
10						
11	No1 died December - 1901: proof of death filed Dec 16, 1902					
12	No.1 died Dec. – 1901. Enrollment cancelled by Department July 8, 1904					
13						
14						
15						
16					Date of Application for Enrollment	Apr 28/99
17						

145

Choctaw By Blood Enrollment Cards 1898-1914

RESIDENCE: Bok Tuklo	COUNTY.							
POST OFFICE: Lukfata, I.T.	**Choctaw Nation**			**Choctaw Roll** (Not Including Freedmen)		CARD NO.		
						FIELD NO.	**1046**	

Dawes' Roll No.	NAME	Relationship to Person First Named	AGE	SEX	BLOOD	TRIBAL ENROLLMENT		
						Year	County	No.
2781	1 Anderson, John 28	First Named	25	M	Full	1896	Bok Tuklo	245
2782	2 " Wysie 30	Wife	27	F	"	1896	" "	246
2783	3 " Jacob DIED PRIOR TO SEPTEMBER 25, 1902	Son	3	M	"	1896	" "	247
2784	4 " Lasen	Dau	2mo	F	"			
*2785	5 Carn, Elias 16	S.Dau	13	M F	"	1896	Bok Tuklo	2571
2786	6 " Lena 14	S.Dau	11	F	F	1896	"	2572
15395	7 Anderson, Jackman 1	Son	2	M	Full			
	8	ENROLLMENT						
	9	OF NOS. 12345 and 6 HEREON APPROVED BY THE SECRETARY						
	10	OF INTERIOR Dec 12 1902						
	11	6-20-30-						
	12	* Sex changed from "M" to "F" – See letter of May 20, 1930. (D-2578-30)						
	13	ENROLLMENT					6-26-36-JDF	
	14	OF NOS. ~~~ 7 ~~~ HEREON APPROVED BY THE SECRETARY						
	15	OF INTERIOR May 9 1904						
	16							
	17	For child of Nos 1&2 see NB(Apr 26-06) Card #485						

TRIBAL ENROLLMENT OF PARENTS

	Name of Father	Year	County	Name of Mother	Year	County
1	Mishe-mah-tubbee	Dead	Bok Tuklo	Mary Anderson	1896	Bok Tuklo
2	Wilson Thomas	"	" "	Ah-no-le-hema	Dead	" "
3	No 1			No 2		
4	No 1			No 2		
5	Wilmon Carn	Dead	Bok Tuklo	No 2		
6	" "	"	" "	No 2		
7	No 1			No 2		
8						
9	No1 on 1896 roll as Johny Anderson.					
10	No6 " 1896 " " Liney Carn					
11	No2 " 1896 " " Wycie Anderson					
	No3 died July 28, 1902: proof of death filed Dec 13 1902					
12	N°7 Born Jany 12, 1902. Application received June 13, 1902 and returned					
13	for correction. Returned, corrected an[sic] N°7 enrolled Feby 20, 1904					
14	No. 3 died July 28,1902: Enrollment cancelled by Department July 8, 1904					#1 to 6
15						Date of Application for Enrollment.
16						Apr 28/99
17						

146

Choctaw By Blood Enrollment Cards 1898-1914

RESIDENCE: Bok Tuklo   COUNTY.   **Choctaw Nation**   Choctaw Roll   CARD NO.

POST OFFICE: Lukfata I.T.   *(Not Including Freedmen)*   FIELD NO. **1047**

Dawes' Roll No.	NAME		Relationship to Person	AGE	SEX	BLOOD	TRIBAL ENROLLMENT		
							Year	County	No.
2787	1 Colbert, Charles	38	First Named	35	M	Full	1896	Bok Tuklo	2577
2788	2 " Julia Anna	42	Wife	39	F	"	1896	" "	2578
2789	3 " Frances	11	Dau	8	"	"	1896	" "	2579
2790	4 " Herndon	6	Son	3	M	"	1896	" "	2580
14634	5 " Charley	1	Son	4mo	M	"			
	6								
	7	ENROLLMENT							
	8	OF NOS. 1 2 3 and 4 HEREON APPROVED BY THE SECRETARY							
	9	OF INTERIOR Dec 12, 1902							
	10	ENROLLMENT							
	11	OF NOS. 5 HEREON APPROVED BY THE SECRETARY							
	12	OF INTERIOR May 20, 1903							
	13								
	14								
	15								
	16								
	17								

TRIBAL ENROLLMENT OF PARENTS

	Name of Father	Year	County	Name of Mother	Year	County
1	Louie Colbert	Dead	Red River	E-la-po-shema	Dead	Bok Tuklo
2	Ben Tissho	"	Bok Tuklo	Man-to-na	"	" " "
3	No 1			No 2		
4	No 1			No 2		
5	No 1			No 2		
6						
7						
8						
9						
10						
11	No1 on 1896 roll as Charleston Colbert					
12	No2 " 1896 " " Jurianna "					
13	No4 " 1896 " " Hyington "					
14	No5 born August 2, 1902; enrolled Dec. 13, 1902				#1 to 4 inc	
15					Date of Application for Enrollment.	
16					Apr 28/99	
17						

Choctaw By Blood Enrollment Cards 1898-1914

RESIDENCE: Bok Tuklo	COUNTY.								
POST OFFICE: Lukfata, I.T.	**Choctaw Nation**			Choctaw Roll *(Not Including Freedmen)*		CARD NO. FIELD NO. **1048**			

Dawes' Roll No.	NAME	Relationship to Person Named	AGE	SEX	BLOOD	TRIBAL ENROLLMENT		
						Year	County	No.
2791	1 Colbert, Acy ²¹	First Named	18	F	Full	1896	Red River	12299
14887	2 Washington, Nelson ¹	Son	6mo	M	Full			
	3							
	4	ENROLLMENT OF NOS. 1 HEREON APPROVED BY THE SECRETARY OF INTERIOR Dec. 12, 1902						
	5							
	6							
	7							
	8	ENROLLMENT OF NOS. 2 HEREON APPROVED BY THE SECRETARY OF INTERIOR May 21, 1903						
	9							
	10							
	11							
	12							
	13							
	14							
	15							
	16							
	17							

TRIBAL ENROLLMENT OF PARENTS

Name of Father	Year	County	Name of Mother	Year	County
1 Louis Colbert	Dead	Red River	Nancy Colbert	Dead	Red River
2 Ben Washington		Choctaw Roll	No 1		
3					
4					
5					
6					
7	On 1896 roll as Asa Thomas				
8	No1 now wife of Ben Washington on Choc Card #697				
9	No2 born May 24, 1902: enrolled Dec. 2, 1902				
	For child of No1 see N.B. (March 3, 1905) #964				
10					
11					
12					
13					
14				#1		
15				Date of Application for Enrollment.		
16				Apr 28/99		
17 P.O. Garvin I.T. 12/2/1902						

148

Choctaw By Blood Enrollment Cards 1898-1914

RESIDENCE: Eagle COUNTY.
POST OFFICE: Eagletown, I.T.

Choctaw Nation

Choctaw Roll
(Not Including Freedmen)

CARD No.
FIELD No. **1049**

Dawes' Roll No.	NAME		Relationship to Person First Named	AGE	SEX	BLOOD	TRIBAL ENROLLMENT		
							Year	County	No.
2792	1 Tonihka, John	25	First Named	22	M	Full	1893	Eagle	P.R. 1531
2793	2 " Betsy	24	Wife	21	F	"	1896	"	12228
DEAD	3 " ~~Wilamos~~		~~Son~~	~~4~~	~~M~~	~~"~~	~~1896~~	~~"~~	~~12221~~
2794	4 " Rogers	5	"	1	"	"			
2795	5 " Norris	2	Son	9mo	M	"			
	6								
	7	ENROLLMENT							
	8	OF NOS. 1 2 4 and 5 HEREON APPROVED BY THE SECRETARY							
	9	OF INTERIOR Dec 12 1902							
	10								
	11	No. 3 Hereon dismissed under order							
	12	of the Commission to the Five Civilized Tribes of March 31, 1905.							
	13								
	14								
	15								
	16								
	17								

TRIBAL ENROLLMENT OF PARENTS

	Name of Father	Year	County	Name of Mother	Year	County
1	Silas Tonihka	Dead	Eagle	Ellen Mambi	1896	Eagle
2	John Hotubbee	"	"	Selina Johnson	1896	"
3	~~No 1~~			~~No 2~~		
4	No 1			No 2		
5	No 1			No 2		
6						
7	No3 on 1896 roll as Williston Tonihka					
8	No1 " 1893 Pay roll as John Toneka No 531, Eagle Co					
9	No5 Enrolled March 29, 1901					
10	~~No3 Died October 12, 1900 Evidence of death filed April 27, 1901~~					
	For child of Nos 1&2 see N.B. (March 3, 1905) #932					
11						
12						
13						
14				#1 to 4 Date of Application for Enrollment.		
15						
16				Apr 28/99		
17						

RESIDENCE: Red River   COUNTY.   **Choctaw Nation**   **Choctaw Roll**   CARD NO.
POST OFFICE: Goodwater, I.T.   *(Not Including Freedmen)*   FIELD NO.   **1050**

Dawes' Roll No.	NAME	Relationship to Person First Named	AGE	SEX	BLOOD	TRIBAL ENROLLMENT Year	TRIBAL ENROLLMENT County	TRIBAL ENROLLMENT No.
2796	1 Thornton, Sallie 29	First Named	26	F	1/4	1896	Red River	12320
2797	2 " Van 6	Son	3	M	1/8	1896	" "	12321
2798	3 " Anna 4	Dau	4mo	F	1/8			
2799	4 " Tony 2	Son	6mo	M	1/8			
2800	5 " Dovie May 1	Dau	5mo	F	1/8			
I.W. 175	6 " Joseph E.	husband	39	M	I.W.			

DIED PRIOR TO SEPTEMBER 25, 1902

7

8   ENROLLMENT
  OF NOS. 1 2 3 4 and 5 HEREON
  APPROVED BY THE SECRETARY   No2 on 1896 roll as Ben Thornton
9   OF INTERIOR Dec 12 1902

10   No3 Affidavit of birth to be supplied. Rec'd May 17/99

11 Nº6 on 1896 Choctaw census roll as Joe Thornton
12 Nº6 admitted by Dawes Commission in 1896 as
  an intermarried citizen Choctaw citizenship case   ENROLLMENT
13 #1387. No appeal.   OF NOS. ～～ 6 ～～ HEREON
    APPROVED BY THE SECRETARY
14 Nº6 transferred from Choctaw card #D133. See   OF INTERIOR Jun 13 1903
15 decision of May 1, 1903

16

17

TRIBAL ENROLLMENT OF PARENTS

	Name of Father	Year	County	Name of Mother	Year	County
1	Van Nash	Dead	Non Citz	Sarah Harris	Dead	Red River
2	J.E. Thornton	1896	" "	No 1		
3	" "	1896	" "	No 1		
4	" "		" "	No 1		
5	" "		" "	No 1		
6	Joe Thornton	1896	" "	Martha Thornton	1896	non-citz.
7						
8	Husband of No1 and father of her children on Card D 133					
9	No.4 Enrolled February 26, 1901.					
10	No.5 Born Nov. 18, 1901. Enrolled April 9, 1902.					
11	No4 died August 4, 1901: proof of death filed Dec 2, 1902.					
12	No.4 died Aug. 4, 1901: Enrollment cancelled by Department July 8, 1904.					
13						
14					#1 to 3 inc	
15					Date of Application for Enrollment.	
16					Apr 28/99	
17	P.O. Arkinda Ark. 11/27/02					

Choctaw By Blood Enrollment Cards 1898-1914

Choctaw Nation

Choctaw Roll
(Not Including Freedmen)

CARD NO.
FIELD NO. **1051**

Dawes' Roll No.	NAME		Relationship to Person First Named	AGE	SEX	BLOOD	TRIBAL ENROLLMENT		
							Year	County	No.
2801	1 Hotubbi, Salina	43	First Named	40	F	Full	1896	Eagle	5649
2802	2 " Elam	23	Son	20	M	"	1896	"	5639
2803	3 Billy, Easter	19	Dau	16	F	"	1896	"	5640
2804	4 Hotubbi, Kissy	17	"	14	"	"	1896	"	5619
2805	5 " Salean	10	"	7	"	"	1896	"	5642
2806	6 " Mary	15	Ward	12	"	"	1896	"	5641
2807	7 Billy, Selin	1	Dau of No3	1	F	"			
	8								
	9	ENROLLMENT							
	10	OF NOS. 1 2 3 4 5 6 and 7 HEREON APPROVED BY THE SECRETARY							
	11	OF INTERIOR Dec. 12, 1902							
	12								
	13	For child of No3 see N.B.(Mar. 3-05) #975							
	14								
	15								
	16								
	17								

TRIBAL ENROLLMENT OF PARENTS

Name of Father	Year	County	Name of Mother	Year	County
1 A-cha-tubbee	Dead	Eagle	Louisa Achatubbee	1896	Eagle
2 Johnson Hotubbee	"	"	No 1		
3 " "	"	"	No 1		
4 " "	"	"	No 1		
5 Ansil Amos	"	"	No1		
6 " "	"	"	Sarah Amos	Dead	Eagle
7 Always Billy on Choctaw card 1039			No 3		
8					
9 For child of No4 see N.B. (Apr. 26-06) Card #585					
10 No3 on 1896 roll as Easter Hotubbe					
No2 on 1896 roll as Elum Hotubbi					
11 No6 " 1896 " " Mele Hotubbe					
12 No5 " 1896 " " Seline Hotubbi					
13 No.3 now the wife of Always Billy on Choctaw card #1039 Evidence of marriage filed July 14th 1902					
No7 Born July 4th 1901: Enrolled July 14th 1902			#1 to 6		
14 No2 in penitentiary for 10 years sent 1898			Date of Application for Enrollment.		
15 No4 is now wife of Craven Ashalintubbe on					
16 Choc. card #1108 Evidence of marriage to be supplied			Apr 28/99		
17					

Choctaw By Blood Enrollment Cards 1898-1914

RESIDENCE: Bok Tuklo   COUNTY.   **Choctaw Nation**   **Choctaw Roll**   CARD NO.

POST OFFICE: Lukfata, I.T.   (Not Including Freedmen)   FIELD NO.   1052

Dawes' Roll No.	NAME	Relationship to Person First Named	AGE	SEX	BLOOD	TRIBAL ENROLLMENT		
						Year	County	No.
2808	1 Anderson, Daniel ²³		20	M	Full	1896	Bok Tuklo	243
	2							
	3	ENROLLMENT						
	4	OF NOS. 1 HEREON APPROVED BY THE SECRETARY						
	5	OF INTERIOR DEC 12 1902						
	6							
	7							
	8							
	9							
	10							
	11							
	12							
	13							
	14							
	15							
	16							
	17							

TRIBAL ENROLLMENT OF PARENTS

	Name of Father	Year	County	Name of Mother	Year	County
1	Barney Anderson	Dead	Bok Tuklo	Cillin Anderson	Dead	Bok Tuklo
2						
3						
4						
5	No1 now the Husband of Winey Anderson on Choctaw Card #1280: Evidence of marriage filed June 28" 1902					
6						
7						
8						
9						
10						
11						
12						
13						
14				Date of Application for Enrollment.		
15						
16				Apr 28/99		
17						

Choctaw By Blood Enrollment Cards 1898-1914

RESIDENCE: Bok Tuklo   COUNTY.   **Choctaw Nation**   Choctaw Roll   CARD NO.
POST OFFICE: Lukfata, I.T.   *(Not Including Freedmen)*   FIELD NO. **1053**

Dawes' Roll No.	NAME		Relationship to Person	AGE	SEX	BLOOD	TRIBAL ENROLLMENT		
							Year	County	No.
2809	1 Davis, Sylvester	43	First Named	40	M	Full	1896	Bok Tuklo	3395
2810	2 " Louisa	48	Wife	45	F	"	1896	" "	3396
	3								
	4								
	5								
	6	ENROLLMENT							
	7	OF NOS. 1 and 2 HEREON APPROVED BY THE SECRETARY							
	8	OF INTERIOR Dec 12, 1902							
	9								
	10								
	11								
	12								
	13								
	14								
	15	No 1 on 1896 roll as Silvester Davis							
	16								
	17								

TRIBAL ENROLLMENT OF PARENTS

Name of Father	Year	County	Name of Mother	Year	County
1 O-na-hubbee	Dead	Blue	E-ba-na-huna	Dead	Bok Tuklo
2 Way-tubbee	"	Red River	O-nan-to-na	"	" "
3					
4					
5					
6					
7					
8					
9					
10					
11					
12					
13					
14				Date of application for Enrollment.		
15						
16				Apr 28/96		
17						

153

Choctaw By Blood Enrollment Cards 1898-1914

RESIDENCE: Nashoba   COUNTY.   **Choctaw Nation**   **Choctaw Roll**   CARD NO.

POST OFFICE: Alikchi, I.T.   (Not Including Freedmen)   FIELD NO. **1054**

Dawes' Roll No.	NAME	Relationship to Person First Named	AGE	SEX	BLOOD	TRIBAL ENROLLMENT Year	County	No.
2811	1 Jefferson, Madison E 50	First Named	47	M	Full	1896	Nashoba	6845
2812	2 " Sukey 48	Wife	45	F	"	1896	"	6846
2813	3 Hicks, Jefferson 17	Ward	14	M	"	1896	"	5532
	4							
	5							
	6							
	7							
	8							
	9							
	10							
	11							
	12							
	13							
	14							
	15							
	16							
	17							

ENROLLMENT OF NOS. 1 2 and 3 HEREON APPROVED BY THE SECRETARY OF INTERIOR Dec 12 1902

TRIBAL ENROLLMENT OF PARENTS

Name of Father	Year	County	Name of Mother	Year	County
1 Ma-la-cha	Dead	Nashoba	Pa-ho-te-ma	Dead	Nashoba
2 E-la-nuley	"	"	Ish-te-ma	"	"
3 Jack Hicks	"	"	Jennie Hicks	"	"
4					
5					
6					
7	No 1 on 1896 roll as Madison Jefferson				
8					
9	No3 also on 1896 roll, Nashoba Co. Page 168				
10	No 6847, as Hicks Jefferson				
11					
12					
13					
14					
15				Date of Application for Enrollment.	
16					Apr 28/99
17					

154

Choctaw By Blood Enrollment Cards 1898-1914

RESIDENCE: Nashoba COUNTY. **Choctaw Nation** Choctaw Roll *(Not Including Freedmen)* CARD NO. FIELD NO. **1055**
POST OFFICE: Alikchi, I.T.

Dawes' Roll No.	NAME		Relationship to Person First Named	AGE	SEX	BLOOD	TRIBAL ENROLLMENT		
							Year	County	No.
Dead	1	Noahobi, Foster		28	M	Full	1896	Nashoba	9672
2814	2	" Sophie 48	Wife	45	F	"	1896	"	9673
	3								
	4								
	5								
	6								
	7								
	8	No. 1 hereon dismissed under order of							
	9	the Commission to the Five Civilized							
	10	Tribes of March 31, 1905.							
	11								
	12								
	13								
	14								
	15								
	16								
	17								

ENROLLMENT OF NOS. 2 HEREON APPROVED BY THE SECRETARY OF INTERIOR Dec 12 1902

TRIBAL ENROLLMENT OF PARENTS

	Name of Father	Year	County	Name of Mother	Year	County
1	Noah-o-bi	Dead	Nashoba	Eli-yo-tema	1896	Nashoba
2	Ma-la-cha	"	"	Pa-ha-te-ma	Dead	"
3						
4						
5						
6						
7	No2 is now the wife of Almon Carterby Choc card #874					
8						
9						
10	No1 died July 18, 1898. Proof of death filed Jan 30, 1905.					
11						
12						
13						
14						
15				Date of Application for Enrollment.		
16				Apr. 28/99		
17						

Choctaw By Blood Enrollment Cards 1898-1914

RESIDENCE: Red River COUNTY. **Choctaw Nation** **Choctaw Roll** (Not Including Freedmen) CARD NO.
POST OFFICE: Shawneetown, I.T. FIELD NO. **1056**

Dawes' Roll No.	NAME	Relationship to Person First Named	AGE	SEX	BLOOD	TRIBAL ENROLLMENT		
						Year	County	No.
2815	1 Kaniatobe, Gibson 25	First Named	22	M	Full	1896	Red River	7570
2816	2 " Sely 25	Wife	22	F	"	1896	" "	7571
2817	3 " Sissie 7	Dau	4	"	"	1896	" "	7572
2818	4 " Annie 6	"	3	"	"	1896	" "	7573
2819	5 " Sidney 4	Son	4mo	M	"			
2820	6 " Walter 1	Son	8mo	M	"			
	7							
	8							
	9							
	10	ENROLLMENT OF NOS. 12345and6 HEREON APPROVED BY THE SECRETARY OF INTERIOR Dec. 12, 1902						
	11							
	12							
	13							
	14							
	15							
	16							
	17							

TRIBAL ENROLLMENT OF PARENTS

	Name of Father	Year	County	Name of Mother	Year	County
1	Davis Kaniatobe	1896	Red River	Sarabel Kaniatobe	Dead	Red River
2	Robert Taylor	1896	" "	Bicey Taylor	1896	" "
3	No 1			No 2		
4	No 1			No 2		
5	No 1			No 2		
6	No 1			No 2		
7						
8						
9			No 2 on 1896 roll as Cilia Kaniatobe			
10			No 3 " 1896 " " Cissy "			
11			No 6 Born Dec. 24, 1901; enrolled Aug. 28, 1902			
12			For child of Nos 1&2 see N.B. (Apr. 26-06) Card #464			
13			" " " " " " " (Mar 3-05) " #899			
14					#1 to 5	
15					Date of Application for Enrollment.	
16					Apr 28/99	
17	P.O. Idabel I.T. 4/12/05					

156

RESIDENCE: **Red River** COUNTY. **Choctaw Nation** **Choctaw Roll** CARD NO.
POST OFFICE: **Goodwater, I.T.** *(Not Including Freedmen)* FIELD NO. **1057**

Dawes' Roll No.	NAME		Relationship to Person First Named	AGE	SEX	BLOOD	TRIBAL ENROLLMENT		
							Year	County	No.
2821	1 Sampson, Thomas	36	First Named	33	M	Full	1896	Red River	11460
2822	2 Wall, Nicy	20	Dau	17	F	"	1896	" "	11462
~~2823~~	~~3 Sampson, Bicy~~ DIED PRIOR TO SEPTEMBER 25, 1902		~~"~~	~~15~~	~~"~~	~~"~~	~~1896~~	~~" "~~	~~11463~~
2824	4 " Colbert	14	Son	11	M	"	1896	" "	11464
2825	5 " Mary	8	Dau	5	F	"	1896	" "	11465
~~2826~~	~~6 Edna~~ DIED PRIOR TO SEPTEMBER 25, 1902		~~"~~	~~4~~	~~"~~	~~"~~	~~1896~~	~~" "~~	~~11466~~
14635	7 Wall, Lickton		Gr Son	2mo	M	"			
	8								
	9	ENROLLMENT OF NOS. 12345and6 HEREON APPROVED BY THE SECRETARY OF INTERIOR Dec 12 1902							
	10								
	11								

No3 died Nov – 1900: No6 died Nov – 1900: Enrollment cancelled by Department Sept. 16 – 1904

	13	ENROLLMENT OF NOS. 7 HEREON APPROVED BY THE SECRETARY OF INTERIOR May 20 1903							
	14								
	15								
	16								
	17								

TRIBAL ENROLLMENT OF PARENTS

	Name of Father	Year	County	Name of Mother	Year	County
1	Sampson	Dead	Red River		Dead	Eagle
2	No 1			Rhoda Sampson	"	"
3	No 1			" "	"	"
4	No 1			" "	"	"
5	No 1			" "	"	"
6	No 1			" "	"	"
7	Joe Wall	1896	Eagle	No 2		
8	No1 on 1896 roll as Loman Sampson.					
9	No6 " 1896 " " Anthon "					
10	No 2 is now the wife of Joe Wall on Choctaw card #776. Evidence of marriage filed Sept. 24, 1902.					
11	No 7 Born July 13, 1902, enrolled Sept. 24, 1902					
12	No3 died Nov. 1900: proof of death filed Dec. 3, 1902.					
13	No6 " Nov. 1900: " " " " " "					
14	No1 is now husband of Winey Colbert Choc 540					
15					Date of Application for Enrollment. #1 to 6	
16					Apr 28/99	
17						

RESIDENCE: Nashoba   COUNTY.   **Choctaw Nation**   Choctaw Roll   CARD NO.

POST OFFICE: Alikchi, I.T.   (Not Including Freedmen)   FIELD NO.   **1058**

Dawes' Roll No.	NAME	Relationship to Person First Named	AGE	SEX	BLOOD	TRIBAL ENROLLMENT		
						Year	County	No.
DEAD	1 Winship, Narcissa **DEAD**		31	F	Full	1896	Nashoba	13351
	2							
	3							
	4							
	5							
	6							
	7							
	8							
	9							
	10							
	11							
	12							
	13							
	14							
	15	Husband on Card No D 134						
	16	No.1 died January 1, 1900: Evidence of death rec'd Dec. 7, 1901						
	17							

TRIBAL ENROLLMENT OF PARENTS

	Name of Father	Year	County		Name of Mother	Year	County
1	Sol Williams		Nashoba		Wicey Williams		Nashoba
2							
3							
4							
5							
6							
7							
8							
9							
10							
11							
12							
13							
14							
15							
16				Date of Application for Enrollment.	April 28/99		
17							

CANCELLED

Died prior to Sept. 25, '02

Choctaw By Blood Enrollment Cards 1898-1914

RESIDENCE: Red River COUNTY. **Choctaw Nation** Choctaw Roll *(Not Including Freedmen)* CARD NO. FIELD NO. **1059**

POST OFFICE: Kullituklo, I.T.

Dawes' Roll No.	NAME	Relationship to Person First Named	AGE	SEX	BLOOD	TRIBAL ENROLLMENT		
						Year	County	No.
2827	1 Kaniatobe, Wilburn 27	First Named	24	M	Full	1896	Red River	7574
	2							
	3							
	4							
	5							
	6							
	7							
	8							
	9							
	10							
	11							
	12							
	13							
	14							
	15							
	16							
	17							

ENROLLMENT OF NOS. 1 HEREON APPROVED BY THE SECRETARY OF INTERIOR Dec. 12, 1902

TRIBAL ENROLLMENT OF PARENTS

Name of Father	Year	County	Name of Mother	Year	County
1 Davis Kaniatobe	1896	Red River	Sarabel Kaniatobe	Dead	Red River
2					
3					
4					
5					
6					
7	No 2 is now the husband of Rosa Williston on Choctaw Card #516, May 17, 1901				
8	No1 is also known as "Flax" Kaniatobe.				
9	For child of No.1 see N.B. (March 3, 1905) #929				
10	" " " No 1 " " (April 26, 1906) #466				
11					
12					
13					
14					
15			Date of Application for Enrollment.		
16				Apr. 28/99	
17					

Choctaw By Blood Enrollment Cards 1898-1914

Dawes' Roll No.	NAME	Relationship to Person First Named	AGE	SEX	BLOOD	TRIBAL ENROLLMENT		
						Year	County	No.
15396	1 Logan, Loman 38	First Named	35	M	Full	1896	Red River	8074
2828	2 " Lina 24	Wife	21	F	"	1896	" "	13681
	3							
	4	ENROLLMENT						
	5	OF NOS. 2 HEREON APPROVED BY THE SECRETARY						
	6	OF INTERIOR Dec. 12, 1902						
	7							
	8							
	9	ENROLLMENT						
	10	OF NOS. ~~~ 1 ~~~ HEREON APPROVED BY THE SECRETARY						
	11	OF INTERIOR May 9, 1904						
	12							
	13							
	14							
	15							
	16							
	17							

TRIBAL ENROLLMENT OF PARENTS

	Name of Father	Year	County	Name of Mother	Year	County
1	Bob Logan	Dead	Red River		Dead	Red River
2	Impson Winship	"	" " "	Selina Winship	"	" " "
3						
4						
5						
6						
7	No 2 on 1896 roll as Slaine Winship					
8						
9	No1 reported dead: no proof filed Nov. 20 '03. He is alive put on schedule					
10						
11						
12						
13						
14						
15					Date of Application for Enrollment.	
16						Apr. 28/99
17						

Choctaw By Blood Enrollment Cards 1898-1914

RESIDENCE: Nashoba   COUNTY.   **Choctaw Nation**   Choctaw Roll   CARD NO.

POST OFFICE: Alikchi I.T.   *(Not Including Freedmen)*   FIELD NO. **1061**

Dawes' Roll No.	NAME		Relationship to Person First Named	AGE	SEX	BLOOD	TRIBAL ENROLLMENT		
							Year	County	No.
2829	1 King, Allington	50	First Named	47	M	Full	1896	Nashoba	7539
2830	2 " Mary	49	Wife	46	F	"	1896	"	7540
2831	3 " Isa	19	Dau	16	"	"	1896	"	7542
2832	4 " Easton	18	Son	15	M	"	1896	"	7543
2833	5 " Hinson	16	"	13	"	"	1896	"	7544
2834	6 " Stalen	11	"	8	"	"	1896	"	7545
2835	7 John, Norris	14	Ward	11	F	"	1893	"	P.R. 680
	8								
	9								
	10								
	11								
	12								
	13								
	14								
	15								
	16								
	17								

ENROLLMENT OF NOS. 1 2 3 4 5 6 and 7 HEREON APPROVED BY THE SECRETARY OF INTERIOR Dec. 12, 1902

TRIBAL ENROLLMENT OF PARENTS

	Name of Father	Year	County	Name of Mother	Year	County
1	Joseph King	Dead	Nashoba	Bicey King	Dead	Nashoba
2	Ta-nih-cha	"	"	Ape-sa-ho-ma	"	"
3	No 1			No 2		
4	No 1			No 2		
5	No 1			No 2		
6	No 1			No 2		
7	Thomas John	Dead	Nashoba	Amy John	Dead	Nashoba
8						
9	No3 on 1896 roll as Aisie King					
10	No4 " 1896 " " Iston "					
11	No7 " 1893 Pay roll as Norris "					
	No7 also on 1896 Choctaw census roll as Nailes Johnson page 168 #6853					
12	No.7 is a female, see letter of Williamson Noahabi #14458-1902 Gen Off Files copy of					
13	same filed herein Sept. 8, 1902					
14	No5 is now husband of Frances Battiest on Choc #1267					
	For child of No5 see N.B. (Apr. 26 '06) #1271					
15						
16						
17	No 5 Bethel I.T.					

161

Choctaw By Blood Enrollment Cards 1898-1914

RESIDENCE: Red River   COUNTY.   **Choctaw Nation**   Choctaw Roll   CARD NO.

POST OFFICE: Kullituklo, I.T.   *(Not Including Freedmen)*   FIELD NO. **1062**

Dawes' Roll No.	NAME	Relationship to Person First Named	AGE	SEX	BLOOD	TRIBAL ENROLLMENT		
						Year	County	No.
2836	1 Cogswell[sic], Ida 33	First Named	30	F	Full	1893	Red River	P.R. 73
2837	2 Boyd, Jacob 11	Son	8	M	"	1896	" "	1345
2838	3 Williston, Frances 6	Dau	3	F	"	1896	" "	9321
*2839	4 Fobb, Oracy 4	"	1mo	M F	"			
2840	5 Cogswell, Herndon 1	Son	10mo	M	"			
	6	ENROLLMENT OF NOS. 1 2 3 4 and 5 HEREON APPROVED BY THE SECRETARY OF INTERIOR Dec 12 1902						
	7							
	8							
	9							
	8-6-32 * Sex of No.4 changed from letter "M" to "F" by order of Departmental letter of 8/2/32. (See letter 7/25/32)							
	11							
	12							
	13							
	14							
	15							
	16							
	17							

TRIBAL ENROLLMENT OF PARENTS

Name of Father	Year	County	Name of Mother	Year	County
1 Henry McIntosh	Dead	Red River	La-te-ma	Dead	Red River
2 Sam Boyd	"	" "	No. 1		
3 Chas Williston	"	" "	No. 1		
4 Ismon Fobb	"	" "	No. 1		
5 Johnson Coxwell	1896	" "	No. 1		
6					
7					
8					
9 No.1 on 1894 Pay roll as Illie Boyd.					
10					
11 No.1 also on 1896 roll Page 234, No 9320, as Ila McIntosh Red River Co.					
12 No.3 on 1896 roll as Frances McIntosh					
13 No.1 is now the wife of Johnson Coxwell on Choctaw card #1316. Evidence					
14 of marriage filed July 25, 1901: Surname of father appears in marriage certificate as "Cogswell".				#1 to 4
15 No.5 Born Sept. 29, 1901: enrolled July 25, 1902.				Date of Application for Enrollment.
16 For child of No.1 see NB (March 3, 1905) #1465				April 28/99
17					

Choctaw By Blood Enrollment Cards 1898-1914

RESIDENCE: Bok Tuklo   COUNTY.   **Choctaw Nation**   Choctaw Roll   CARD NO.
POST OFFICE: Lukfata, I.T.   *(Not Including Freedmen)*   FIELD NO. **1063**

Dawes' Roll No.	NAME		Relationship to Person First Named	AGE	SEX	BLOOD	TRIBAL ENROLLMENT		
							Year	County	No.
2841	1 Nakishi, Alfred	39	First Named	36	M	Full	1896	Bok Tuklo	9716
2842	2 " Selina	30	Wife	27	F	"	1896	" "	3401
2843	3 " Osborne	12	Son	9	M	"	1896	" "	9718
2844	4 Durant, Jane	10	S.Dau	7	F	"	1896	" "	3402
	5								
	6								
	7	ENROLLMENT OF NOS. 1 2 3 and 4 HEREON APPROVED BY THE SECRETARY							
	8	OF INTERIOR Dec 12 1902							
	9								
	10								
	11								
	12								
	13								
	14								
	15								
	16								
	17								

TRIBAL ENROLLMENT OF PARENTS

	Name of Father	Year	County	Name of Mother	Year	County
1	Davis Nakishi	Dead	Bok Tuklo	Cillin Nakishi	Dead	Bok Tuklo
2	Wilson Thomas	"	" " "	Martha Cornelius	1896	" "
3	No. 1			Mulsey Nakishi	Dead	" "
4	Thomas Durant	Dead	Bok Tuklo	No. 2		
5						
6						
7	No 4 on 1896 roll as James Durant					
8	No.2 " 1896 " " Selina "					
9	No 1 and 2 are divorced					
	No.2 is now wife of Joe James Choc #1314.					
10						
11	For child of No.2 see NB. (Mar 3-1905) #19.					
12						
13						
14					Date of Application for Enrollment.	
15						
16					Apr. 28/99	
17	Chula, I.T. 11/26/02.					

Choctaw By Blood Enrollment Cards 1898-1914

RESIDENCE: Red River   COUNTY.   **Choctaw Nation**   **Choctaw Roll** CARD No.
POST OFFICE: Kullituklo, I.T.   *(Not Including Freedmen)*   FIELD No. **1064**

Dawes' Roll No.	NAME	Relationship to Person	AGE	SEX	BLOOD	TRIBAL ENROLLMENT		
						Year	County	No.
I.W. 1602	1 Peter, Minnie ³⁰	First Named	28	F	I.W.			
14923	2 " , Arthur ¹	Son	5mo	M	1/2			
14924	3 " , Lela ¹	Dau	5mo	F	1/2			
	4							
	5 ENROLLMENT							
	6 OF NOS. 2 and 3 HEREON APPROVED BY THE SECRETARY							
	7 OF INTERIOR Oct 15 1903							
	8 Take no further action relative to enroll-							
	9 ment of No1. Protest of Attys for Choctaw							
	10 and Chickasaw Nations Jan 23/04							
	11							
	12 ENROLLMENT							
	13 OF NOS. 1 HEREON APPROVED BY THE SECRETARY							
	14 OF INTERIOR Feb 12 1907							
	15							
	16							
	17 No1 Granted Oct 17 1906							

TRIBAL ENROLLMENT OF PARENTS

Name of Father	Year	County	Name of Mother	Year	County
1 Wᵐ Dickerson	Dead	Non Citz	Mary A. Dickerson	Dead	Non Citz
2 Pitman Peter	1896	Red River	№ 1		
3 " "	1896	" "	No 1		
4					
5 No1 originally enrolled on this card as Minnie Tambe changed to Peter Aug 29 '04					
6 No1's name is now Minnie Peter 11/26/02 Was wife of					
7 Pitman Peter Choctaw card '503 Roll 1012 who has been divorced from her.					
8 Nos 2 and 3 proof of birth recd 11/26/02 and returned for proof of marriage Certificate of marriage filed March 9, 1903					
9 №2 Born June 16, 1902, application made Dec 3, 1902. Proof of birth filed March 10, 03.					
10 №3 Born June 16, 1902, application " Dec 3, 1902. " " " " " 10, 03. №s 2 and 3 are twins.					
11 No1 now seems to be Minnie Jackson					
12 Notify P.T. Hamilton, Cornish I.T. of decision 3/13/06					
13 " F.P. Branson, Muskogee " " 3/10/06					
14					
15					
16			Date of Application for Enrollment.	#1 Apr 28/99	
17					

164

Choctaw By Blood Enrollment Cards 1898-1914

Choctaw Nation

Choctaw Roll (Not Including Freedmen)

CARD NO. FIELD NO. **1065**

Dawes' Roll No.	NAME	Relationship to Person First Named	AGE	SEX	BLOOD	TRIBAL ENROLLMENT Year	County	No.
2845	1 Jacob, Houston B. 32	First Named	29	M	Full	1896	Towson	6764
2846	2 Leflore, Narcissa 27	Wife	24	F	"	1896	"	7926
2847	3 Lond, Melissa 7	S Dau	4	"	"	1896	"	7927
2848	4 Leflore, Ada 2	Dau of No. 2	7mo	F	"			
	5							
	6 ENROLLMENT							
	7 OF NOS. 1, 2,3 and 4 HEREON APPROVED BY THE SECRETARY							
	8 OF INTERIOR Dec 12 1902							
	9							
	10							
	11							
	12							
	13							
	14							
	15							
	16							
	17							

TRIBAL ENROLLMENT OF PARENTS

	Name of Father	Year	County	Name of Mother	Year	County
1	Grayson Jacob	Dead	Towson	Silncy[sic] Jacob	Dead	Towson
2	Chicca	"	"	Amy Chicca	1896	"
3	Charles Lond	"	"	No. 2		
4	James LeFlore	1896	Red River	No. 2		
5						
6	No.2 on 1896 roll as Narcissa Lond.					
7	No.3 " 1896 " " Malissy "					
8	Nos. 1 and 2 have been divorced and No.2 is now the wife of James Leflore on Choctaw Card #1042, Aug. 3, 1901. Evidence of divorce filed Sept 16, 1906					
9	No.4 Enrolled Sept 16, 1901					
10	Evidence of marriage of No.2 and James Leflore filed November 1, 1901.					
11	No.1 is now the husband of Rhoda Austin on Choctaw card #1207 - Aug-1, 1902					
12	Nos 1 and 2 divorced.					
13						
14						
15				#1 to 3 inc Date of Application for Enrollment.		
16				Apr. 28/99		
17						

| RESIDENCE: | Red River | COUNTY. | **Choctaw Nation** | **Choctaw Roll** | CARD NO. | |
| POST OFFICE: | Janis, I.T. | | | *(Not Including Freedmen)* | FIELD NO. | **1066** |

Dawes' Roll No.	NAME	Relationship to Person	AGE	SEX	BLOOD	TRIBAL ENROLLMENT		
						Year	County	No.
2849	1 Harris, J. Emmet ²⁴	First Named	21	M	1/8	1896	Red River	5721
I.W. 222	2 " Maggie E. ²⁵	Wife	21	F	I.W.			
	3							
	4	ENROLLMENT OF NOS. 1 HEREON APPROVED BY THE SECRETARY OF INTERIOR Dec 12 1902						
	5							
	6							
	7	ENROLLMENT OF NOS. 2 HEREON APPROVED BY THE SECRETARY OF INTERIOR Sep 12 1903						
	8							
	9							
	10							
	11							
	12							
	13							
	14							
	15	No.1 on 1896 roll as Emmuet Harris						
	16							
	17							

TRIBAL ENROLLMENT OF PARENTS

	Name of Father	Year	County	Name of Mother	Year	County
1	John G. Harris	1896	Red River	Mary F. Harris	1896	Intermarried
2	Geo. Mannings[sic]	Dead	Non Citz	Lyzie[sic] Mannings	1896	Non Citz
3						
4						
5						
6						
7						
8						
9						
10						
11						
12						
13						
14						
15				Date of Application for Enrollment		Apr. 28/99
16						
17	P.O. Arkinda, Ark. 4/6/03					

Choctaw By Blood Enrollment Cards 1898-1914

RESIDENCE: Bok Tuklo COUNTY. **Choctaw Nation** Choctaw Roll CARD NO.
POST OFFICE: Lukfata, I.T. *(Not Including Freedmen)* FIELD NO. **1067**

Dawes' Roll No.	NAME	Relationship to Person First Named	AGE	SEX	BLOOD	TRIBAL ENROLLMENT Year	County	No.
2850	1 Cornelius, Martha 44	First Named	41	F	Full	1893	Bok Tuklo	P.R. 140
2851	2 Jones, Frances 18	Dau	15	"	"	1893	" "	141
	3							
	4							
	5							
	6							
	7							
	8							
	9							
	10							
	11							
	12							
	13							
	14							
	15							
	16							
	17							

ENROLLMENT
OF NOS. 1 and 2 HEREON
APPROVED BY THE SECRETARY
OF INTERIOR Dec 12 1902

TRIBAL ENROLLMENT OF PARENTS

Name of Father	Year	County	Name of Mother	Year	County
1 Ho-pa-con-oby	Dead	Bok Tuklo	Hokla-ho-na	Dead	Bok Tuklo
2 Jacoway Jones	"	" "	No. 1		
3					
4					
5					
6					
7	No. 1 on 1893 Pay roll as Mathew Cornelius.				
8					
9	No.2 also on 1896 roll, Bok Tuklo Co. Page 170, No. 6922.				
10					
11					
12					
13					
14					
15					
16				Date of Application for Enrollment Apr. 28/99		
17						

Choctaw By Blood Enrollment Cards 1898-1914

RESIDENCE: Bok Tuklo	COUNTY.	**Choctaw Nation**	**Choctaw Roll**	CARD No.
POST OFFICE: Lukfata, I.T.			*(Not Including Freedmen)*	FIELD No. 1068

Dawes' Roll No.	NAME	Relationship to Person First Named	AGE	SEX	BLOOD	TRIBAL ENROLLMENT Year	County	No.
2852	1 Cornelius, Mary *DIED PRIOR TO SEPTEMBER 25, 1902*		52	F	Full	1893	Bok Tuklo	P.R. 139
	2							
	3							
	4	ENROLLMENT OF NOS. 1 HEREON APPROVED BY THE SECRETARY OF INTERIOR DEC 12 1902						
	5							
	6							
	7							
	8							
	9							
	10							
	11							
	12							
	13							
	14							
	15							
	16							
	17							

TRIBAL ENROLLMENT OF PARENTS

	Name of Father	Year	County	Name of Mother	Year	County
1	Ho-pa-kon-aby	Dead	Bok Tuklo	Hokla-ho-na	Dead	Bok Tuklo
2						
3						
4						
5						
6						
7	No 1 died April 8, 1900; proof of death filed Dec 3, 1902.					
8	No 1 died April 8, 1900; Enrollment cancelled by Department July 8, 1904					
9						
10						
11						
12						
13						
14						
15						
16					Date of Application for Enrollment Apr. 28/99	
17						

168

Choctaw By Blood Enrollment Cards 1898-1914

RESIDENCE: Cedar   COUNTY.   **Choctaw Nation**   Choctaw Roll   CARD No.
POST OFFICE: Doaksville, I.T.   *(Not Including Freedmen)*   FIELD No. **1069**

Dawes' Roll No.	NAME	Relationship to Person First Named	AGE	SEX	BLOOD	TRIBAL ENROLLMENT		
						Year	County	No.
2853	1 Campbell, Sallie Ann 52		49	F	Full	1896	Cedar	2406
2854	2 Reason DIED PRIOR TO SEPTEMBER 25, 1902	Son	10	M	"	1896	"	2408
2855	3 " Louis 21	"	18	"	"	1896	"	2409
DEAD	4 " John DEAD	"	14	"	"	1896	"	2410
DEAD Dead	5 " Frank DEAD	"	12	"	"	1896	"	2411
	6							
	7							
	8 ENROLLMENT OF NOS. 1 2 and 3 HEREON APPROVED BY THE SECRETARY OF INTERIOR Dec 12 1902							
	9							
	10							
	11 No. 4&5 hereon dismissed under order							
	12 of the Commission to the Five Civilized							
	13 Tribes of March 31, 1905.							
	14							
	15							
	16							
	17							

TRIBAL ENROLLMENT OF PARENTS

	Name of Father	Year	County	Name of Mother	Year	County
1	Cha-pa-tubbee	Dead	Cedar	E-ma-sha-huna	Dead	Cedar
2	Solomon Campbell	"	"	No. 1		
3	"	"	"	"	No. 1	
4	"	"	"	"	No. 1	
5	"	"	"	"	No. 1	
6						
7	No. 1 on 1896 roll as Sally Ann Campbell					
8	No. 4 on 1896 roll as Johnny Campbell.					
9	No.5 died August 1, 1899 Proof of death filed July 20, 1901.					
10	No.4 died June 11, 1901. Proof of death filed July 20, 1901.					
11	No.3 is now the husband of Martha Frazier on Choctaw Card 1299; Nov 15, 1901.					
12	No.2 died Dec – 1901; proof of death filed Dec. 5, 1902.					
13	No 2 died Feb. 26, 1902; Enrollment cancelled by Department July 8, 1904					
14						
15					Date of Application for Enrollment.	
16					Apr. 28/99	
17						

Choctaw By Blood Enrollment Cards 1898-1914

RESIDENCE: Towson	COUNTY.							
POST OFFICE: Fowlerville, I.T.								

Choctaw Nation

Choctaw Roll (Not Including Freedmen)

CARD No. FIELD No. 1070

Dawes' Roll No.	NAME	Relationship to Person First Named	AGE	SEX	BLOOD	TRIBAL ENROLLMENT		
						Year	County	No.
2856	1 Wilson, Elizabeth		35	F	Full	1893	Nashoba	P.R. 776
2857	2 Christy, Eastman ²¹	Nephew	18	M	"	1893	Towson	67
2858	3 Hickman, Cephus ¹⁰	"	7	"	"	1893	"	68
	4							
	5							
	6 ENROLLMENT							
	7 OF NOS. 1, 2 and 3 HEREON APPROVED BY THE SECRETARY							
	8 OF INTERIOR DEC 12 1902							
	9							
	10							
	11							
	12							
	13							
	14							
	15							
	16							
	17							

TRIBAL ENROLLMENT OF PARENTS

	Name of Father	Year	County	Name of Mother	Year	County
1	Una ha ko by	Dead	Towson	Po tah	Dead	Towson
2	Edward Christy	"	"	Mollie Christy	"	"
3	Coleman Hickman	1896	Bok Tuklo	Mollie Christy	"	"
4						
5						
6						
7	No3 on 1896 roll Towson Co. Page 133.					
8	No 5475					
9						
10	No1 died Dec 4 - 1901: proof of death filed Dec 3 – 1902					
11	No1 died Dec 4-1901: Enrollment cancelled by Department July 8, 1904					
12						
13						
14						
15						
16				Date of Application for Enrollment	Apr. 28/99	
17						

RESIDENCE: Bok Tuklo COUNTY. **Choctaw Nation** **Choctaw Roll** *(Not Including Freedmen)* CARD NO.
POST OFFICE: Lukfata, I.T. FIELD NO. 1071

Dawes' Roll No.		NAME	Relationship to Person First Named	AGE	SEX	BLOOD	TRIBAL ENROLLMENT Year	County	No.
2859	1	DIED PRIOR TO SEPTEMBER 25, 1902 ~~Charley, Thomas~~ 49	~~Named~~	~~46~~	~~M~~	~~Full~~	~~1896~~	~~Bok Tuklo~~	~~2559~~
2860	2	" Sina 43	Wife	10	F	"	1896	" "	2560
2861	3	" Elam 19	Son	16	M	"	1896	" "	2562
	4								
	5	ENROLLMENT OF NOS. 1 2 and 3 HEREON APPROVED BY THE SECRETARY OF INTERIOR DEC 12 1902							
	6								
	7								
	8								
	9								
	10								
	11								
	12								
	13								
	14								
	15								
	16								
	17								

TRIBAL ENROLLMENT OF PARENTS

	Name of Father	Year	County	Name of Mother	Year	County
1	~~Chas. Yokotubbee~~	~~Dead~~	~~Bok Tuklo~~	~~Sallie Charley~~	~~Dead~~	~~Bok Tuklo~~
2	Carson	"	Nashoba	Sillis Carson	"	Nashoba
3	No 1			No 2		
4						
5						
6						
7						
8						
9						
10						
11						
12						
13						
14						
15						
16						
17						

No2 on 1896 roll as Liney Charley
No3 " 1896 " " Elam "
No.3 is now husband of Ester Anderson on Choctaw Card #916 May 13, 1901
~~No1 died Jan 20, 1900: proof of death filed Dec 5, 1902.~~
No.1 died Jan.20, 1900: Enrollment cancelled by Department [remainder illegible]

Date of Application for Enrollment.
Apr. 28/99

Choctaw By Blood Enrollment Cards 1898-1914

RESIDENCE: Red River	COUNTY.	**Choctaw Nation**	**Choctaw Roll**	CARD NO.
POST OFFICE: Garvin, I.T.			*(Not Including Freedmen)*	FIELD NO. **1072**

Dawes' Roll No.	NAME	Relationship to Person First Named	AGE	SEX	BLOOD	TRIBAL ENROLLMENT Year	County	No.
2862	1 McAfee, Melvina *DIED PRIOR TO SEPTEMBER 25, 1902* 38		35	F	Full	1893	Red River	P.R. 522
2863	2 Jones, Armon *DIED PRIOR TO SEPTEMBER 25, 1902*	Son	19	M	"	1893	" "	329
2864	3 McAfee, Josephine 18	Dau	15	F	"	1893	" "	410
2865	4 " Alice 16	"	13	"	"	1893	" "	11
2866	5 " Selina 10	"	7	"	"	1893	" "	411
14636	6 " Hettie 7 3-19-1896	"	3	"	"			

7
8 ENROLLMENT OF NOS. 1 2 3 4 and 5 HEREON
9 APPROVED BY THE SECRETARY OF INTERIOR Dec 12 1902
10 No 1 died Nov. 1898: proof of death
11 filed Dec. 3, 1902.
12 No.2 died Nov. 1898: proof of death filed Dec. 3, 1902.
13 For child of No3 see NB (Mar 3'05) #885
14 ENROLLMENT OF NOS. 6 HEREON
15 APPROVED BY THE SECRETARY OF INTERIOR May 20 1903
16 No. 3,4&5 live with Louie M Leflore
17 guardianship papers to be supplied

TRIBAL ENROLLMENT OF PARENTS

	Name of Father	Year	County	Name of Mother	Year	County
1	Abraham McAfee	Dead	Red River	Lucy McAfee	Dead	Red River
2	Thomas Jones	"	" "	No. 1		
3	Louie LeFlore	1896	" "	No. 1		
4	" "	1896	" "	No. 1		
5	" "	1896	" "	No. 1		
6	" "	1896	" "	No. 1		

7
8
9 No.2 died Nov. – 1898: Enrollment cancelled by Department Sept. 16, 1904.
10 No.3 on 1893 Pay roll as Josephine Leflore
11 No.4 " 1893 " " Alis McAfee
12 No.5 " 1893 " " Salina Leflore
13 No.1 " 1893 " " Melvina McAfee
No.1 also on 1896 roll, Page 234, No 9330 as Melvinas McField
14 No.2 also on 1896 roll, Page 173, 7037
No.3 " 1896 " " 234, No.9327 as Josephine McField
15 No.4 " 1896 " " 234, No.9328 as Ella McField
16 No.5 " 1896 " " 234, No 9329 as Cerena "

Date of Application for Enrollment. Apr 28/99

17 No.1 died Nov. – 1898: Enrollment cancelled by Department July 8, 1904.

Choctaw By Blood Enrollment Cards 1898-1914

RESIDENCE: Red River COUNTY. POST OFFICE: Garvin, I.T.	**Choctaw Nation**	Choctaw Roll (Not Including Freedmen)	CARD NO. FIELD NO. **1073**

Dawes' Roll No.	NAME	Relationship to Person First Named	AGE	SEX	BLOOD	TRIBAL ENROLLMENT		
						Year	County	No.
2867	1 McAfee, Wilmon 53		50	M	Full	1893	Red River	P.R. 520
	2							
	3	ENROLLMENT						
	4	OF NOS. I HEREON APPROVED BY THE SECRETARY						
	5	OF INTERIOR Dec 12, 1902						
	6							
	7							
	8							
	9							
	10							
	11							
	12							
	13							
	14							
	15							
	16							
	17							

TRIBAL ENROLLMENT OF PARENTS

	Name of Father	Year	County	Name of Mother	Year	County
1		Dead	Towson		Dead	Towson
2						
3						
4						
5						
6						
7	On 1893 Pay roll as Wilburn McAfee					
8						
9	On 1896 Roll Page 234, No. 9325 as					
10	Wilburn McField.					
11	No.1 now husband of Sophia Homer on Choc 1146.					
12						
13						
14					Date of Application	
15					for Enrollment.	
16					Apr 28/99	
17						

Choctaw By Blood Enrollment Cards 1898-1914

RESIDENCE: Nashoba   COUNTY.   **Choctaw Nation**   **Choctaw Roll**   CARD NO.
POST OFFICE: Alikchi, I.T.   *(Not Including Freedmen)*   FIELD NO.   **1074**

Dawes' Roll No.	NAME	Relationship to Person	AGE	SEX	BLOOD	TRIBAL ENROLLMENT		
						Year	County	No.
2868	1 John, Carney ²⁵	First Named	22	M	Full	1896	Nashoba	6876
2869	2 " Burris ⁴	Son	1	"	"			
	3							
	4	ENROLLMENT						
	5	OF NOS. 1 and 2 HEREON APPROVED BY THE SECRETARY						
	6	OF INTERIOR Dec 12 1902						
	7							
	8							
	9							
	10							
	11							
	12							
	13							
	14							
	15							
	16							
	17							

TRIBAL ENROLLMENT OF PARENTS

	Name of Father	Year	County	Name of Mother	Year	County
1	Lake John	Dead	Nashoba	Aknie John	Dead	Nashoba
2	No. 1			Lena John	1896	"
3						
4						
5						
6						
7		No.1 is now the husband of Esa Lowman				
8		on Choctaw Card No. 658. February 12, 1901.				
9						
10						
11						
12						
13						
14					Date of Application for Enrollment.	
15						
16					Apr. 28/99	
17						

174

Choctaw By Blood Enrollment Cards 1898-1914

RESIDENCE: Cedar   COUNTY.   **Choctaw Nation**   Choctaw Roll   CARD No.
POST OFFICE: Doaksville, I.T.   (Not Including Freedmen)   FIELD No. 1075

Dawes' Roll No.	NAME	Relationship to Person First Named	AGE	SEX	BLOOD	TRIBAL ENROLLMENT		
						Year	County	No.
2870	1 Choate, Sophia ⁴⁸	First Named	45	F	Full	1893	Cedar	P.R. 105
	2							
	3	ENROLLMENT						
	4	OF NOS. 1 HEREON APPROVED BY THE SECRETARY						
	5	OF INTERIOR DEC 12 1902						
	6							
	7							
	8							
	9							
	10							
	11							
	12							
	13							
	14							
	15							
	16							
	17							

TRIBAL ENROLLMENT OF PARENTS

	Name of Father	Year	County	Name of Mother	Year	County
1	Nicholas	Dead	Cedar		Dead	Cedar
2						
3						
4						
5						
6						
7		On 1896 roll Page 345, No 13133, Sophia				
8		Nicholas, Cedar Co.				
9		N°1 was married to Paul Homma Choctaw card #1826, Feby 9, 1901. See				
10		testimony of Selin Taylor and Reason Hopson of May 22, 1903, and also evidence of marriage filed herein.				
11						
12						
13						
14						
15						
16				Date of Application for Enrollment	Apr. 28/99	
17						

Choctaw By Blood Enrollment Cards 1898-1914

RESIDENCE: Red River   COUNTY.   **Choctaw Nation**   **Choctaw Roll**   CARD NO.

POST OFFICE: Kullituklo, I.T.   *(Not Including Freedmen)*   FIELD NO.   1076

Dawes' Roll No.	NAME		Relationship to Person First Named	AGE	SEX	BLOOD	TRIBAL ENROLLMENT		
							Year	County	No.
2871	1 Cash, Wallace	73	First Named	70	M	Full	1896	Red River	2678
2872	2 " Sophia	19	Dau	16	F	"	1896	" "	2679
	3								
	4	ENROLLMENT							
	5	OF NOS. 1 and 2 HEREON APPROVED BY THE SECRETARY							
	6	OF INTERIOR DEC 2 1902							
	7								
	8								
	9								
	10								
	11								
	12								
	13								
	14								
	15								
	16								
	17								

TRIBAL ENROLLMENT OF PARENTS

	Name of Father	Year	County	Name of Mother	Year	County
1		Dead			Dead	in Mississippi
2	No 1			Isho-na	"	Red River
3						
4						
5						
6						
7						
8						
9						
10						
11						
12						
13						
14					Date of Application for Enrollment.	
15						
16					April 28/99	
17						

Choctaw By Blood Enrollment Cards 1898-1914

RESIDENCE: Nashoba COUNTY. **Choctaw Nation** Choctaw Roll CARD NO.
POST OFFICE: Alikchi, I.T. *(Not Including Freedmen)* FIELD NO. 1077

Dawes' Roll No.	NAME		Relationship to Person	AGE	SEX	BLOOD	TRIBAL ENROLLMENT		
							Year	County	No.
2873	1 John, Museton	24	First Named	21	M	Full	1893	Nashoba	P.R. 442
2874	2 " Lena	23	Wife	20	F	"	1896	"	6877
2875	3 " Rencey	3	Dau	1mo	F	"			
14637	4 " Jashin	1	Son	5mo	M	"			
	5								
	6 ENROLLMENT OF NOS. 1 2 and 3 HEREON APPROVED BY THE SECRETARY OF INTERIOR DEC 2 1902								
	7								
	8								
	9								
	10								
	11								
	12 ENROLLMENT OF NOS. 4 HEREON APPROVED BY THE SECRETARY OF INTERIOR MAY 20 1903								
	13								
	14								
	15								
	16								
	17								

TRIBAL ENROLLMENT OF PARENTS

	Name of Father	Year	County	Name of Mother	Year	County
1	E-cha-lich-tubbee	Dead	Nashoba	Mary King	1896	Nashoba
2	John Cephus	"	"	Adeline Cephus	1896	"
3	No 1			No 2		
4	Nº1			Nº2		
5						
6						
7	No1 on 1893 Pay roll as Meyostan Kin					
8						
9	No1 also on 1896 roll as Meyoster Johnson					
10	Page 169, No 6875					
11	Nº4 Born July 8, 1902. Enrolled Dec. 24, 1902 For child of Nos 1&2 see NB (March 3 1905) #891					
12						
13						
14						
15					#1&2	
16				Date of Application for Enrollment Apr. 28/99		
17	Bethel I.T.			No3 enrolled Nov 1/99		

177

Choctaw By Blood Enrollment Cards 1898-1914

| RESIDENCE: Towson COUNTY. | POST OFFICE: Garvin, I.T. | **Choctaw Nation** | **Choctaw Roll** (Not Including Freedmen) | CARD NO. FIELD NO. 1078 |

Dawes' Roll No.	NAME	Relationship to Person First Named	AGE	SEX	BLOOD	TRIBAL ENROLLMENT		
						Year	County	No.
2876	1 Choate, Lonie 26		23	M	3/4	1896	Towson	21457
2877	2 " Jency 38	Wife	35	F	Full	1896	"	6799
	3							
	4	ENROLLMENT						
	5	OF NOS. 1 and 2 HEREON APPROVED BY THE SECRETARY						
	6	OF INTERIOR DEC 12 1902						
	7							
	8							
	9							
	10							
	11							
	12							
	13							
	14							
	15							
	16							
	17							

TRIBAL ENROLLMENT OF PARENTS

Name of Father	Year	County	Name of Mother	Year	County
1 John Anderson	De'd	Red River (Tex)	Sally Choate	1896	Towson
2 William Little	"	Bok Tuklo	Wacy Little	De'd	Bok Tuklo
3					
4					
5					
6					
7	No 2 on 1896 Roll as Jency John.				
8	No 1 on 1896 roll as Luvis Choate				
9					
10					
11					
12					
13					
14					
15				Date of Application for Enrollment.	
16				Apr. 28/99	
17					

178

Choctaw By Blood Enrollment Cards 1898-1914

RESIDENCE: Bok Tuklo COUNTY. **Choctaw Nation** **Choctaw Roll** CARD No.
POST OFFICE: Luk-Fa-tah I.T. *(Not Including Freedmen)* FIELD No. 1079

Dawes' Roll No.	NAME	Relationship to Person First Named	AGE	SEX	BLOOD	TRIBAL ENROLLMENT		
						Year	County	No.
2878	1 Sealy 53	First Named	50	F	Full	1893	Bok-Tuklo	P.R. 224
	2							
	3							
	4	ENROLLMENT OF NOS. 1 HEREON						
	5	APPROVED BY THE SECRETARY OF INTERIOR DEC 12 1902						
	6							
	7							
	8							
	9							
	10							
	11							
	12							
	13							
	14							
	15							
	16							
	17							

TRIBAL ENROLLMENT OF PARENTS

	Name of Father	Year	County	Name of Mother	Year	County
1		Ded		Eli-yo-ca-ta-na	De'd	Bok Tuklo
2						
3						
4						
5						
6						
7	On 1893 Pay roll as Selen also on 1896 roll as					
8	Silen Frazier, Page 101, No 4159, Bok Tuklo Co.					
9						
10						
11						
12						
13						
14						
15					DATE OF APPLICATION	
16					FOR ENROLLMENT. Apr. 28'99	
17						

Choctaw By Blood Enrollment Cards 1898-1914

RESIDENCE: Cedar COUNTY. **Choctaw Nation** **Choctaw Roll** CARD No.
POST OFFICE: Doaksville I.T. *(Not Including Freedmen)* FIELD No. 1080

Dawes' Roll No.	NAME	Relationship to Person First Named	AGE	SEX	BLOOD	TRIBAL ENROLLMENT		
						Year	County	No.
2879	₁ Nail, Phoebe ⁵³	First Named	50	F	Full	1893	Cedar	373
2880	₂ " Simeon ¹⁴	Son	11	M	"	1893	"	374
	3							
	4	ENROLLMENT						
	5	OF NOS. 1 and 2 HEREON APPROVED BY THE SECRETARY						
	6	OF INTERIOR DEC 12 1902						
	7							
	8							
	9							
	10							
	11							
	12							
	13							
	14							
	15							
	16							
	17							

TRIBAL ENROLLMENT OF PARENTS

	Name of Father	Year	County	Name of Mother	Year	County
1	Nak-ni-la	Ded	Wade	Elaimuna	De'd	Cedar
2	Joseph Nail	"	Cedar	No 1		
3						
4						
5						
6						
7		No 2 also on 1896 roll Page 244,				
8		No 9646 as Simeon Nale				
9						
10						
11						
12						
13						
14					Date of Application for Enrollment.	
15				Date of Application for Enrollment.		
16					Apr. 28/99	
17						

180

Choctaw By Blood Enrollment Cards 1898-1914

	RESIDENCE: Towson COUNTY.	POST OFFICE: Fowlersville I.T.

Choctaw Nation

Choctaw Roll *(Not Including Freedmen)*

CARD NO.

FIELD NO. **1081**

Dawes' Roll No.	NAME		Relationship to Person First Named	AGE	SEX	BLOOD	TRIBAL ENROLLMENT		
							Year	County	No.
2881	1 Choate Sallie	58	First Named	55	F	Full	1893	Towson	434
	2								
	3	ENROLLMENT							
	4	OF NOS. 1 HEREON APPROVED BY THE SECRETARY							
	5	OF INTERIOR DEC 12 1902							
	6								
	7								
	8								
	9								
	10								
	11								
	12								
	13								
	14								
	15								
	16								
	17								

TRIBAL ENROLLMENT OF PARENTS

	Name of Father	Year	County	Name of Mother	Year	County
1	Kan-che-hom-be	De'd	Sans Bois	Winnie	De'd	Towson
2						
3						
4						
5						
6						
7	On 1893 Pay roll as Sally Choat					
8	No1 is now wife of Gibson Cobb on Choctaw card #584: evidence of					
9	marriage filed December 3 1902					
10						
11						
12						
13						
14				Date of Application for Enrollment.		
15						
16				Apr. 28/99		
17						

181

Choctaw By Blood Enrollment Cards 1898-1914

| RESIDENCE: Bok Tuklo | COUNTY. | Choctaw Nation | Choctaw Roll | CARD No. |
| POST OFFICE: Lukfata, I.T. | | | (Not Including Freedmen) | FIELD No. 1082 |

Dawes' Roll No.	NAME	Relationship to Person First Named	AGE	SEX	BLOOD	TRIBAL ENROLLMENT		
						Year	County	No.
DEAD.	1 Kamashambe Harrison	Named	27	M	Full	1896	Bok Tuklo	7551
15569	2 Phoebe [ED PRIOR TO SEPTEMBER 25, 1902]	Wife	35	F	"	1896	" "	7552
2882	3 Carn, Harlis 21	S.Son	18	M	"	1896	" "	2570
	4							
	5 ENROLLMENT							
	6 OF NOS. 3 HEREON APPROVED BY THE SECRETARY							
	7 OF INTERIOR DEC 12 1902							
	8							
	9 ENROLLMENT							
	10 OF NOS. 2 HEREON APPROVED BY THE SECRETARY							
	11 OF INTERIOR SEP 22 1904							
	12							
	13 No. 1 HEREON DISMISSED UNDER							
	14 ORDER OF THE COMMISSION TO THE FIVE							
	15 CIVILIZED TRIBES OF MARCH 31, 1905.							
	16							
	17							

		TRIBAL ENROLLMENT OF PARENTS				
Name of Father	Year	County	Name of Mother	Year	County	
1 Kamashambe	Dead	Bok Tuklo	Eli a ma	Dead	Bok Tuklo	
2 Geo. Tikbombe	"	" "	Ah no le hema	"	" "	
3 Wilmon Carn	"	" "	No 2			
4						
5						
6						
7 Surnames on 1896 roll for Nos 1-2, Kanashambe						
8 Nº1 Died Aug 28, 1900, proof of death filed Nov 29, 1904						
9						
10						
11 No2 died in Dec. 1900 or Jan. 1901: Enrollment cancelled by Department Jan. 18, 1907						
12						
13						
14						
15						
16				Date of Application for Enrollment	Apr. 28/99	
17						

Choctaw By Blood Enrollment Cards 1898-1914

RESIDENCE: Red River COUNTY.
POST OFFICE: Goodwater I.T.

Choctaw Nation

Choctaw Roll (Not Including Freedmen)

CARD NO.
FIELD NO. 1083

Dawes' Roll No.	NAME	Relationship to Person First Named	AGE	SEX	BLOOD	TRIBAL ENROLLMENT		
						Year	County	No.
I.W. 64	1 Whiteman, W. J. 33	First Named	29	M	I.W.	1896	Red River	15179
2883	2 " Mattie J. 22	Wife	19	F	1/16	1896	" "	13679
2884	3 " Maggie E. 5	Dau	2	"	1/32		" "	
2885	4 " Mary Lena 2	Dau	4mo	F	1/32			
	5							
	6	ENROLLMENT OF NOS. 2 3 and 4 HEREON APPROVED BY THE SECRETARY OF INTERIOR DEC 12 1902						
	7							
	8							
	9							
	10							
	11							
	12	ENROLLMENT OF NOS. 1 HEREON APPROVED BY THE SECRETARY OF INTERIOR JUN 13 1903						
	13							
	14							
	15							
	16							
	17							

TRIBAL ENROLLMENT OF PARENTS

	Name of Father	Year	County	Name of Mother	Year	County
1	D.C. Whiteman	1896	Non Citz	Mary E. Whiteman	1896	Non Citz
2	H.C. Harris	1896	Red River	Maggie E. Harris	1896	Inter M.
3	No 1			No 2		
4	No 1			No 2		
5						
6						
7	No1 Admitted as intermarried citizen by Dawes					
8	Commission #537 – No appeal. Evidence of mar-					
9	riage filed with Dawes Commission – See Same					
	No3 – Affidavit of birth to be supplied. Recd May 9/99					
10	No2 Daughter of H.C. Harris – card No 763					
11	Evidence of his marriage to non citizen wife					
12	Maggie Harris on file and in office of					
	Dawes Commission Muskogee I.T.					
13	No.4 Enrolled July 24, 1901.					
14	For child of Nos. 1&2 see NB (Mar 3'05) #601					
15					Date of Application for Enrollment.	
16					4-28-99	
17						

Choctaw By Blood Enrollment Cards 1898-1914

			COUNTY. n, I.T.	Relationship to Person	AGE	SEX	BLOOD	TRIBAL ENROLLMENT		
								Year	County	No.
2886	1	McAfee, Frank	32	First Named	29	M	7/8	1893	Red River	P.R. 517
2887	2	" Selina	21	Wife	18	F	Full	1896	" "	7918
2888	3	McAfee Josephine	1	Dau	4mo	F	15/16			
	4									
	5									
	6	ENROLLMENT								
	7	OF NOS. 1 2 and 3 HEREON APPROVED BY THE SECRETARY OF INTERIOR								
	8									
	9									
	10									
	11									
	12									
	13									
	14									
	15									
	16									
	17									

Choctaw Nation
Choctaw Roll (Not Including Freedmen)

TRIBAL ENROLLMENT OF PARENTS

	Name of Father	Year	County	Name of Mother	Year	County
1	Abel McAfee	Dead	Red River	Louisa McAfee	Dead	Red River
2	Felin LeFlore	1896	Jackson	Jincy Choate	1896	" "
3	No.1			No 2		
4						
5						
6						
7						
8						
9						
10	No2 on 1896 roll as Selina LeFlore					
11	" 1 " 1893 " " Frank McAlfee					
12	No1 on 1896 roll, Page 234, No 9322 as Frank McField.					
13	No.3 Enrolled Sept 16, 1901. Born 5-12-01					
14	Nos 1 and 2 have seperated[sic]. No1 is now husband of Sena					
15	Hotenlubbee Choc #725 11/26/02					
16	No2 is now wife of Charles James on Choc #1302 11/27/02					
17	For child of No.1 see NB (March 3,1905) #880					
	" " " No 2 " " " " #1464					

Date of Application for Enrollment.
Apr. 28/99
[illegible]

184

Choctaw By Blood Enrollment Cards 1898-1914

RESIDENCE: Bok Tuklo   COUNTY.   **Choctaw Nation**

POST OFFICE: Lukfata, I.T.   *(Not Including Freedmen)*   FIELD NO. **1085**

Dawes' Roll No.	NAME	Relationship to Person First Named	AGE	SEX	BLOOD	TRIBAL ENROLLMENT		
						Year	County	No.
2889	1 Jackson, Moses ²⁴							
	2							
	3							
	4							
	5							
	6							
	7							
	8							
	9							
	10							
	11							
	12							
	13							
	14							
	15							
	16							
	17							

ENROLLMENT
OF NOS. 1 HEREON
APPROVED BY THE SECRETARY
OF INTERIOR DEC 12 1902

TRIBAL ENROLLMENT OF PARENTS

	Name of Father	Year	County	Name of Mother	Year	C
1	Amos Jackson	Dead	Bok Tuklo	Nancy Jackson	De'd	Bok
2						
3						
4						
5						
6						
7	No.1 is now the husband of Narcissa Dennis on Choctaw card #1093					
8						Sept.
9						
10						
11						
12						
13						
14						
15						
16					Date of Application for Enrollment	Apr. 28/99
17						

185

Choctaw By Blood Enrollment Cards 1898-1914

	NAME		Relationship to Person First Named	AGE	SEX	BLOOD	TRIBAL ENROLLMENT		
							Year	County	No.
	Webster, Daniel	59		56	M	3/4	1896	Red River	13645
	" Nannie W	30	Wife	30	F	I.W.	1896	" "	15178
2891	" Lizzie	15	Dau	12	"	3/4	1896	" "	13646
2892	" Robert	8	Son	5	M	3/8	1896	" "	13547
2893	" Josiah	7	"	4	"	3/8	1896	" "	13648
2894	" Maggie	4	Dau	16 mon	F	3/8			
2895	" Ida May	3	Dau	13m	F	3/8			
2896	" Wood Kirk	1	Son	2mo	M	3/8			

ENROLLMENT
OF NOS. 1 3 4 5 6 7 and 8 HEREON
APPROVED BY THE SECRETARY
OF INTERIOR DEC 12 1902

ENROLLMENT
OF NOS. 2 HEREON
APPROVED BY THE SECRETARY
OF INTERIOR FEB -8 1904

For child of Nos 1&2 see NB (Apr 26'06) Card #477
" " " " " " " " (Mar 3-05) " #1017

TRIBAL ENROLLMENT OF PARENTS

	Name of Father	Year	County	Name of Mother	Year	County
1	David Webster	Ded	Towson	Pliny Webster	De'd	Red River
2	James Davis	1896	Non Citz	Kate Davis	1896	Non Citz
3	No 1			Susie Webster	Ded	Red River
4	No 1			No 2		
5	No 1			No 2		
6	No 1			No 2		
7	No. 1			No. 2		
8	Nº1			Nº2		
9			No6 Affidavit of birth to be supplied. Rec'd 5/9/99			
10			No.7 Enrolled January 10th 1901.			
11			Nº8 Born Dec. 21, 1901; enrolled May 15, 1902			
12			Marriage certificate between Nos. 1 and 2 filed December 3, 1902			
13			Certified copy of divorce proceedings between Daniel and Melvina			
14			Webster filed March 26, 1903			#1 to 6 inc
15						Date of Application for Enrollment.
16			Date of application for enrollment			Apr. 28-99
17						

Choctaw By Blood Enrollment Cards 1898-1914

RESIDENCE: Nashoba   COUNTY.   **Choctaw Nation**   Choctaw Roll   CARD NO.
POST OFFICE: Garvin I.T.   *(Not Including Freedmen)*   FIELD NO. 1087

Dawes' Roll No.	NAME		Relationship to Person	AGE	SEX	BLOOD	TRIBAL ENROLLMENT		
							Year	County	No.
2897	1 Wright, John	22	First Named	19	M	1/2	1896	Nashoba	13223
2898	2 " Surena	22	Wife	19	F	Full	1893	Towson	P.R. 222
	3								
	4	ENROLLMENT							
	5	OF NOS. 1 and 2 HEREON APPROVED BY THE SECRETARY							
	6	OF INTERIOR DEC 12 1902							
	7								
	8								
	9								
	10								
	11								
	12								
	13								
	14								
	15								
	16								
	17								

TRIBAL ENROLLMENT OF PARENTS

	Name of Father	Year	County	Name of Mother	Year	County
1	Willie Wright	Ded	Red River	Sissy Durant	Ded	Red River
2	Nolen Gardner	De'd	Towson	Mary Ann Gardner	1896	Towson
3						
4						
5						
6						
7			No 1 enrolled on 1896 Roll as Johnny Wright			
8			No 2 " on 93 pay roll for Towson			
9			County as Surena Gardner			
10			Nº1 also on 1896 Choctaw census roll page 365 #13918 as Johnny Wright.			
11						
12						
13			For child of Nos 1&2 see NB (Mar 3rd 1905) Card #98.			
14						
15						
16				Date of Application for Enrollment	Apr. 28/99	
17						

Choctaw By Blood Enrollment Cards 1898-1914

RESIDENCE: COUNTY.
POST OFFICE:

Choctaw Nation
Choctaw R.a.B
(Not Including Freedmen)   FIELD NO.   1088

Dawes' Roll No.	NAME	Relationship to Person First Named	AGE	SEX	BLOOD	TRIBAL ENROLLMENT		
						Year	County	No.
2899	DIED PRIOR TO SEPTEMBER 25, 1902 1 Harkin John		61	M	Full	1896	Red River	5725
2								
3	ENROLLMENT							
4	OF NOS. I HEREON APPROVED BY THE SECRETARY							
5	OF INTERIOR DEC 12 1902							
6								
7								
8								
9								
10								
11								
12								
13								
14								
15								
16								
17								

TRIBAL ENROLLMENT OF PARENTS

	Name of Father	Year	County	Name of Mother	Year	County
1	Helitubbee	De'd	Eagle		Ded	Eagle
2						
3						
4						
5						
6						
7	No 1 died in 1900 or 1901: Enrollment cancelled by Department [remainder illegible]					
8						
9						
10						
11						
12						
13						
14						
15						
16					Date of Application for Enrollment	Apr. 28-99
17						

188

Choctaw By Blood Enrollment Cards 1898-1914

RESIDENCE: Red River COUNTY.		POST OFFICE: Goodwater I.T.		**Choctaw Nation**	Choctaw Roll (Not Including Freedmen)	CARD NO. FIELD NO. 1089	

Dawes' Roll No.	NAME		Relationship to Person First Named	AGE	SEX	BLOOD	TRIBAL ENROLLMENT		
							Year	County	No.
2900	1 Loman Sissy	49		46	F	Full	1896	Red River	8075
2901	2 " Burt	15		12	M	"	1896	" "	8073
2902	3 " Siah	11		8	F	"	1896	" "	8076
	4								
	5	ENROLLMENT OF NOS. 1 2 and 3 HEREON APPROVED BY THE SECRETARY OF INTERIOR DEC 12 1902							
	6								
	7								
	8								
	9								
	10								
	11								
	12								
	13								
	14								
	15								
	16								
	17								

TRIBAL ENROLLMENT OF PARENTS

Name of Father	Year	County	Name of Mother	Year	County
1 He-lit-ub-bee	De'd	Eagle		Ded	Eagle
2 Eastman Loman	Ded	Red River	No 1		
3 " "	"	" "	No 1		
4					
5					
6					
7			No3 on 1896 roll as Josiah Loman		
8			No2 " " " " Loman		
9			No1 is now wife of Alfred Going on Choctaw #1120.		
10					
11					
12					
13					
14					
15					
16				Date of Application for Enrollment	Apr. 28/99
17					

RESIDENCE: Red River   COUNTY.   **Choctaw Nation**   Choctaw Roll   CARD NO.
POST OFFICE: Harris, I.T.   *(Not Including Freedmen)*   FIELD NO.   1090

Dawes' Roll No.	NAME	Relationship to Person	AGE	SEX	BLOOD	TRIBAL ENROLLMENT Year	County	No.
2903	₁ Harris, Walter C. ³²	First Named	29	M	1/8	1896	Red River	5691
DEAD.	₂ " Sallie C DEAD.	Wife	27	F	Full	1896	" "	5692
2904	₃ " Henry C ¹²	Son	9	M	9/16	1896	" "	5693
2905	₄ " Maggie E ¹¹	Dau	8	F	9/16	1896	" "	5694
2906	₅ " William ⁹	Son	6	M	9/16	1896	" "	5695
2907	₆ " Mattie M ⁷	Dau	4	F	9/16	1896	" "	5696
2908	₇ " Bessie L ⁴	"	1	"	9/16			
DEAD.	₈ " Walter W. DEAD.	Son	4mo	M	9/16			
I.W. 890	₉ " Sarah E. ⁽¹⁸⁾	Wife	16	F	I.W.			
2909	₁₀ " Nettie Ella ¹	Dau	3mo	F				
	₁₁							
	₁₂ No.1 married to Sarah E. Warren,					Father of No 10 is No 1		
	₁₃ April 29, 1900					Mother of No 10 is No 9		
	₁₄ Father of No.9 Robert R Warren, non citz							
	Mother of No.9 Mary E Warren " "							
	₁₅ For proof of death of Nos 2 and 8	June 4,1900						
	₁₆ see testimony of No1 taken at	No. 2 and 8 HEREON DISMISSED UNDER						
	₁₇ Atoka I.T. June 4, 1900.	ORDER OF THE COMMISSION TO THE FIVE CIVILIZED TRIBES OF MARCH 31, 1905.						

TRIBAL ENROLLMENT OF PARENTS

	Name of Father	Year	County	Name of Mother	Year	County
₁	H. C. Harris	1896	Red River	Maggie E. Harris	1896	Non Citz
₂	Sik-ken Washington	Ded	Towson	Mary Washington	1896	Towson
₃	No 1			No 2		
₄	No 1	ENROLLMENT OF NOS. 134567and10 HEREON		No 2		
₅	No 1	APPROVED BY THE SECRETARY OF INTERIOR DEC 12 1902		No 2		
₆	No 1			No 2		
₇	No 1			No 2		
₈	No. 1			No. 2		
₉	No1 enrolled on 1896 Roll as Walter Harris					
₁₀	He is a son of Judge H.C. Harris – Card					
₁₁	No 764 whose evidence of marriage to		ENROLLMENT			
	non citizen wife Maggie Harris is on file		OF NOS. 9 HEREON			
₁₂	with Dawes Commission at Muskogee I.T.		APPROVED BY THE SECRETARY			
₁₃	No7 Affidavit of birth to be supplied. Recd May 9/99		OF INTERIOR AUG 3 1904			
₁₄	No4 on 1896 roll as Maggie Harris					
	No.8 Enrolled May 24, 1900					
₁₅					#1 to 7 inc	
₁₆	For child of No 1&9 see Choctaw NB (Act Apr 26,06) No. 112.		Date of Application for Enrollment. Apr. 28/99			
₁₇	" " " " " " "	" " " " Mar 3-05) " 1243				

Choctaw By Blood Enrollment Cards 1898-1914

RESIDENCE: **Nashoba** COUNTY. **Choctaw Nation** **Choctaw Roll** CARD NO.
POST OFFICE: **Alikchi** I.T. *(Not Including Freedmen)* FIELD NO. **1091**

Dawes' Roll No.	NAME		Relationship to Person	AGE	SEX	BLOOD	TRIBAL ENROLLMENT		
							Year	County	No.
2910	1 Houston, Isaac	61	First Named	58	M	Full	1896	Nashoba	5483
2911	2 " Emma	28	Wife	25	F	"	1896	"	5484
	3								
	4	ENROLLMENT							
	5	OF NOS. 1 and 2 HEREON APPROVED BY THE SECRETARY							
	6	OF INTERIOR DEC 12 1902							
	7								
	8								
	9								
	10								
	11								
	12								
	13								
	14								
	15								
	16								
	17								

TRIBAL ENROLLMENT OF PARENTS

	Name of Father	Year	County	Name of Mother	Year	County
1	Emo-no-hub-bee	De'd	Cedar	Sally	De'd	Towson
2	Jim Lowman	Ded	Towson	Elizabeth Lowman	1896	Nashoba
3						
4						
5						
6						
7						
8						
9						
10						
11						
12						
13						
14						
15						
16						
17						

Date of Application for Enrollment Apr. 28/99

191

Choctaw By Blood Enrollment Cards 1898-1914

POST OFFICE: Lukfata, I.T.	██████ lo COUNTY.	**Choctaw Nation**	Choctaw Roll *(Not Including Freedmen)*	CARD NO. FIELD NO. 1092

Dawes' Roll No.	NAME	Relationship to Person Named	AGE	SEX	BLOOD	TRIBAL ENROLLMENT		
						Year	County	No.
2912	1 Dennis, Simpson ⁵²	First Named	49	M	Full	1896	Bok Tuklo	3389
2913	2 ~~Sillis~~ DIED PRIOR TO SEPTEMBER 25, 1902	Wife	44	F	"	1896	" "	3390
2914	3 " Sophie ¹⁸	S.Dau	15	"	"	1896	" "	3391
	4							
	5	ENROLLMENT OF NOS. 1 2 and 3 HEREON						
	6	APPROVED BY THE SECRETARY						
	7	OF INTERIOR DEC 12 1902						
	8							
	9							
	10							
	11							
	12							
	13							
	14							
	15							
	16							
	17							

TRIBAL ENROLLMENT OF PARENTS

Name of Father	Year	County	Name of Mother	Year	County
1 Un-te-ma-ba	Dead	Bok Tuklo	Noh-ka	Dead	Bok Tuklo
2 ~~Min te hi ya~~	"	" "	~~Ah hu na~~	1896	" "
3 Sam'l Wallen	"	" "	No 2		
4					
5					
6					
7	No1 on 1896 roll as Sampson Dines				
8	No2 " 1896 " " Sillis "				
9	No3 " 1896 " " Sophie "				
	For child of No.3 see NB (March 3, 1905) #963				
10	No2 died January 1, 1900: proof of death filed Dec 3, 1902.				
11	No.2 died Jan. 1, 1900: Enrollment cancelled by Department Sept 16 1904				
12					
13					
14					
15				Date of Application for Enrollment.	Apr. 28/99
16					
17	No 3 P.O. Garvin I.T. 4/10/03				

Choctaw By Blood Enrollment Cards 1898-1914

RESIDENCE: Bok Tuklo   COUNTY.   **Choctaw Nation**   **Choctaw Roll**   CARD NO.
POST OFFICE: Lukfata, I.T.   *(Not Including Freedmen)*   FIELD NO.   1093

Dawes' Roll No.	NAME	Relationship to Person	AGE	SEX	BLOOD	TRIBAL ENROLLMENT		
						Year	County	No.
2915	1 Jackson, Narcissa ²³	First Named	20	F	Full	1896	Bok Tuklo	3394
2916	2 Jackson, Semean ²	Son	8mo	M	"			
	3							
	4							
	5	ENROLLMENT						
	6	OF NOS. 1 and 2 HEREON APPROVED BY THE SECRETARY						
	7	OF INTERIOR DEC 12 1902						
	8							
	9							
	10							
	11							
	12							
	13							
	14							
	15							
	16							
	17							

TRIBAL ENROLLMENT OF PARENTS

	Name of Father	Year	County	Name of Mother	Year	County
1	Dompson Dennis	1896	Bok Tuklo	Marie Dennis	Dead	Bok Tuklo
2	Moses Jackson		Bok Tuklo	No 1		
3						
4						
5						
6						
7	No.1 On 1896 roll as Narcissa Dines					
8	No.2 is now the wife of Moses Jackson on Choctaw card #1085.					
9	No.2 Enrolled Sept 26ᵗʰ, 1900.					
10						
11						
12						
13						
14						#1
15					Date of Application for Enrollment.	
16					Apr. 28/99	
17						

Choctaw By Blood Enrollment Cards 1898-1914

RESIDENCE: Nashoba COUNTY. **Choctaw Nation** Choctaw Roll CARD NO.
POST OFFICE: Alikchi, I.T. (Not Including Freedmen) FIELD NO. 1094

Dawes' Roll No.	NAME	Relationship to Person First Named	AGE	SEX	BLOOD	TRIBAL ENROLLMENT Year	County	No.
2917	1 Holmes, Archibald 31	First Named	28	M	Full	1896	Nashoba	5529
2918	2 " Mima 32	Wife	29	F	"	1896	"	5530
2919	3 " Littie 13	Dau	10	"	"	1896	"	5531
2920	4 " Came 10	Ward	7	M	"	1896	"	5539
	5							
	6 ENROLLMENT							
	7 OF NOS. 1 2 3 and 4 HEREON APPROVED BY THE SECRETARY							
	8 OF INTERIOR DEC 12 1902							
	9							
	10							
	11							
	12							
	13							
	14							
	15							
	16							
	17							

TRIBAL ENROLLMENT OF PARENTS

	Name of Father	Year	County	Name of Mother	Year	County
1	James Holmes	Dead	Nashoba	Susan Holmes	Dead	Nashoba
2	Thompson Morrison	"	"	Aleas Morrison	1896	"
3	Levi Holmes			No 2		
4	Wallace Carney	Dead	Nashoba	Silean Carney	Dead	Nashoba
5						
6						
7	No2 on 1896 roll as Maimie Holmes					
8	No3 " 1896 " " Lithe "					
9	No4 " 1896 " " Gaines "					
10						
11						
12						
13						
14						
15						
16					Date of Application for Enrollment Apr. 28/99	
17						

194

Choctaw By Blood Enrollment Cards 1898-1914

Choctaw Nation

Choctaw Roll
(Not Including Freedmen)   FIELD NO. 1095

Dawes' Roll No.	NAME	Relationship to Person First Named	AGE	SEX	BLOOD	TRIBAL ENROLLMENT		
						Year	County	No.
2921	DIED PRIOR TO SEPTEMBER 25, 1902 1 Wright, Soella		56	F	Full	1893	Eagle	P.R. 454
	2							
	3	ENROLLMENT						
	4	OF NOS. 1 HEREON APPROVED BY THE SECRETARY						
	5	OF INTERIOR DEC 12 1902						
	6							
	7							
	8							
	9							
	10							
	11							
	12							
	13							
	14							
	15							
	16							
	17							

TRIBAL ENROLLMENT OF PARENTS

	Name of Father	Year	County	Name of Mother	Year	County
1	Ar-tom-e-by	Dead	Red River		Dead	Eagle
2						
3						
4						
5						
6						
7	On 1893 Pay roll as Sowely Johnson					
8						
9						
10						
11	No.1 died in November 1900: Enrollment cancelled by Department Oct 19 1906					
12						
13						
14						
15						
16				Date of Application for Enrollment. Apr. 28/99		
17						

Choctaw By Blood Enrollment Cards 1898-1914

RESIDENCE: Nashoba COUNTY. **Choctaw Nation** **Choctaw Roll** CARD NO.
POST OFFICE: Alikchi I.T. *(Not Including Freedmen)* FIELD NO. 1096

Dawes' Roll No.	NAME	Relationship to Person First Named	AGE	SEX	BLOOD	TRIBAL ENROLLMENT		
						Year	County	No.
2922	1 Loman Elizabeth 51	First Named	48	F	Full	1896	Cedar	7914
2923	2 " Agnes 30	Dau	27	"	"	1896	"	7915
	3							
	4	ENROLLMENT						
	5	OF NOS. 1 and 2 HEREON APPROVED BY THE SECRETARY						
	6	OF INTERIOR DEC 12 1902						
	7							
	8							
	9							
	10							
	11							
	12							
	13							
	14							
	15							
	16							
	17							

TRIBAL ENROLLMENT OF PARENTS

	Name of Father	Year	County	Name of Mother	Year	County
1	Thomas	De'd	Cedar	Betsy Thomas	Ded	Cedar
2	Jim Loman	"	Towson	No 1		
3						
4						
5						
6						
7	No 2 enrolled on 1896 Roll as Etnie Loman					
8						
9						
10						
11						
12						
13						
14					Date of Application for Enrollment.	
15						
16					Apr 28/99	
17						

196

Choctaw By Blood Enrollment Cards 1898-1914

RESIDENCE: Red River   COUNTY.   **Choctaw Nation**   **Choctaw Roll**   CARD NO.
POST OFFICE: Goodwater, I.T.   (Not Including Freedmen)   FIELD NO. **1097**

Dawes' Roll No.	NAME	Relationship to Person First Named	AGE	SEX	BLOOD	TRIBAL ENROLLMENT Year	County	No.
2924	1 Prudhume, Charles J ⁵⁵	First Named	52	M	Full	1896	Red River	10422
2925	2 " Mary ⁶⁸	Wife	65	F	"	1896	" "	10424
2926	3 Wade, Nancy ¹²	Ward	9	"	"	1896	" "	13696
2927	4 " Sissy ⁹	"	6	"	"	1896	" "	13697
	5							
	6	ENROLLMENT						
	7	OF NOS. 1,2,3, and 4 HEREON APPROVED BY THE SECRETARY						
	8	OF INTERIOR Dec 12 1902						
	9							
	10							
	11							
	12							
	13							
	14							
	15							
	16							
	17							

TRIBAL ENROLLMENT OF PARENTS

	Name of Father	Year	County	Name of Mother	Year	County
1	Fa-la-mon-tuby	Dead	Eagle	Nancy	Dead	Eagle
2	Hah-pa-tah	"	"		"	"
3	Aaron Wade	"	Red River	Ellen Wade	"	Red River
4	" "	"	" "	" "	"	" "
5						
6						
7	No 1 on 1896 roll as C. J. Prudham					
8	No 2 " 1896 " " Mary "					
9	No 4 " 1896 " " Cissy Wade					
10						
11						
12						
13						
14					Date of Application for Enrollment.	
15						
16					Apr. 28/99	
17						

197

Choctaw By Blood Enrollment Cards 1898-1914

RESIDENCE: Bok Tuklo	COUNTY.	**Choctaw Nation**	**Choctaw Roll**	CARD No.	
POST OFFICE: Lukfata, I.T.			(Not Including Freedmen)	FIELD No. 1098	

Dawes' Roll No.	NAME	Relationship to Person First Named	AGE	SEX	BLOOD	TRIBAL ENROLLMENT		
						Year	County	No.
2028	DIED PRIOR TO SEPTEMBER 25, 1902 1 Pislin, James		24	M	Full	1893	Bok Tuklo	P.R. 177
	2							
	3							
	4	ENROLLMENT						
	5	OF NOS. 1 HEREON APPROVED BY THE SECRETARY						
	6	OF INTERIOR DEC 12 1902						
	7							
	8							
	9							
	10							
	11							
	12							
	13							
	14							
	15							
	16							
	17							

TRIBAL ENROLLMENT OF PARENTS

Name of Father	Year	County	Name of Mother	Year	County
1 Pislin	Dead	Bok Tuklo	Sincy Pislin	Dead	Bok Tuklo
2					
3					
4					
5					
6					
7		On 1893 Pay roll as James Kanashambe			
8					
9					
10		No 1 died Oct 13, 1901; proof of death filed Dec 5, 1902			
11		No.1 died Oct 13 1901: Enrollment cancelled by Department July 8 1904			
12					
13					
14					
15					
16				Date of Application for Enrollment.	Apr. 28/99
17					

198

RESIDENCE: Red River	COUNTY.	**Choctaw Nation**	Choctaw Roll	CARD NO.
POST OFFICE: Janis, I.T.			*(Not Including Freedmen)*	FIELD NO. 1099

Dawes' Roll No.	NAME	Relationship to Person First Named	AGE	SEX	BLOOD	TRIBAL ENROLLMENT		
						Year	County	No.
2929	1 McClure, Elliston 55	First Named	52	M	Full	1896	Red River	9333
DEAD X	2 " Malis	Wife	35	F	"	1896	" "	9334
2930	3 DIED PRIOR TO SEPTEMBER 25, 1902 Susie	Dau	18	"	"	1896	" "	9336
2931	4 " Gibson 15	Son	12	M	"	1896	" "	9337
2932	5 " Minnie 12	Dau	9	F	"	1896	" "	9338
2933	6 DIED PRIOR TO SEPTEMBER 25, 1902 Semie	"	4	"	"	1896	" "	9339
2934	7 Collin, Bittie 20	S.Dau	17	"	"	1896	" "	9335
2935	8 " Annie 19	"	16	"	"	1896	" "	2668
2936	9 DIED PRIOR TO SEPTEMBER 25, 1902 James	S.Son	10	M	"	1896	" "	2669
2937	10 " Ed 11	"	8	"	"	1896	" "	2670
2938	11 " Esther 3	G.S.Dau	1mo	F	"	ENROLLMENT		
2939	12 McClure, Sam 3	Son	4mo	M	"	OF NOS. 13 HEREON APPROVED BY THE SECRETARY		
14675	13 Stewart, Nancy 1	Dau of No.8	5mo	F	"	OF INTERIOR May 20 1903		

No.3 died Feb-1900: Enrollment cancelled by Department July 8. 1904
No1 died Jan or Feb 1900:proof of death filed Dec 3,1902
No6 #5 Aug 7,1902: " " " " " "   No.11 is child of Annie Collin on Choctaw card #2249
No9 #6 Feb – 1901: " " " " " "   No.11 died March13,1901-See testimony in
No6 died Aug 7,1901:No9 died Feb-1901: Enrollment   jacket 1099.
cancelled by Department July 8, 1904   No2 Died Feb 19"1901:Evidence of death filed July 14"1902

TRIBAL ENROLLMENT OF PARENTS

	Name of Father	Year	County	Name of Mother	Year	County
1	Wallace McClure	Dead	Red River	Isabelle McClure	1896	Red River
2	Thos. Lawachubbee	"	Eagle	Yoh-ka	Dead	" "
3	No1			Elsie McClure	"	" "
4	No1		ENROLLMENT OF NOS. 1,3,4,5,6,7,8,9,10,11 and 12 HEREON	"	"	" "
5	No1		APPROVED BY THE SECRETARY	"	"	" "
6	No1		OF INTERIOR Dec 12 1902	"	"	" "
7	Robert Collin	Dead	Red River	No2		" "
8	" "	"	" "	No2		" "
9	" "	"	" "	No2		" "
10	" "	"	" "	No2		" "
11	Robert Anderson		Choctaw	No8		
12	No1		No.12 Enrolled June 23d, 1900	No2		

For child of No8 see No 7

13 No1 on 1896 roll as Allison McClure | Father of No.13 is Levi Stewart on Choctaw Card
14 No2 " 1896 " " Nalis   No.911: Mother is No.8
No6 " 1896 " " Cemie   No13 born Aug 27-1901:application made 12/15/02
15 No7 " 1896 " " Littie   No11 enrolled Nov.24/99
16 No8 " 1896 " " Anna Collin   Date of application for enrollment Apr 28/99
17 No8 is now wife of Levi Stewart Choctaw card #911. Evidence of marriage filed Dec 24,1902

Goodwater I.T. 11/28/02 Proof of birth of No13 filed Jan. 30,1903 No2 hereon dismissed under order of the
Commission of the Five Civilized Tribes of March 31, 1905

Choctaw By Blood Enrollment Cards 1898-1914

POST OFFICE: Luklata, I.T.   COUNTY. **Choctaw Nation**   **Choctaw Roll** (Not Including Freedmen)   CARD No.   FIELD NO. 1100

Dawes' Roll No.	NAME	Relationship to Person	AGE	SEX	BLOOD	TRIBAL ENROLLMENT		
						Year	County	No.
2940	1 Willis, Eastman H ⁵⁶	First Named	53	M	Full	1896	Bok Tuklo	13435
2941	2 " Mary J	Wife	29	F	"	1896	" "	13436
2942	3 " Frances ¹³	Dau	10	"	"	1896	" "	13438
2943	4 " Robinson ¹⁰	Son	7	M	"	1896	" "	13439
2944	5 " Rotey ⁷	Dau	4	F	"	1896	" "	13440
	6							
	7 ENROLLMENT							
	8 OF NOS. 1 2 3 4 and 5 HEREON APPROVED BY THE SECRETARY							
	9 OF INTERIOR DEC 12 1902							
	10							
	11							
	12							
	13							
	14							
	15							
	16							
	17							

(Row 2941 is struck through; "DIED PRIOR TO SEPTEMBER 25, 1902" noted)

TRIBAL ENROLLMENT OF PARENTS

	Name of Father	Year	County	Name of Mother	Year	County
1	He-ke-tom-be	Dead	Bok Tuklo	Na-yo-ka	Dea	Bok Tuklo
2	Losimo Christy	"	Towson	Lisana Christy	"	Towson
3	No1			No2		
4	No1			No2		
5	No1			No2		
6						
7						
8	No1 on 1896 roll as E. H. Willis					
9	No2 died Nov. 15, 1899: proof of death filed Dec 5, 1902					
10	No.2 died Nov. 15, 1899: Enrollment cancelled by Department July 8, 1904					
11						
12						
13						
14					Date of Application for Enrollment.	
15						
16					Apr. 28/99	
17						

Choctaw By Blood Enrollment Cards 1898-1914

RESIDENCE: Red River COUNTY.	POST OFFICE: Goodwater I.T.	**Choctaw Nation**	Choctaw Roll (Not Including Freedmen)	CARD NO. FIELD NO. **1101**

Dawes' Roll No.	NAME		Relationship to Person First Named	AGE	SEX	BLOOD	TRIBAL ENROLLMENT		
							Year	County	No.
2945	1 Butter, Abel	43	First Named	40	M	Full	1896	Red River	1399
2946	2 " Aly	38	Wife	35	F	"	1896	" "	1400
2947	3 " Silas	11	Son	8	M	"	1896	" "	1401
2948	4 " Dwight	9	"	6	"	"	1896	" "	1402
2949	5 " Ellis	6	"	2	"	"			
2950	6 Byington, Elizabeth	21	Ward	18	F	"	1893	Eagle	353
2951	7 Butter, Jimmie		Son	1 mo	M	"			
	8								
	9 No 6 also on 1896 roll as Isabelle								
	10 Byington, Page 32, No 1281, Eagle Co.								
	11								
	12								
	13								
	14								
	15 For child of Nos 1&2 see NB (March 3, 1905) #1394								
	16								
	17								

DIED PRIOR TO SEPTEMBER 25, 1902 (stamp over row 7)

ENROLLMENT OF NOS. 123456 and 7 HEREON APPROVED BY THE SECRETARY OF INTERIOR Dec 12, 1903 (stamp)

TRIBAL ENROLLMENT OF PARENTS

	Name of Father	Year	County	Name of Mother	Year	County
1	John Butter					
2	Ashalintubbee	Ded	Eagle	Timis	De'd	Eagle
3	No 1			No 2		
4	No 1			No 2		
5	No 1			No 2		
6	Aleck Byington	Ded	Eagle	Louisa Byington	Ded	Eagle
7	No 1			No 2		
8						
9						
10	No1 Enrolled on 1896 Roll as Abel Butler					
11	No2 " " " " " Ila Butler					
	No3 " " " " " Sissy Butler					
12	No4 " " " " " Lewis Butler					
13	No5 " " " " " Ellis Butler					
14	No6 " " 1893 Pay roll for Eagle County					
15	as Lisby Homma – orphan child					
	No7 enrolled Nov. 24/99					
16	No7 died April.1900: proof of death filed Dec.3,1902. No5 Affidavit of birth to be supplied Recd Apr 28/99					
17	No7 died April – 1900: Enrollment cancelled by Department July 8, 1904					

DATE OF APPLICATION FOR ENROLLMENT. April 28/99

#1 to 6

201

Choctaw By Blood Enrollment Cards 1898-1914

RESIDENCE: Eagle   COUNTY.   **Choctaw Nation**   Choctaw Roll   CARD NO.

POST OFFICE: Eagle Town I.T.   *(Not Including Freedmen)*   FIELD NO. **1102**

Dawes' Roll No.	NAME		Relationship to Person	AGE	SEX	BLOOD	TRIBAL ENROLLMENT		
							Year	County	No.
2952	1 Anna	Santa 51	First Named	48	M	Full	1896	Eagle	300
2953	2 "	Lisne 23	Wife	30	F	"	1896	"	291
2954	3 "	Melville 15	Son	12	M	"	1896	"	295
2955	4 "	Kolisten 10	"	7	"	"	1896	"	286
2956	5 "	Mary 8	Dau	5	F	"	1896	"	296
2957	6 "	Tecumseh 6	Son	3	M	"	1896	"	303
2958	7 "	Thompson 4	"	6mo	"	"			
16047	8 "	Silvanie	Dau	2	F	"			
	9 ENROLLMENT								
	OF NOS. 1 2 3 4 5 6 and 7 HEREON APPROVED BY THE SECRETARY								
	OF INTERIOR Dec 12, 1902								
	11								
	12 ENROLLMENT								
	OF NOS. ~~~ 8 ~~~ HEREON APPROVED BY THE SECRETARY								
	OF INTERIOR Aug 22, 1906								
	15								
	16								
	17								

TRIBAL ENROLLMENT OF PARENTS

	Name of Father	Year	County	Name of Mother	Year	County
1	Achuk-ma-tubbee	Ded	Eagle	Tahoyo	Ded	Eagle
2	Ta-ma-hil-a-bi	Ded	"	No yahima	1896	"
3	No 1			No 2		
4	No 1			No 2		
5	No 1			No 2		
6	No 1			No 2		
7	No 1			No 2		
8	No 1			No 2		
9						
10			No6 on 1896 Roll as Ticineah Anna			
11			No8 was born Jan. 19, 1901; application was received and No8 placed on this card March 4, 1905, under Act of Congress			
12			approved March 3, 1905			
13			For child of Nos 1&2 see N.B. (Apr. 26-06) Card #914			
14				Santa Anna		
15						
16	Santa Anna, Francis				#1 to 7 inc	
17				Date of Application for Enrollment		April 28/99

202

Choctaw By Blood Enrollment Cards 1898-1914

RESIDENCE: Eagle COUNTY.
POST OFFICE: Eagle Town I.T.

Choctaw Nation

Choctaw Roll
(Not Including Freedmen)

CARD NO.
FIELD NO. **1103**

Dawes' Roll No.	NAME	Relationship to Person First Named	AGE	SEX	BLOOD	TRIBAL ENROLLMENT		
						Year	County	No.
2959	1 Jackson, Toto 58	First Named	55	M	Full	1896	Eagle	12230
2960	2 " Salin 43	Wife	40	F	"	1896	"	12231
2961	3 McGee, Elizabeth 20	Ward	17	"	"	1896	"	9298
	4							
	5 ENROLLMENT							
	6 OF NOS. 1 2 and 3 HEREON APPROVED BY THE SECRETARY							
	7 OF INTERIOR Dec. 12, 1902							
	8							
	9							
	10							
	11							
	12							
	13							
	14							
	15							
	16							
	17							

TRIBAL ENROLLMENT OF PARENTS

	Name of Father	Year	County	Name of Mother	Year	County
1	Jackson	De'd	Eagle		De'd	
2	Billy	Ded	Buk[sic]-Tuk-lo	E-lan-te-ma	"	Eagle
3	Billy McGee	Ded	Eagle	Mollie McGee	"	"
4						
5						
6						
7	No1 on 1896 roll as Toto					
8	No2 " " " " Selin Toto					
9	No3 Orphan					
10						
11						
12						
13						
14						
15					Date of Application for Enrollment.	
16						
17					Apr 28 "99	

Choctaw By Blood Enrollment Cards 1898-1914

RESIDENCE: Red River   COUNTY.   **Choctaw Nation**   **Choctaw Roll**   CARD NO.
POST OFFICE: Cerro Gordo, Ark.   *(Not Including Freedmen)*   FIELD NO.   **1104**

Dawes' Roll No.	NAME	Relationship to Person First Named	AGE	SEX	BLOOD	TRIBAL ENROLLMENT		
						Year	County	No.
2962	1 Loman Josan	DIED PRIOR TO SEPTEMBER 25, 1902	45	M	Full	1896	Red River	8036
2963	2 " Lucy Ann 21	Wife	18	F	"	1896	" "	1396
2964	3 " Louis	DIED PRIOR TO SEPTEMBER 25, 1902 Son	9	M	"	1896	" "	8037
2965	4 " Lena 10	Dau	7	F	"	1896	" "	8038
2966	5 " Febre	DIED PRIOR TO SEPTEMBER 25, 1902 Dau	6mo	F	"			
	6							
	7							
	8							
	9							
	10							
	11							
	12	No.1 died – – , 1900: No. 3 died						
	13	– – , 1900: No 5 died Sept. 7, 1902:						
	14	Enrollment cancelled by Department July 8, 1904.						
	15							
	16							
	17							

ENROLLMENT OF NOS. 1 2 3 4 and 5 HEREON APPROVED BY THE SECRETARY OF INTERIOR Dec. 12, 1902

TRIBAL ENROLLMENT OF PARENTS

Name of Father	Year	County	Name of Mother	Year	County
1 Eastman Loman	Ded	Red River	On tia ho na	Ded	Red River
2 Davis McClure	"	" "	Sally Billy	1896	" "
3 No 1			Nice Loman	Ded	" "
4 No 1		" "		"	" "
5 No 1			No 2		
6					
7					
8					
9			For child of No 2 see N.B. (March 3, 1905) #1000		
10			No 2 Enrolled as Lucy Ann Billy on 1896 roll.		
11			No.5 Enrolled Aug. 6th 1900		
12			No 2 also on 1896 Choctaw census roll, page 296, No 11450, as Lucy Stephenson.		
13			No 5 Died September 7-1902 Proof of death filed October 25, 1902		
14			No 1 died in 1900; proof of death filed Dec. 3, 1902.		
15			No 3 " " 1900 " " " " " " " "		
16			No 2 now wife of Samuel McKinney on Choctaw card #805: Evidence of marriage filed Dec. 6, 1902.		
17			Date of Application for Enrollment. Apr. 28/99		

Choctaw By Blood Enrollment Cards 1898-1914

RESIDENCE: Red River   COUNTY.   **Choctaw Nation**   Choctaw Roll   CARD NO.
POST OFFICE: Harris I.T.   (Not Including Freedmen)   FIELD NO. **1105**

Dawes' Roll No.	NAME		Relationship to Person First Named	AGE	SEX	BLOOD	TRIBAL ENROLLMENT		
							Year	County	No.
2967	1 Morris, Solon	28	First Named	25	M	1/16	1896	Red River	8684
I.W. 65	2 " Arreathy	22	Wife	19	F	I.W.	1896	"Non Citz"	14823
2968	3 " Almer	4	Dau	1	"	1/32			
2969	4 " Elmer Otis DIED PRIOR TO SEPTEMBER 25, 1902		Son	3 mo	M	1/32			
	5								
	6								
	7	ENROLLMENT OF NOS. 1, 3 and 4 HEREON							
	8	APPROVED BY THE SECRETARY OF INTERIOR Dec. 12, 1902							
	9								
	10								
	11	ENROLLMENT OF NOS. ~ 2 ~ HEREON							
	12	APPROVED BY THE SECRETARY OF INTERIOR Jun 13, 1903							
	13								
	14								
	15								
	16								
	17								

TRIBAL ENROLLMENT OF PARENTS

	Name of Father	Year	County	Name of Mother	Year	County
1	Calvin Morris	Ded	Non Citz	Carrie Hampton	1896	Red River
2	Mathew Randolph	1896	Non Citz	Anna Randolph	1896	Red River (Tex)
3	No 1			No 2		
4	No 1			No 2		
5						
6						
7						
8						
9	No 2 Admitted as inter married citizen by Dawes Commission					
10	#1278, as Arreothy Morris – No appeal					
11	No 2 on 1896 roll as Ralphy Morris					
	No 4 born July 13th 1901. Enrolled Nov. 1st 1901					
12	For child of Nos. 1 and 2 see N.B. (Apr 26-06) No 539					
13	No 4 died August 27, 1902, proof of death filed Dec 3, 1902					
14	No4 died Aug. 27, 1902. Enrollment cancelled by Department July 8, 1904					
15	For child of Nos 1&2 see N.B. (March 3, 1905) #1061				#1 to 3.	
16					Date of Application for Enrollment	
17	P.O. Idabel I.T. 4/12/05				4-28-99	

205

RESIDENCE: Eagle COUNTY.	**Choctaw Nation**	Choctaw Roll	CARD No.
POST OFFICE: Eagletown, I.T.		(Not Including Freedmen)	FIELD No. **1106**

Dawes' Roll No.	NAME		Relationship to Person First Named	AGE	SEX	BLOOD	TRIBAL ENROLLMENT		
							Year	County	No.
2970	1 McGee, Jesse	33	First Named	30	M	Full	1896	Eagle	9293
2971	2 " Licksey	30	Wife	27	F	"	1896	"	9294
2972	3 " Ennie	11	Dau	8	"	"	1896	"	9295
2973	4 " Wattie	9	Son	6	M	"	1896	"	9296
2974	5 " Josie	6	Dau	3	F	"	1896	"	9297
2975	6 " Sissy	4	"	6mo	"	"			
15570	7 " Selin	15	Niece	12	"	"	1893	"	P.R. 261
2976	8 " Linney	1	Dau	3wks	F	"			
	9								
	10	ENROLLMENT OF NOS. 123456and8 HEREON APPROVED BY THE SECRETARY OF INTERIOR Dec. 2, 1902							
	11								
	12								
	13	ENROLLMENT OF NOS. ~7~ HEREON APPROVED BY THE SECRETARY OF INTERIOR Sep. 22, 1904							
	14								
	15								
	16								
	17								

TRIBAL ENROLLMENT OF PARENTS

	Name of Father	Year	County	Name of Mother	Year	County
1	Austin McGee	1896	Bok Tuklo	Po-pone	Dead	Eagle
2	Ta-ma-he-laby	Dead	Eagle	No-wa-he-ma	1896	"
3	No 1			No 2		
4	No 1			No 2		
5	No 1			No 2		
6	No 1			No 2		
7	Butler McGee	Dead	Eagle	Emiline McGee	Dead	Eagle
8	No 1			No 2		
9						
10						
11		No3 on 1896 roll as Emma McGee				
12		No4 " 1896 " " Watty "				
13		No7 " 1893 Pay roll as Selin Forb.				
14		No8 Born Aug. 5, 1902; enrolled Aug. 22, 1902. For child of Nos. 1&2 see N.B. (March 3, 1905) #1145				
15	See additional testimony as to No.7 of Dec. 5, 1902			Refer to No 2 on		#1 to 7
16	See also testimony relative to No.7 taken at Atoka IT May 13 1904			7-8-21	Date of Application for Enrollment.	
17						Apr.28/99

Choctaw By Blood Enrollment Cards 1898-1914

RESIDENCE: Eagle   COUNTY.   **Choctaw Nation**   Choctaw Roll   CARD NO.
POST OFFICE: Eagletown, I.T.   *(Not Including Freedmen)*   FIELD NO. **1107**

Dawes' Roll No.	NAME		Relationship to Person First Named	AGE	SEX	BLOOD	TRIBAL ENROLLMENT		
							Year	County	No.
2977	₁ Ben, Louisa	40	Named	37	F	Full	1896	Bok Tuklo	4157
2978	₂ Amos, Eastman	17	Son	14	M	"	1896	" "	314
2979	₃ " Nellis	16	Dau	13	F	"	1893	Eagle	P.R. 247
2980	₄ Cooper, Sisty	13	"	10	"	"	1896	Bok Tuklo	2563
2981	₅ Going, John	10	Son	7	M	"	1896	" "	4778
2982	₆ Ben, Elias	4	Son	8mo	M	"			
	₇								
	₈	ENROLLMENT							
	₉	OF NOS. 12345and6 HEREON APPROVED BY THE SECRETARY							
	₁₀	OF INTERIOR Dec. 12, 1902							
	₁₁								
	₁₂								
	₁₃								
	₁₄								
	₁₅								
	₁₆								
	₁₇								

TRIBAL ENROLLMENT OF PARENTS

Name of Father	Year	County	Name of Mother	Year	County
₁ Forbit	Dead	Eagle	Ah-no-ah-ka	Dead	Eagle
₂ Sam Amos	"	"	No 1		
₃ " "	"	"	No 1		
₄ William Cooper	"	"	No 1		
₅ Bunton Going	"	"	No 1		
₆ Joe Ben	1896	"	No 1		
₇					
₈					
₉	No 2 on 1896 roll as E. Amos				
₁₀	No 4 ' 1896 " " Listie Cooper				
₁₁	No 2 also on 1896 roll, Bok Tuklo Co., Page 90, No 3740, as Eastman Emus				
₁₂	No 3 also on 1896 roll. Bok Tuklo Col..				
₁₃	Page 90, No 3741 as Nellis Emus				
₁₄	No.1 is now the wife of Joe Ben on Choctaw card #1109. Evidence of marriage				
₁₅	filed July 15, 190				#1 to 5
₁₆	No. 6 Enrolled July 15, 1901			Date of Application for Enrollment.	
₁₇				Apr. 28/99	

Choctaw By Blood Enrollment Cards 1898-1914

RESIDENCE: Red River COUNTY.
POST OFFICE: Goodwater, I.T.

Choctaw Nation

Choctaw Roll
(Not Including Freedmen)

CARD No.
FIELD No. 1108

Dawes' Roll No.	NAME	Relationship to Person First Named	AGE	SEX	BLOOD	TRIBAL ENROLLMENT		
						Year	County	No.
2983	1 Ashshalintubbi, Quitman 20	First Named	17	M	Full	1896	Eagle	297
2984	2 " Craven 16	Bro	13	"	"	1896	"	278
	3							
	4 ENROLLMENT							
	5 OF NOS. 1 and 2 HEREON APPROVED BY THE SECRETARY							
	6 OF INTERIOR DEC 12 1902							
	7							
	8							
	9							
	10							
	11							
	12							
	13							
	14							
	15							
	16							
	17							

TRIBAL ENROLLMENT OF PARENTS

	Name of Father	Year	County	Name of Mother	Year	County
1	Alex Ashshalintubbi	Dead	Eagle	Nicey Ashshalintubbi	Dead	Eagle
2	" "	"	"	" "	"	"
3						
4						
5	No2 on 1896 roll as Graven Ashshalintubbi					
6	No2 also on 1896 roll as Craven Wilson page 355 #13528 Dec 8, 1902					
7	No2 is now the husband of Kissy Hotubbee on Choc card #1051 2/9/02					
8						
9						
10						
11						
12						
13						
14						
15					Date of Application for Enrollment.	
16					Apr. 28/99	
17						

Choctaw By Blood Enrollment Cards 1898-1914

Choctaw Nation

Choctaw Roll
(Not Including Freedmen)

CARD No.
FIELD No. 1109

Dawes' Roll No.	NAME		Relationship to Person First Named	AGE	SEX	BLOOD	TRIBAL ENROLLMENT		
							Year	County	No.
2985	1 Ben, Joe	40	First Named	37	M	Full	1896	Eagle	1336
DEAD.	2 " Salena	DEAD.	Wife	38	F	"	1896	"	1312
	3								
	4	ENROLLMENT							
	5	OF NOS. 1 HEREON APPROVED BY THE SECRETARY							
	6	OF INTERIOR DEC 12 1902							
	7								
	8	No. 2 HEREON DISMISSED UNDER							
	9	ORDER OF THE COMMISSION TO THE FIVE							
	10	CIVILIZED TRIBES OF MARCH 31, 1905.							
	11								
	12								
	13								
	14								
	15								
	16								
	17								

TRIBAL ENROLLMENT OF PARENTS

	Name of Father	Year	County	Name of Mother	Year	County
1	Ben	Dead	Eagle	E-la-ka-ma	Dead	Eagle
2	Ya-ho-ta-by	"	Nashoba	Ho-ta-che-ho-na	"	"
3						
4						
5						
6			No2 on 1896 roll as Selina Ben			
7			No.1 is now husband of Louisa Forbit on Choctaw Card #1107, July 15, 1901			
8			No 2 died November 20, 1900. Proof of death filed Aug 16, 1901.			
9						
10						
11						
12						
13						
14						
15						
16				Date of Application for Enrollment.		Apr 28/99
17						

Choctaw By Blood Enrollment Cards 1898-1914

RESIDENCE: Bok Tuklo   COUNTY.   **Choctaw Nation**   Choctaw Roll   CARD NO.
POST OFFICE: Lukfata, I.T.   *(Not Including Freedmen)*   FIELD NO.   1110

Dawes' Roll No.	NAME	Relationship to Person First Named	AGE	SEX	BLOOD	TRIBAL ENROLLMENT		
						Year	County	No.
DEAD.	1 Thomas, Tobias DEAD.		24	M	Full	1896	Bok Tuklo	12198
2986	2 " Louisa 22	Wife	19	F	"	1896	" "	12199
DEAD.	3 " Grinton DEAD.	Dau	6mo	"	"			
DEAD.	4 " Joseph DEAD.	Son	7wks	M	"			
	5							
	6	ENROLLMENT						
	7	OF NOS. 2 HEREON APPROVED BY THE SECRETARY						
	8	OF INTERIOR DEC 12 1902						
	9							
	10	No. 1-3-4 HEREON DISMISSED UNDER ORDER OF THE COMMISSION TO THE FIVE						
	11	CIVILIZED TRIBES OF MARCH 31, 1905.						
	12							
	13							
	14							
	15							
	16							
	17							

TRIBAL ENROLLMENT OF PARENTS

	Name of Father	Year	County	Name of Mother	Year	County
1	Washington Thomas	Dead	Bok Tuklo	Phoebe Thomas	1896	Bok Tuklo
2	Harlison Lawitaia	"	" "	Siss Lawitaia	Dead	" "
3	No 1			No 2		
4	No.1			No.2		
5						
6			No.4 Enrolled May 6, 1901.			
7						
8						
9			No1 died in 1900: proof of death filed Dec 3, 1902.			
10			No3 " " 1900: " " " " " "			
11			No4 " in Spring of 1902: proof of death filed Dec 3, 1902			
12			No2 is wife of Silas Tushka on Choc 1149.			
13			For child of No 2 see NB (March 3 1905) #903			
14					#1 to 3	
15				Date of Application for Enrollment.		
16				Apr 28/99		
17						

Choctaw By Blood Enrollment Cards 1898-1914

RESIDENCE: Bok Tuklo   COUNTY.   **Choctaw Nation**   **Choctaw Roll**   CARD NO.
POST OFFICE: Lukfata, I.T.   (Not Including Freedmen)   FIELD NO.   **1111**

Dawes' Roll No.	NAME		Relationship to Person First Named	AGE	SEX	BLOOD	TRIBAL ENROLLMENT		
							Year	County	No.
2987	₁ Ishcomer, Eve	34	First Named	31	F	Full	1896	Bok Tuklo	6287
2988	₂ Harley, Manford	17	Son	14	M	"	1893	" "	P.R. 54
2989	₃ Billy, Frances	13	Dau	10	F	"	1896	" "	1255
2990	₄ " Sophina	11	"	8	"	"	1896	" "	1256
2991	₅ " Robert	9	"	6	"	"	1896	" "	1257
14638	₆ Willis, Selena	1	Dau	13mo	F	"			
	₇								
	₈	ENROLLMENT							
	₉	OF NOS. 1 2 3 4 and 5 HEREON APPROVED BY THE SECRETARY							
	₁₀	OF INTERIOR Dec. 12, 1902							
	₁₁								
	₁₂	ENROLLMENT							
	₁₃	OF NOS. 6 HEREON APPROVED BY THE SECRETARY							
	₁₄	OF INTERIOR May 20, 1903							
	₁₅								
	₁₆								
	₁₇								

TRIBAL ENROLLMENT OF PARENTS

	Name of Father	Year	County	Name of Mother	Year	County
₁	Nelson Ishcomer	Dead	Bok Tuklo	Ish-ti-oke	Dead	Bok Tuklo
₂	Tecumseh Harley	"	" "	No 1		
₃	Morris Billy	"	" "	No 1		
₄	" "	"	" "	No 1		
₅	" "	"	" "	No 1		
₆	Sampson Willis	1896	" "	No 1		
₇						
₈						
₉						
₁₀	No 4 on 1896 roll as Sapheyney Billy					
₁₁	No 1 " 1896 " " Eve Ishcommar					
₁₂	No 2 " 1893 Pay roll as Manford Horly No6 Born Nov. 21, 1901 enrolled Dec. 24, 1902.					
₁₃	No2 is now husbnd of Enos Tontubbee on Choc card #728 Nov 28/03					
₁₄	For child of No2 see NB (March 3, 1905) #1136					
₁₅					#1 to 5	
₁₆					Date of Application for Enrollment	April 28, 1899
₁₇						

Choctaw By Blood Enrollment Cards 1898-1914

RESIDENCE: Red River COUNTY. **Choctaw Nation** Choctaw Roll CARD NO.
POST OFFICE: Harris, I.T. (Not Including Freedmen) FIELD NO. 1112

Dawes' Roll No.	NAME	Relationship to Person	AGE	SEX	BLOOD	TRIBAL ENROLLMENT		
						Year	County	No.
2992	1 Harris, Jack 36	First Named	33	M	1/16	1896	Red River	5699
I.W. 66	2 " Amanda A 31	Wife	28	F	I.W.	1896	" "	14627
2993	3 " Lena J 11	Dau	8	"	1/32	1896	" "	5700
2994	4 " Frank 5	Son	1½	M	1/32			
2995	5 " Dewy Lee 2	Son	1mo	M	1/32			
	6							
	7	ENROLLMENT						
	8	OF NOS. 1,3,4 and 5 HEREON APPROVED BY THE SECRETARY						
	9	OF INTERIOR DEC 12 1902						
	10							
	11							
	12	ENROLLMENT						
	13	OF NOS. ~~2~~ HEREON APPROVED BY THE SECRETARY						
	14	OF INTERIOR JUN 13 1903						
	15							
	16							
	17							

TRIBAL ENROLLMENT OF PARENTS

	Name of Father	Year	County	Name of Mother	Year	County
1	H. C. Harris	1896	Red River	Maggie Harris	1896	Intermarried
2	Frank McDonald	Dead	Non Citz	Nancy McDonald	1896	Non Citz
3	No 1			No 2		
4	No 1			No 2		
5	No.1			No.2		
6						
7						
8	No2 on 1896 roll as Amanda Harris					
9	No2 was admitted by the Dawes Commission as an intermarried					
10	citizen, as Amanda A. Harris, Case No 1373. No appeal. Evidence of marriage on file in office of Dawes Commission,					
11	Muskogee, I.T.					
12						
13	Evidence of marriage of parents of No1 are on file in office					
14	of Dawes Commission, Muskogee, I.T.			#1 to 4 inc		
15				Date of Application for Enrollment.		
16	No4 Affidavit of birth to be supplied. Recd May 6/99			Apr. 28/99		
17	No.5 Enrolled Oct. 30th, 1900.					

212

Choctaw By Blood Enrollment Cards 1898-1914

RESIDENCE: Red River   COUNTY.   **Choctaw Nation**   **Choctaw Roll** *(Not Including Freedmen)*   CARD NO.

POST OFFICE: Harris, I.T.   FIELD NO. 1113

Dawes' Roll No.	NAME	Relationship to Person First Named	AGE	SEX	BLOOD	TRIBAL ENROLLMENT		
						Year	County	No.
I.W. 1288	1 Kirby, Wyatte T. ⁶⁰	First Named	56	M	I.W.	1896	Red River	14726
2996	2 " Ed ²⁰	Son	17	"	1/16	1896	" "	7583
See 5350	3 " ~~Sallie~~[sic]	"	~~14~~	"	~~1/16~~	~~1896~~	" "	~~7582~~
I.W. 809	4 Kirby, Lizzie ⑯	Wife of No 2	16	F	I.W.			
	5							
	6 ENROLLMENT OF NOS. 2 HEREON APPROVED BY THE SECRETARY OF INTERIOR DEC 12 1902							
	7							
	8							
	9							
	10 ENROLLMENT OF NOS. 4 HEREON APPROVED BY THE SECRETARY OF INTERIOR MAY 21 1904							
	11							
	12							
	13 ENROLLMENT OF NOS. 1 HEREON APPROVED BY THE SECRETARY OF INTERIOR MAR 14 1905							
	14							
	15							
	16							
	17							

TRIBAL ENROLLMENT OF PARENTS

Name of Father	Year	County	Name of Mother	Year	County
1 Richard Kirby	Dead	Non Citz	Pollie Kirby	Dead	Non Citz
2 No 1			Kizzie Kirby	"	Red River
3 ~~No 1~~			" "	"	" " "
4 John Wheeler		noncitizen	Sibby Wheeler		noncitizen
5					
6 No. 1 formerly husband of Kizzie Kirby, 1885 Red River, No 765,					
7 who died in 1887					
8 No1 on 1896 roll as Wyatte Kirby No3 " 1896 " " Sallie E "					
9 For child of Nos. 2&4 see N.B. (Apr. 26, 1906) Card No. 106					
10 No1 was married to Kizzie Harris a Choctaw Citizen, in 1872,					
11 under the laws of Arkansas For child of Nos 2&4 see NB (March 3 1905) #1144					
12 ~~No. 3 transferred to Choctaw card #5350 with her husband, Henry C Stanford~~					
13			~~Dec. 6, 1900~~		
14 No 4 transferred from Choctaw card D945 April 15, 1904. See decision of March 15, 1904					
15					
16			Date of Application for Enrollment.	#103inc Apr. 28/99	
17					

213

Choctaw By Blood Enrollment Cards 1898-1914

RESIDENCE: Towson COUNTY.   **Choctaw Nation**   Choctaw Roll CARD NO.
POST OFFICE: Fowlerville, I.T.   (Not Including Freedmen)   FIELD NO. 1114

Dawes' Roll No.	NAME	Relationship to Person First Named	AGE	SEX	BLOOD	TRIBAL ENROLLMENT		
						Year	County	No.
2997	1 Jackson, Nicholas 44	First Named	41	M	Full	1896	Towson	6767
2998	2 " Susan 21	Wife	18	F	"	1896	"	5505
2999	3 Jacob, Emma 5	S.Dau	1½	"	"			
	4							
	5 ENROLLMENT							
	6 OF NOS. 1 2 and 3 HEREON APPROVED BY THE SECRETARY							
	7 OF INTERIOR DEC 12 1902							
	8							
	9							
	10							
	11							
	12							
	13							
	14							
	15							
	16							
	17							

TRIBAL ENROLLMENT OF PARENTS

	Name of Father	Year	County	Name of Mother	Year	County
1	Tak-lan-tubbee	Dead	Towson	No-wah-tee	Dead	Towson
2	Joseph Hokabe	1896	"	Litey Hokabe	"	"
3	Gleason Jacob	Dead	"	No 2		
4						
5						
6	No2 on 1896 roll as Susan Hokabe					
7	For child of No.1, see N.B. (Apr. 26, 1906) Card No. 202					
8						
9						
10	See card T-604					
11						
12						
13						
14				Date of Application for Enrollment.		
15						
16				Apr. 28/99		
17						

RESIDENCE: Towson	COUNTY.	**Choctaw Nation**		Choctaw Roll	CARD NO.
POST OFFICE: Alikchi, I.T.				*(Not Including Freedmen)*	FIELD NO. 1115

Dawes' Roll No.	NAME	Relationship to Person First Named	AGE	SEX	BLOOD	TRIBAL ENROLLMENT		
						Year	County	No.
3000	1 Hoyopatubbi, Wash ⁴²	First Named	39	M	Full	1896	Towson	5492
DEAD.	2 " Narcissa	Wife	34	F	"	1896	"	5493
3001	3 " Sallie *DIED PRIOR TO SEPTEMBER 25, 1902*	Dau	14	"	"	1896	"	5494
3002	4 " Lettie ¹⁰	"	7	"	"	1896	"	5495
3003	5 " Jincy	"	4	"	"	1896	"	5496
DEAD.	6 " Isabella	"	4½ mo	"	"			
	7							
	8							
	9							
	10							
	11							
	12							
	13							
	14							
	15							
	16							
	17							

ENROLLMENT
OF NOS. 1 3 4 and 5 HEREON
APPROVED BY THE SECRETARY
OF INTERIOR DEC 12 1902

No. 2 and 6 HEREON DISMISSED UNDER
ORDER OF THE COMMISSION TO THE FIVE
CIVILIZED TRIBES OF MARCH 31, 1905.

TRIBAL ENROLLMENT OF PARENTS

	Name of Father	Year	County	Name of Mother	Year	County
1	Abel Hoyopatubbi	Dead	Towson	Isabelle Hoyopatubbi	Dead	Red River
2	Ellis Cobb	"	Nashoba	Martha Cobb	"	Nashoba
3	No 1			No 2		
4	No 1			No 2		
5	No 1			No 2		
6	No 1			No 2		
7						
8	No4 on 1896 roll as Rhoda Hoyopatubbi					
9						
10	No6 enrolled Dec 19/99. Affidavit					
11	irregular and returned for correction					
12	No.2 Died October 15, 1899. See letter of No1, filed April 25, 1901.					
13	No.1 is now husband of Sarah James on Choctaw Card 574, April 25, 1901					
14						
15						Date of Application for Enrollment.
16	No6 Died Oct 4, 1900, proof of death filed Jany. 21, 1903.					Apr. 28/99
17	No.3 died – – 1900: Enrollment cancelled by Department July 8 1904					

Choctaw By Blood Enrollment Cards 1898-1914

Dawes' Roll No.	NAME		Relationship to Person First Named	AGE	SEX	BLOOD	TRIBAL ENROLLMENT		
							Year	County	No.
3004	1 Jones Edward	36	First Named	33	M	Full	1896	Red River	7053
3005	2 " Winsey	26	Wife	23	F	"	1896	" "	7054
3006	3 " Nellis	9	Son	6	M	"	"	" "	7055
3007	4 " Sibbie	5	Dau "[sic]	1	F	"			
3008	5 Wade Sarbit	18	Ward	15	"	"	1896	" "	13686
3009	6 McClure Selfin	16	Bro.	13	M	"	1896	" "	9345
3010	7 Jones, Ensie	3	Dau	1	F	"			
	8								
	9								
	10								
	11								
	12								
	13								
	14								
	15								
	16								
	17								

ENROLLMENT
OF NOS. 1,2,3,4,5,6 and 7 HEREON
APPROVED BY THE SECRETARY
OF INTERIOR DEC 12 1902

TRIBAL ENROLLMENT OF PARENTS

	Name of Father	Year	County	Name of Mother	Year	County
1	Noel Jones	Ded	Red River	Sallie Jones	Ded	Red River
2	Levi Sampson	1896	" "	Elizabeth Sampson	Ded	Eagle
3	No 1			No 2		
4	No 1			No 2		
5	No 1			No 2		
6	No 1			No 2		
7	No 1			No 2		
8						
9	No 2 on 1896 roll as Jincey Jones					
10	No 3 " " " " Ellis "					
11	No 6 " " " " Sulphe McClure					
12						
13	No.7 Enrolled, June 8, 1900					
14	For child of No. 5 see N.B. (Apr. 26, 1906) Card No. 138.					
15	" " " Nos 1&2 " " " " " 306.			#1 to 6		
16				Date of Application for Enrollment Apr. 29"99		
17						

216

Choctaw By Blood Enrollment Cards 1898-1914

RESIDENCE: Red River COUNTY.
POST OFFICE: Shawnee Town, I.T.

Choctaw Nation

Choctaw Roll
(Not Including Freedmen)

CARD NO.
FIELD NO. **1117**

Dawes' Roll No.	NAME	Relationship to Person First Named	AGE	SEX	BLOOD	Year	County	No.
3011	1 Tushka, Impson W. 39	First Named	36	M	Full	1896	Red River	12269
3012	2 " Nellie 39	Wife	36	F	"	1896	" "	12270
3013	3 " Alfred 20	Son	17	M	"	1896	" "	12271
3014	4 DIED PRIOR TO SEPTEMBER 25, 1902 Minerva	Dau	13	F	"	1896	" "	12272
3015	5 DIED PRIOR TO SEPTEMBER 25, 1902 Sillen	"	11	"	"	1896	" "	12273
3016	6 " Isaac 12	Son	9	M	"	1896	" "	12274
3017	7 " Lowie 10	"	7	"	"	1896	" "	12275
3018	8 " Mary 6	Dau	3	F	"	1896	" "	12276
3019	9 " Benjamin 5	Son	1	M	"			
	10							
	11	ENROLLMENT						
	12	OF NOS.12345678and9 HEREON APPROVED BY THE SECRETARY						
	13	OF INTERIOR Dec. 12, 1902						
	14 No.5 died April 16, 1902:							
	15 Enrollment cancelled							
	16 by Department Sept. 16, 1904.							
	17							

TRIBAL ENROLLMENT OF PARENTS

	Name of Father	Year	County	Name of Mother	Year	County
1	Wallis Tushka	1896	Red River	Lissy Tushka	1896	Red River
2	Bok Tamahika	Ded	" "	Emey Tamahika	1896	" "
3	No 1			No 2		
4	No 1			No 2		
5	No 1			No 2		
6	No 1			No 2		
7	No 1			No 2		
8	No 1			No 2		
9	No 1			No 2		
10			No5 on 1896 roll as Cillin Tushka			
11			No7 " " " " Levi "			
12			No1 " " " " I.W. "			
13	For child of Nos1&2 see NB (Mar.3'05) #927					
14	No.4 died April 8, 1900: Proof of death filed Dec. 3, 1902. No.5 " April16,1902: " " " " " " "					
15	No.4 died April8,1900:Enrollment cancelled by Department July 8,1904.			Date of Application for Enrollment.		
16	No.3 husband of Viney Fisher on 7-1326			Apr. 29 "99		
17	P.O. Idabel I.T. 4/11/05					

Choctaw By Blood Enrollment Cards 1898-1914

RESIDENCE: Red River COUNTY.		Choctaw Nation		Choctaw Roll (Not Including Freedmen)		CARD NO.	
POST OFFICE: Harris, I.T.						FIELD NO. 1118	

Dawes' Roll No.	NAME	Relationship to Person First Named	AGE	SEX	BLOOD	TRIBAL ENROLLMENT		
						Year	County	No.
3020	1 Kirby, Robert 29	First Named	26	M	1/16	1896	Red River	7585
I.W. 67	2 " Emma 25	Wife	22	F	I.W.	1896	" "	14725
3021	3 " Kate 6	Dau	3	"	1/32	1896	" "	7586
3022 DIED PRIOR TO SEPTEMBER 25, 1902	4 " Ben	Son	1	M	1/32			
DEAD.	5 " Maud Henrietta	Dau.	4mo	F	1/32			
	6							
	7	ENROLLMENT OF NOS. 1 3 and 4 HEREON APPROVED BY THE SECRETARY OF INTERIOR DEC 12 1902						
	8							
	9							
	10	ENROLLMENT OF NOS ~ 2 ~ HEREON APPROVED BY THE SECRETARY OF INTERIOR JUN 13 1903						
	11							
	12							
	13							
	14	No. 5 HEREON DISMISSED UNDER ORDER OF THE COMMISSION TO THE FIVE CIVILIZED TRIBES OF MARCH 31, 1905.						
	15							
	16							
	17							

TRIBAL ENROLLMENT OF PARENTS

	Name of Father	Year	County	Name of Mother	Year	County
1	Wyatt Kirby	1896	Non Citz	Kizzie Kirby	Ded	Red River
2	Ben Know	Ded	" "		Ded	Non Citz
3	No 1			No 2		
4	No 1			No 2		
5	No.1			No.2		
6						
7				1896		
8			No 2 admitted by Dawes Commission as inter			
9			married citizen 1201 – Admitted as Emma			
10			Kirby – No appeal			
11			No.5 born Oct. 10, 1902: Enrolled Feby. 14, 1902.			
12			Nº5 Died March 19, 1902: proof of death filed June 13, 1902.			
13			No 4 died Nov. 18, 1898: proof of death filed Dec 6, 1902.			
14			No 4 died Nov. 18, 1898: Enrollment cancelled by Department July 8, 1904			
15					#1 to 4	
16					DATE OF APPLICATION FOR ENROLLMENT. Apr. 28-99	
17						

218

Choctaw By Blood Enrollment Cards 1898-1914

RESIDENCE: Bok Tuk-lo COUNTY.
POST OFFICE: Lu-fa-tah I T.

Choctaw Nation

Choctaw Roll
(Not Including Freedmen)

CARD NO.
FIELD NO. 1119

Dawes' Roll No.	NAME	Relationship to Person First Named	AGE	SEX	BLOOD	TRIBAL ENROLLMENT		
						Year	County	No.
3023	1 Thomas Phoebe 53	First Named	50	F	Full	1896	Red River	12204
	2							
	3	ENROLLMENT						
	4	OF NOS. 1 HEREON APPROVED BY THE SECRETARY						
	5	OF INTERIOR DEC 12 1902						
	6							
	7							
	8							
	9							
	10							
	11							
	12							
	13							
	14							
	15							
	16							
	17							

TRIBAL ENROLLMENT OF PARENTS

	Name of Father	Year	County	Name of Mother	Year	County
1						
2						
3						
4						
5						
6						
7						
8						
9						
10						
11						
12						
13						
14					Date of Application for Enrollment.	
15						
16					Apr. 28-99	
17						

Choctaw By Blood Enrollment Cards 1898-1914

RESIDENCE: Red River COUNTY.
POST OFFICE: Goodwater I.T.

Choctaw Nation

Choctaw Roll (Not Including Freedmen)

CARD NO.
FIELD NO. 1120

Dawes' Roll No.	NAME	Relationship to Person First Named	AGE	SEX	BLOOD	TRIBAL ENROLLMENT Year	County	No.
3024	1 Going, Alfred 48	First Named	45	M	Full	1896	Red River	4797
3025	2 Eliza DIED PRIOR TO SEPTEMBER 25, 1902	Wife	56	F	"	1896	" "	4798
3026	3 " Ben 22	Son	19	M	"	1896	" "	4800
3027	4 McKinney Minerva 20	Dau	17	F	"	1896	" "	4801
3028	5 Going Ellen 18	"	15	"	"	1896	" "	4802
3029	6 " Sissy 15	"	12	"	"	1896	" "	4803
3030	7 McKinney, Paul 1	Gr Son	6mo	M	"			
	8	ENROLLMENT						
	9	OF NOS. 123456and7HEREON APPROVED BY THE SECRETARY						
	10	OF INTERIOR DEC 12 1902						
	11	For child of No.3 see NB (March 3 1905) #961						
	12	" " " " " " " (April 26 1906) #422						
	13	" " " " " " " (March 3 1905) #1184						
		No.2 died Feb. 2, 1900 Enrollment cancelled by Department July 8, 1904						
	14	No3 was husband of Frances Thompson on Choctaw card #979 at the time she died						
	15							
	16	No2 died Feb 2, 1900, proof of death filed Dec. 3/02						
	17							

TRIBAL ENROLLMENT OF PARENTS

Name of Father	Year	County	Name of Mother	Year	County
1 Ebaf-ok-ka	De'd	Eagle		De'd	Eagle
2 George Graham	"	Red River		De'd	Red River
3	No 1		No 2		
4	No 1		No 2		
5	No 1		No 2		
6	No 1		No 2		
7 David McKinney	1896	Red River	No 4		
8					
9		No 1 on 1896 roll as Alfred Ghoing			
10		No 2 " " " " Eliza "			
11		No 3 " " " " Ben "			
12		No 4 " " " " Minerva "			
13		No 5 " " " " Ellen "			
		No 6 " " " " Cissy "			#1 to 6
14	No4 is now the wife of David McKinney on Choctaw card No810. Evidence of				Date of Application for Enrollment.
15	marriage filed June 9, 1902. No.1 is now husband of Sissy Loman on Choc #1089				Apr. 28"99
16	No7 Born Nov. 24, 1901: enrolled June 9, 1902.				
17					

Choctaw By Blood Enrollment Cards 1898-1914

RESIDENCE: Red River COUNTY. **Choctaw Nation** Choctaw Roll CARD NO.
POST OFFICE: Kully Tuk-lo I.T. *(Not Including Freedmen)* FIELD NO. 1121

Dawes' Roll No.	NAME		Relationship to Person	AGE	SEX	BLOOD	TRIBAL ENROLLMENT		
							Year	County	No.
3031	1 John, Morris	50	First Named	47	M	Full	1896	Red River	6986
3032	2 " Eliza	33	Wife	30	F	"	1896	" "	6987
3033	3 " James	19	Son	16	M	"	1896	" "	6988
3034	4 " Amos	14	"	11	"	"	1896	" "	6989
3035	5 ~~" Lucian~~ DIED PRIOR TO SEPTEMBER 25, 1902		~~Dau~~	~~9~~	~~F~~	~~"~~	~~1896~~	~~" "~~	~~6990~~
3036	6 " Edna	10	"	7	"	"	1896	" "	6991
3037	7 " Israel	7	Son	4	M	"	1896	" "	6992
3038	8 " Sophina	5	Dau	1	F	"			
3039	9 " Henry	1	Son	10m	M	"			
	10								
	11	ENROLLMENT OF NOS. 12345678and9 HEREON APPROVED BY THE SECRETARY OF INTERIOR DEC 12 1902							
	12								
	13								
	14								
	15								
	16								
	17								

TRIBAL ENROLLMENT OF PARENTS

	Name of Father	Year	County	Name of Mother	Year	County
1	"John"	De'd	Bok-Tuk-lo	Fle-chi-ho-ke	Ded	Bok-Tuk-lo
2	~~Alfred Shoney~~	~~Ded~~	~~Red River~~	~~Elsie Shoney~~	~~Ded~~	~~Red River~~
3	No 1			Saney John	"	" " "
4	No 1			No 2		
5	No 1			No 2		
6	No 1			No 2		
7	No 1			No 2		
8	No 1			No 2		
9	No 1			No 2		
10						
11						
12			No 6 on 1896 roll as Etta John			
13			No5 " 1896 " " Lucin "			
14	No9 Born Aug 28th 1901: Enrolled June 19th 1902					#1 to 8 inc
15	No5 died Dec 30, 1901: proof of death filed Dec 3, 1902					Date of Application for Enrollment.
16	No.5 died Dec.30,1901: Enrollment cancelled by Department July 8 1904					Apr. 28"99
	For child of Nos 1&2 see NB (Apr 26-06) Card No 758					
17						

Choctaw By Blood Enrollment Cards 1898-1914

RESIDENCE: Red River COUNTY.							
POST OFFICE: Goodwater I.T.	**Choctaw Nation**	Choctaw Roll (Not Including Freedmen)			CARD NO.	FIELD NO. 1122	

Dawes' Roll No.	NAME	Relationship to Person First Named	AGE	SEX	BLOOD	TRIBAL ENROLLMENT Year	County	No.
3040	1 Wilson Willis 52	First Named	49	M	Full	1896	Red River	13673
3041	2 " Anna 47	Wife	46	F	"	1896	" "	13674
3042	3 " Martha 23	Dau	20	"	"	1896	" "	13675
3043	4 " Darius 18	Son	15	M	"	1896	" "	13676
3044	5 " Sillis 14	Dau	11	F	"	1896	" "	13677
3045	6 " Jubel 9	Son	6	M	"	1896	" "	13678
	7							
	8 ENROLLMENT							
	9 OF NOS. 12345and6 HEREON APPROVED BY THE SECRETARY OF INTERIOR							
	10							
	11							
	12							
	13							
	14							
	15							
	16							
	17							

TRIBAL ENROLLMENT OF PARENTS

Name of Father	Year	County	Name of Mother	Year	County
1 George Wilson	Ded	Red River		De'd	Red River
2 Alfred Shoney	"	" "		"	" "
3 No 1			No 2		
4 No 1			No 2		
5 No 1			No 2		
6 No 1			No 2		
7					
8					
9					
10					
11		No 4 on 1896 roll as Terry Wilson			
12		No 5 " " " " Charles "			
13		No 6 " " " " Jarvis "			
14					
15					
16				Date of Application for Enrollment	Apr. 28"99
17					

222

Choctaw By Blood Enrollment Cards 1898-1914

RESIDENCE: Red River COUNTY.
POST OFFICE: Kully Tuk-lo I.T.

Choctaw Nation

Choctaw Roll
(Not Including Freedmen)

CARD No.
FIELD No. 1123

Dawes' Roll No.	NAME		Relationship to Person First Named	AGE	SEX	BLOOD	TRIBAL ENROLLMENT		
							Year	County	No.
3046	1 Jackson Lester	36	First Named	33	M	Full	1896	Red River	6998
	2								
	3								
	4	ENROLLMENT							
	5	OF NOS. 1 HEREON APPROVED BY THE SECRETARY							
	6	OF INTERIOR DEC 12 1902							
	7								
	8								
	9								
	10								
	11								
	12								
	13								
	14								
	15								
	16								
	17								

TRIBAL ENROLLMENT OF PARENTS

	Name of Father	Year	County	Name of Mother	Year	County
1	Jackson, Nicholas	Ded	Louisana[sic]	Ailis Jackson	Ded	Louisana[sic]
2						
3						
4						
5	Admitted as a Mississippi Choctaw by act of					
6	Council approved October 16" 1895.					
7						
8	Enrolled on 1896 roll as Lastie Jackson					
9						
10						
11						
12						
13						
14						
15						
16				Date of Application for Enrollment	Apr. 29-99	
17						

223

Choctaw By Blood Enrollment Cards 1898-1914

RESIDENCE: Eagle   COUNTY.
POST OFFICE: Eagle Town I.T.

Choctaw Nation

Choctaw Roll
(Not Including Freedmen)

CARD NO.
FIELD NO. 1124

Dawes' Roll No.	NAME	Relationship to Person First Named	AGE	SEX	BLOOD	TRIBAL ENROLLMENT		
						Year	County	No.
3047	1 Anderson Wright ²²		19	M	Full	1896	Eagle	12245
	2							
	3							
	4	ENROLLMENT						
	5	OF NOS. 1 HEREON APPROVED BY THE SECRETARY						
	6	OF INTERIOR DEC 12 1902						
	7							
	8							
	9							
	10							
	11							
	12							
	13							
	14							
	15							
	16							
	17							

TRIBAL ENROLLMENT OF PARENTS

	Name of Father	Year	County	Name of Mother	Year	County
1	Gaffin Anderson	Ded	Bok Tuklo	Celia Anderson	1896	Eagle
2						
3						
4						
5						
6						
7			On 1896 roll as Wright Thomas			
8		No 1 is now husband of Sillis Haiakonobi Choc 529				
9						
10						
11						
12						
13						
14						
15						
16				Date of Application for Enrollment Apr. 29"99		
17						

224

Choctaw By Blood Enrollment Cards 1898-1914

RESIDENCE: Bok Tuk-lo	COUNTY.	**Choctaw Nation**		Choctaw Roll	CARD No.	
POST OFFICE: Luk fa tah I.T.				*(Not Including Freedmen)*	FIELD No.	1125

Dawes' Roll No.	NAME		Relationship to Person	AGE	SEX	BLOOD	TRIBAL ENROLLMENT		
							Year	County	No.
3048	1 James Davis	22	First Named	19	M	Full	1896	Bok Tuklo	6911
	2								
	3								
	4	ENROLLMENT							
	5	OF NOS. 1 HEREON APPROVED BY THE SECRETARY							
	6	OF INTERIOR DEC 12 1902							
	7								
	8								
	9								
	10								
	11								
	12								
	13								
	14								
	15								
	16								
	17								

TRIBAL ENROLLMENT OF PARENTS

Name of Father	Year	County	Name of Mother	Year	County
1 Alfred James	De'd	Bok Tuklo	So-yo Willis	1896	Bok Tuklo
2					
3					
4					
5					
6					
7		No 1 husband of No 8 on 7-1183.			
8					
9					
10					
11					
12					
13					
14					
15					
16				Date of Application for Enrollment	Apr. 29"99
17					

Choctaw By Blood Enrollment Cards 1898-1914

RESIDENCE: Red River COUNTY. POST OFFICE: Goodwater, I.T.

Choctaw Nation

Choctaw Roll (Not Including Freedmen)

CARD NO. FIELD NO. **1126**

Dawes' Roll No.	NAME	Relationship to Person First Named	AGE	SEX	BLOOD	TRIBAL ENROLLMENT		
						Year	County	No.
3049	1 Sampson, Levi 41	First Named	38	M	Full	1896	Red River	11457
3050	2 " , Eyahoke 43	Wife	40	F	"	1896	" "	11458
3051	3 King, Simpson 18	S.Son	15	M	"	1896	" "	7591
3052	4 " , Petty 15	S.Dau	12	F	"	1896	" "	7592
3053	5 Logan, Seley DIED PRIOR TO SEPTEMBER 25, 1902	Ward	7	"	"	1896	" "	8072
	6							
	7							
	8							
	9							
	10							
	11							
	12							
	13							
	14							
	15							
	16							
	17							

ENROLLMENT OF NOS. 1,2,3,4 and 5 HEREON APPROVED BY THE SECRETARY OF INTERIOR Dec. 12, 1902

TRIBAL ENROLLMENT OF PARENTS

	Name of Father	Year	County	Name of Mother	Year	County
1	Sampson	Ded	Red River		Ded	Eagle
2		Ded	" "			
3	Milwit King	"	" "	Eya-ho-ke	1896	Red River
4	" "	"	" "	" " "	1896	" "
5	Griggs Logan	"	" "	Elizabeth Logan	Ded	" "
6						
7						
8						
9						
10			No.2 enrolled as Annie Sampson			
11			No.3 " " Sampson King			
12			No.5 " " Celey Logan			
13	No.5 died May 17, 1901: Proof of death filed Dec 3, 1902.					
14	No.5 died May 17, 1901: Enrollment cancelled by Department July 8, 1904.					
15						
16					Date of Application for Enrollment.	Apr. 29"99
17						

RESIDENCE: Red River   **COUNTY.**   **Choctaw Nation**   **Choctaw Roll** *(Not Including Freedmen)*   **CARD No.**

POST OFFICE: Goodwater I.T.   **FIELD No.** 1127

Dawes' Roll No.	NAME		Relationship to Person First Named	AGE	SEX	BLOOD	TRIBAL ENROLLMENT Year	County	No.
3054	1 Jones, Eastman	41	First Named	38	M	Full	1896	Red River	7017
DEAD.	2 " Melissie DEAD.		Wife	30	F	"	1896	" "	7018
3055	3 " Eliza Ann	6	Dau	3	"	"	1896	" "	7016
3056	4 King Anderson (DIED PRIOR TO SEPTEMBER 25, 1902)		S Son	12	M	"	1896	" "	7567
3057	5 " Missey	10	S Dau	7	F	"	1896	" "	7569
3058	6 " Robin	12	S Son	9	M	"	1896	" "	7568
3059	7 Jones, Celia (DIED PRIOR TO SEPTEMBER 25, 1902)		Dau	12	F	"	1893	" "	343
	8								
	9								
	10								
	11								
	12								
	13								
	14								
	15								
	16								
	17								

ENROLLMENT
OF NOS. 1 3 4 5 6 and 7 HEREON
APPROVED BY THE SECRETARY
OF INTERIOR DEC 12 1902

No. 2 HEREON DISMISSED UNDER ORDER OF THE COMMISSION TO THE FIVE CIVILIZED TRIBES OF MARCH 31, 1905.

No.4 died July – , 1901: No.7 died Sept – ,1900: Enrollment cancelled by Department July 8, 1904

TRIBAL ENROLLMENT OF PARENTS

	Name of Father	Year	County	Name of Mother	Year	County
1	Noel Jones	De'd	Red River	Ano-he Jackson	Ded	Red River
2	John Thomas	"	" "		"	" "
3	No 1			No 2		
4	Silas King	Ded	Red River	No 2		
5	" "	"	" "	No 2		
6	" "	"	" "	No 2		
7	No 1			Betsy Ghoing		Eagle
8						
9			No 2 on 1896 roll as Elizabeth Jones			
10			No 6 " " " " Lobbin King			
11			No7 on 1893 Pay roll, Page 41, No 343, Red River Co. as Selie			
12			Jones, No.1 now husband of Nelis Johnson on 7-847			
13			No 2 died Dec 19, 1901: proof of death filed Dec 3, 1902.			
14			No 4 " July – ,1901: " " " " " " "			#1 to 6
15			No 7 " Sept – 1900: " " " " " " "			Date of Application for Enrollment.
16						Apr. 29"99
17						No 7 enrolled Aug 1/99

Choctaw By Blood Enrollment Cards 1898-1914

RESIDENCE: Red River COUNTY.
POST OFFICE: Good-water I T

Choctaw Nation

Choctaw Roll
(Not Including Freedmen)

CARD NO.
FIELD NO. 1128

Dawes' Roll No.	NAME	Relationship to Person First Named	AGE	SEX	BLOOD	TRIBAL ENROLLMENT		
						Year	County	No.
3060	1 Harner Loring 55	First Named	52	M	Full	1896	Red River	5668
3061	2 " Sallie Ann 53	Wife	50	F	"	1896	" "	5669
	3							
	4	ENROLLMENT OF NOS. 1 and 2 HEREON APPROVED BY THE SECRETARY						
	5	OF INTERIOR DEC 12 1902						
	6							
	7							
	8							
	9							
	10							
	11							
	12							
	13							
	14							
	15							
	16							
	17							

TRIBAL ENROLLMENT OF PARENTS

	Name of Father	Year	County	Name of Mother	Year	County
1	Harner	De'd	Red River	Kamahima	Ded	Red River
2	Tama-ho-na-bi	"	" "	Ela-ho-to-na	"	" "
3						
4						
5						
6						
7			No 2 on 1896 roll as Elizann Harner			
8						
9						
10						
11						
12						
13						
14						
15						
16				Date of Application for Enrollment	Apr. 29"99	
17						

228

Choctaw By Blood Enrollment Cards 1898-1914

RESIDENCE: Bok Tuk-lo COUNTY. **Choctaw Nation** **Choctaw Roll** CARD NO.
POST OFFICE: Luk-fa-tah I.T. (Not Including Freedmen) FIELD NO. 1129

Dawes' Roll No.	NAME	Relationship to Person First Named	AGE	SEX	BLOOD	TRIBAL ENROLLMENT Year	County	No.
3062	1 Homa Franklin 36	First Named	33	M	Full	1896	Bok-Tuk-lo	5563
3063	2 " Louisa 26	wife	23	F	"	1896	" " "	5564
	3							
	4 ENROLLMENT							
	5 OF NOS. 1 and 2 HEREON APPROVED BY THE SECRETARY							
	6 OF INTERIOR DEC 12 1902							
	7							
	8							
	9							
	10							
	11							
	12							
	13							
	14							
	15							
	16							
	17							

TRIBAL ENROLLMENT OF PARENTS

Name of Father	Year	County	Name of Mother	Year	County
1 Ho-shi-sha-ho-ma	De'd	Kiamatia[sic]	Ti-h na ho ke	Ded	Kiamatia[sic]
2 Calvin James	1896	Bok-Tuk-lo	Neise James	"	Towson
3					
4					
5	No.2 Died prior to September 25-1901; not entitled to land or money.				
6	(See Indian Office letter Mch 14, 1911)				
7					
8					
9					
10					
11					
12					
13					
14					
15					
16				Date of Application for Enrollment	Apr. 29-99
17					

Choctaw By Blood Enrollment Cards 1898-1914

RESIDENCE: Red River COUNTY.
POST OFFICE: Good Water I.T.

Choctaw Nation

Choctaw Roll (Not Including Freedmen)

CARD NO. FIELD NO. 1130

Dawes' Roll No.	NAME	Relationship to Person First Named	AGE	SEX	BLOOD	TRIBAL ENROLLMENT Year	County	No.
Dead	1 Wilson Thompson		53	M	Full	1896	Red River	13689
3064	2 Thompson, Sena 16	Dau	13	F	"	1896	" "	12341
	3							
	4							
	5							
	6							
	7							
	8							
	9							
	10							
	11							
	12							
	13							
	14							
	15							
	16							
	17							

ENROLLMENT
OF NOS. ----2---- HEREON
APPROVED BY THE SECRETARY
OF INTERIOR DEC 12 1902

No. 1 HEREON DISMISSED UNDER
ORDER OF THE COMMISSION TO THE FIVE
CIVILIZED TRIBES OF MARCH 31, 1905.

TRIBAL ENROLLMENT OF PARENTS

Name of Father	Year	County	Name of Mother	Year	County
1			Achuk-ma-ho-na	De'd	Red River
2 No 1			Ka-naho-te-ma	"	" "
3					
4					
5					
6					
7		No 2 on 1896 as Cinnie Thompson			
8		No.1 Died August 17, 1899: Evidence of death filed May 16, 1901.			
9		For child of No.2 see NB (March 3, 1905) #1370.			
10					
11					
12					
13					
14					
15			Date of Application for Enrollment		
16					Apr. 29-99
17					

230

Choctaw By Blood Enrollment Cards 1898-1914

RESIDENCE: Red River COUNTY. **Choctaw Nation** Choctaw Roll CARD No.
POST OFFICE: Kully Tuk-lo, I.T. (Not Including Freedmen) FIELD No. 1131

Dawes' Roll No.	NAME		Relationship to Person First Named	AGE	SEX	BLOOD	TRIBAL ENROLLMENT		
							Year	County	No.
3065	1 Victor George	22	First Named	19	M	Full	1896	Red River	12506
	2								
	3		~~ENROLLMENT~~						
	4		OF NOS. 1 HEREON APPROVED BY THE SECRETARY						
	5		OF INTERIOR DEC 12 1902						
	6								
	7								
	8								
	9								
	10								
	11								
	12								
	13								
	14								
	15								
	16								
	17								

TRIBAL ENROLLMENT OF PARENTS

	Name of Father	Year	County	Name of Mother	Year	County
1	Frank Victor	Ded	Red River	Sissy Parker	Ded	Red River
2						
3						
4						
5						
6			For child of No. 1 see NB (March 3 1905) #903			
7						
8						
9						
10						
11						
12						
13						
14						
15					Date of Application for Enrollment.	
16					Apr. 29 '99	
17						

Choctaw By Blood Enrollment Cards 1898-1914

RESIDENCE: Nashoba COUNTY. **Choctaw Nation** Choctaw Roll CARD NO.

POST OFFICE: Octava[sic] I.T. *(Not Including Freedmen)* FIELD NO. 1132

Dawes' Roll No.	NAME		Relationship to Person First Named	AGE	SEX	BLOOD	TRIBAL ENROLLMENT		
							Year	County	No.
I.W. 223	1 Labor Houston	51	First Named	50	M	I.W.	1896	Nashoba	14766
3066	2 " Permelia	45	Wife	42	F	3/4	1896	"	7949
3067	3 " ✓Alexander	22	Son	19	M	3/8	1896	"	7951
3068	4 " ✓Elliston	20	"	17	"	"	1896	"	7952
3069	5 " ✓Sarah J	18	Dau	15	F	"	1896	"	7953
3070	6 " ✓Ida	16	"	13	"	"	1896	"	7954
3071	7 " ✓Phoebe	14	"	11	"	"	1896	"	7955
3072	8 " ✓Ellen	12	"	9	"	"	1896	"	7956
3073	9 " ✓Willie	9	Son	6	M	"	1896	"	7957
	10								
	11	ENROLLMENT							
	12	OF NOS. 2345678and9 HEREON APPROVED BY THE SECRETARY							
	13	OF INTERIOR DEC 12 1902							
	14								
	15	ENROLLMENT							
	16	OF NOS. 1 HEREON APPROVED BY THE SECRETARY							
	17	OF INTERIOR SEP 12 1903							

TRIBAL ENROLLMENT OF PARENTS

	Name of Father	Year	County	Name of Mother	Year	County
1	William Labor	Ded	Non Citz	Preasy Labor	Ded	Non City
2	Wᵐ Watson	"	Nashoba	Betsy Watson	1896	Nashoba
3	No 1			No 2		
4	No 1			No 2		
5	No 1			No 2		
6	No 1			No 2		
7	No 1			No 2		
8	No 1			No 2		
9	No 1			No 2		
10						
11	No 4 on 1896 Roll as Alliston Labor					
12	For child of No4 see NB (Apr 26-06) Card #641					
13	No.1 Admitted by Dawes Commission #855 = No appeal					
14	No1 on 1896 roll as Houston Labor					
15	No5 now wife of W.S. Slaton: evidence of marriage filed Dec. 6, 1902.					
16	For child of No.3 see NB (March 3, 1905) #1107					
17	Bennington I.T.					Apr. 29-99

12/1/02

Choctaw By Blood Enrollment Cards 1898-1914

RESIDENCE: Nashoba   COUNTY.   **Choctaw Nation**   Choctaw Roll   CARD NO.
POST OFFICE: Smithville I.T.   *(Not Including Freedmen)*   FIELD NO.   1133

Dawes' Roll No.	NAME	Relationship to Person First Named	AGE	SEX	BLOOD	TRIBAL ENROLLMENT		
						Year	County	No.
3074	1 Litrell Joseph J. 10	First Named	7	M	3/16	1896	Nashoba	7959
3075	2 " Mary A 7	Sis.	4	F	3/16	1896	"	7960
	3							
	4 ENROLLMENT							
	5 OF NOS. 1 and 2 HEREON APPROVED BY THE SECRETARY							
	6 OF INTERIOR DEC 2 1902							
	7							
	8							
	9							
	10							
	11							
	12							
	13							
	14							
	15							
	16							
	17							

TRIBAL ENROLLMENT OF PARENTS

	Name of Father	Year	County	Name of Mother	Year	County
1	William Littrell[sic]	1896	Non Citz	Mary Littrell	Ded	Nashoba
2	" "	1896	" "	" "	"	"
3						
4						
5	No 1 on 1896 roll as Joseph J Littell					
6	No 2 " " " " Mary A. "					
7						
8						
9						
10						
11						
12						
13						
14					Date of Application for Enrollment.	
15						
16					Apr. 29"99	
17						

Choctaw By Blood Enrollment Cards 1898-1914

RESIDENCE: Towson COUNTY. **Choctaw Nation** **Choctaw Roll** CARD NO.

POST OFFICE: Garvin I.T. (Not Including Freedmen) FIELD NO. 1134

Dawes' Roll No.	NAME		Relationship to Person First Named	AGE	SEX	BLOOD	TRIBAL ENROLLMENT		
							Year	County	No.
3076	1 Jackson Wilson	27	First Named	24	M	Full	1896	Red River	7060
	2								
	3								
	4	ENROLLMENT							
	5	OF NOS. 1 HEREON APPROVED BY THE SECRETARY							
	6	OF INTERIOR DEC 12 1902							
	7								
	8								
	9								
	10								
	11								
	12								
	13								
	14								
	15								
	16								
	17								

TRIBAL ENROLLMENT OF PARENTS

	Name of Father	Year	County	Name of Mother	Year	County
1	Jackson Nicholas	Ded	Louisana[sic]	Sallie Jackson	1896	Towson
2						
3						
4						
5	No.1 on 1896 Choctaw census roll as Wilson Jackson.					
6						
7						
8						
9						
10						
11						
12				Admitted as Mississippi Choctaw		
13				by ^ act of Council approved Oct 16 1895		
14						
15						
16				Date of Application for Enrollment Apr. 29"99		
17						

234

Choctaw By Blood Enrollment Cards 1898-1914

RESIDENCE: Nashoba COUNTY. **Choctaw Nation** **Choctaw Roll** CARD NO.
POST OFFICE: Alikchi, I.T. (Not Including Freedmen) FIELD NO. **1135**

Dawes' Roll No.	NAME		Relationship to Person	AGE	SEX	BLOOD	TRIBAL ENROLLMENT		
							Year	County	No.
3077	1 Choate, Dwight	39	First Named	36	M	Full	1896	Nashoba	2539
3078	2 " , Maud	24	Wife	21	F	1/2	1896	"	2540
3079	3 " , Green M.	6	Son	3	M	3/4	1896	"	2542
3080	4 " , Ben	8	"	5	"	3/4	1896	"	2541
3081	5 " , Ida	1	Dau	2mo	F	3/4			
	6								
	7	ENROLLMENT							
	8	OF NOS. 1 2 3 4 and 5 HEREON APPROVED BY THE SECRETARY							
	9	OF INTERIOR Dec 12, 1902							
	10								
	11								
	12								
	13								
	14								
	15								
	16								
	17								

TRIBAL ENROLLMENT OF PARENTS

	Name of Father	Year	County	Name of Mother	Year	County
1	Ben Choate	De'd	Cedar	Emily Choate	De'd	Cedar
2	Ben Watkins	1896	Inter Married		"	Bok Tuklo
3	No 1			No 2		
4	No 1			No 2		
5	No 1			No 2		
6						
7			No 4 enrolled as Ben W. Choate			
8			No 3 " " MᶜCurtain			
9			No 5 enrolled Sept. 7, 1901			
10						
11						
12						
13						
14					#1 to 4 inc	
15					Date of Application for Enrollment.	
16					Apr. 29/99	
17						

Choctaw By Blood Enrollment Cards 1898-1914

RESIDENCE: Red River COUNTY. **Choctaw Nation** Choctaw Roll CARD NO.
POST OFFICE: Goodwater, I.T.   (Not Including Freedmen)   FIELD NO. **1136**

Dawes' Roll No.	NAME	Relationship to Person First Named	AGE	SEX	BLOOD	TRIBAL ENROLLMENT		
						Year	County	No.
3082	1 Phillips, Sissie ²⁹	First Named	26	F	Full	1896	Red River	5717
3083	2 Lela DIED PRIOR TO SEPTEMBER 25, 1902	Dau	6wk	"	1/2			
3084	3 Hunter, Silas ¹⁴	Son	11	M	Full	1896	Red River	5718
3085	4 " , Siney ⁷	Dau	4	F	"	1896	" "	5719
3086	5 Phillips, Micheal[sic] R ²	Son	1mo	M	1/2			
3087	6 " , Lizer ¹	Dau	3mo	F	1/2			
I.W. 176	7 " , Charley	Husband	27	M	I.W.			
	8							
	9 ENROLLMENT OF NOS. 12345and6 HEREON APPROVED BY THE SECRETARY OF INTERIOR Dec. 12, 1902							
	10							
	11							
	12 No7 transferred from Choctaw card #D136. See decision of May 1, 1903.							
	13 ENROLLMENT OF NOS. ~~~ 7 ~~~ HEREON APPROVED BY THE SECRETARY OF INTERIOR Jun 13, 1903							
	14							
	15							
	16 No.2 died May, 1901 Proof of death filed Dec 3, 1902							
	17 No.2 died May 1, 1901: Enrollment cancelled by Department July 8, 1904							

TRIBAL ENROLLMENT OF PARENTS

Name of Father	Year	County	Name of Mother	Year	County
1 Payson Hunter	Ded	Red River	Lila Hunter	Ded	Red River
2 Charley Phillips	1896	Inter Married	No 1		
3 Julius Jefferson	1896	Red River	No 1		
4 Smith Wilson	1896	" "	No 1		
5 Charley Phillips		Inter Married	No 1		
6 " "		" "	No 1		
7 Bob Phillips	Dead	Non-Citizen	Sallie Phillips	1896	Non-Citz
8					
9		Proof of marriage to Charley Phillips Must be			
10		supplied, Recd. May 17/99. Attached to Card D136			
11		No.1 enrolled as Sissie Hunter			
12		No.1 is wife of Charlie Phillips White man on Card D136.			
13		No.5 Enrolled Nov. 6th 1900.			
14		No.6 Born Feby. 27, 1902: Enrolled May 19, 1902.			
15					#1 to 4 inc
16			Date of Application for Enrollment		Apr. 29"99
17					

Choctaw By Blood Enrollment Cards 1898-1914

RESIDENCE: Bok Tuk-lo   COUNTY.   **Choctaw Nation**   **Choctaw Roll** *(Not Including Freedmen)*   CARD NO.

POST OFFICE: Luk-fa-tah I.T.   FIELD NO. 1137

Dawes' Roll No.	NAME	Relationship to Person First Named	AGE	SEX	BLOOD	TRIBAL ENROLLMENT		
						Year	County	No.
3088	1 Willis Garben ²¹	First Named	18	M	Full	1896	Bok Tuklo	13419
	2							
	3 ENROLLMENT							
	4 OF NOS. 1 HEREON APPROVED BY THE SECRETARY							
	5 OF INTERIOR DEC 12 1902							
	6							
	7							
	8							
	9							
	10							
	11							
	12							
	13							
	14							
	15							
	16							
	17							

TRIBAL ENROLLMENT OF PARENTS

Name of Father	Year	County	Name of Mother	Year	County
1 Ampson Chika	Ded	Towson	Ellen Anderson	Ded	Bok Tuklo
2					
3					
4					
5					
6					
7					
8					
9					
10					
11					
12					
13					
14				Date of Application for Enrollment.	
15					
16				Apr. 29"99	
17					

237

Choctaw By Blood Enrollment Cards 1898-1914

RESIDENCE: Towson COUNTY.
POST OFFICE: Fowlersville I.T.

Choctaw Nation
Choctaw Roll
(Not Including Freedmen)

CARD NO.
FIELD NO. 1138

Dawes' Roll No.	NAME	Relationship to Person First Named	AGE	SEX	BLOOD	TRIBAL ENROLLMENT		
						Year	County	No.
3089	₁ Bobb Johnson		41	M	Full	1896	Towson	1095
3090	₂ " Sophie ³⁹	Wife	36	F	3/4	1896	"	1696
	3							
	4	ENROLLMENT						
	5	OF NOS. 1 and 2 HEREON APPROVED BY THE SECRETARY						
	6	OF INTERIOR DEC 12 1902						
	7							
	8							
	9							
	10							
	11							
	12							
	13							
	14							
	15							
	16							
	17							

TRIBAL ENROLLMENT OF PARENTS

	Name of Father	Year	County	Name of Mother	Year	County
1	Bob Hla-oh-ta-bi	De'd	Towson	Ho-chi-fo	Ded	Towson
2	King Perkin[sic]	Ded	Blue	Edna Perkins	"	Blue
3						
4						
5						
6						
7						
8						
9			No 1 died Dec 30, 1899; proof of death filed Dec 18, 1902.			
10			No 1 died Dec. 30, 1899; Enrollment cancelled by Department July 8, 1904			
11						
12						
13						
14						Date of Application for Enrollment.
15						
16						Apr. 29 99
17	No 2 – Doaksville I.T	12/18/02.				

238

Choctaw By Blood Enrollment Cards 1898-1914

RESIDENCE: Red River COUNTY. **Choctaw Nation** Choctaw Roll CARD NO.
POST OFFICE: Good-water I.T. *(Not Including Freedmen)* FIELD NO. 1139

Dawes' Roll No.	NAME	Relationship to Person	AGE	SEX	BLOOD	TRIBAL ENROLLMENT		
						Year	County	No.
3091	1 Wade Esickey 51	First Named	48	M	Full	1896	Red River	13683
14639	2 " Chiffie 51	Wife	48	F	"	1896	" "	13684
	3							
	4 ENROLLMENT OF NOS. 1 HEREON APPROVED BY THE SECRETARY OF INTERIOR DEC 12 1902							
	5							
	6							
	7							
	8 ENROLLMENT OF NOS. 2 HEREON APPROVED BY THE SECRETARY OF INTERIOR MAY 20 1903							
	9							
	10							
	11							
	12							
	13							
	14							
	15							
	16							
	17							

TRIBAL ENROLLMENT OF PARENTS

Name of Father	Year	County	Name of Mother	Year	County
1 Ahlioha	Ded	Eagle	Ishtia	Ded	Eagle
2 John Logan	"	Red River	Mahala Logan	"	"
3					
4					
5					
6					
7					
8					
9					
10					
11					
12					
13					
14					
15					
16				Date of Application for Enrollment Apr. 29"99		
17						

239

Choctaw By Blood Enrollment Cards 1898-1914

RESIDENCE: Red River COUNTY.	**Choctaw Nation**	**Choctaw Roll** (Not Including Freedmen)	CARD NO.
POST OFFICE: Kully Tuk-lo I.T.			FIELD NO. **1140**

Dawes' Roll No.	NAME	Relationship to Person First Named	AGE	SEX	BLOOD	TRIBAL ENROLLMENT		
						Year	County	No.
3092	1 Wright, Hampton 40	First Named	37	M	Full	1896	Red River	13584
	2							
	3							
	4	ENROLLMENT OF NOS. 1 HEREON APPROVED BY THE SECRETARY OF INTERIOR Dec. 12 1902						
	5							
	6							
	7							
	8							
	9							
	10							
	11							
	12							
	13							
	14							
	15							
	16							
	17							

TRIBAL ENROLLMENT OF PARENTS

Name of Father	Year	County	Name of Mother	Year	County
1 Ahayohtubbee	Ded	Bok Tuk-lo	Amy	Ded	Red River
2					
3					
4					
5					
6					
7					
8					
9					
10					
11					
12					
13					
14				Date of Application for Enrollment.	
15					
16				Apr. 29, 99	
17					

240

Choctaw By Blood Enrollment Cards 1898-1914

RESIDENCE: Red River   COUNTY.   **Choctaw Nation**   Choctaw Roll   CARD NO.
POST OFFICE: Kully Tuk-lo I.T.   (Not Including Freedmen)   FIELD NO.   1141

Dawes' Roll No.	NAME	Relationship to Person First Named	AGE	SEX	BLOOD	TRIBAL ENROLLMENT		
						Year	County	No.
3093	1 Gardner Wyles 25		22	F	Full	1896	Red River	4810
	2							
	3	ENROLLMENT						
	4	OF NOS. 1 HEREON APPROVED BY THE SECRETARY						
	5	OF INTERIOR DEC 12 1902						
	6							
	7							
	8							
	9							
	10							
	11							
	12							
	13							
	14							
	15							
	16							
	17							

TRIBAL ENROLLMENT OF PARENTS

	Name of Father	Year	County	Name of Mother	Year	County
1	Tennessee	De'd	Eagle	Tolowa	Ded	Eagle
2						
3						
4						
5						
6						
7						
8	No 1 died Sept. 6, 1902; proof of death filed Dec 3, 1902.					
9						
10	No.1 Died prior to September 25, 1902; not entitled to land or money.					
11	See Indian Office Letter April 20, 1908 (I.T. 19830-1908)					
12						
13						
14						
15						
16				Date of Application for Enrollment	Apr. 29 99	
17						

241

Choctaw By Blood Enrollment Cards 1898-1914

RESIDENCE: Bok Tuklo   COUNTY.
POST OFFICE: Luk-Fa-lah, I.T.

Choctaw Nation

CARD NO.
Choctaw Roll   (Not Including Freedmen)   FIELD NO. **1142**

Dawes' Roll No.	Glover NAME		Relationship to Person	AGE	SEX	BLOOD	TRIBAL ENROLLMENT		
							Year	County	No.
I.W. 1654	1 Franklin, John Anderson	52	First Named	49	M	I.W.	1896	Bok Tuklo	14530
3094	2 " , Susan	26	Wife	23	F	Full	1893	Red River	609
3095	3 " , Allen	6	Son	3	M	1/2	1896	" "	4158
3096	4 DIED PRIOR TO SEPTEMBER 25, 1902 , Helen		Dau	1	F	1/2			
3097	5 DIED PRIOR TO SEPTEMBER 25, 1902 , Sanders		Son	16	M	1/2	1896	Red River	1348
	6								
	7								
	8	ENROLLMENT OF NOS. 2 3 4 and 5 HEREON APPROVED BY THE SECRETARY							
	9	OF INTERIOR Dec 12, 1902.							
	10 No.1								
	11 REFUSED Jun 22, 1906.								
	12 RECORD FORWARDED DEPARTMENT Jun 22, 1906								
	13 Nov 23, 1906 Brief of D.W. Yancey as to No.1 forwarded Department								
	14 Feb. 13, 1907. Decision of June 22, 1906 reversed by the Department.								
	15 ENROLLMENT OF NOS. ~~~ 1 ~~~ HEREON								
	16 APPROVED BY THE SECRETARY								
	17 OF INTERIOR Mar 2 — 1907								

TRIBAL ENROLLMENT OF PARENTS

Name of Father	Year	County	Name of Mother	Year	County
1 Harmon Franklin	Ded	Non Citz	Nancy Haley	1896	Non Citz
2 Peter Thomas	Ded	Bok Tuklo		Ded	San Bois
3 No 1			No 2		
4 No 1			No 2		
5 No 1			Easter Franklin	Ded	Red River
6					
7					
8			No.2 on 1893 pay roll for Red River County as Susan Thomas		
9			No.5 on 1896 rolls as Cubby Burney		
10 No.4 died June20,1902: No.5 died April5,1902: Enrollment cancelled by Department July 8, 1904.					
11			No.2 on 1896 roll as Susan Thomas, Page 317		
12		No. 12196, Bok Tuklo Co.			
13 No 4 died June 20, 1902: Proof of death filed Dec 6, 1902					
14 No 5 " April 5, 1902: " " " " " " "				Date of Application for Enrollment.	
15					
16				Apr 29"99	
17 7/12/04 Fort Towson I.T.					

242

Choctaw By Blood Enrollment Cards 1898-1914

RESIDENCE: Red River   COUNTY. **Choctaw Nation**   Choctaw Roll   CARD NO.
POST OFFICE: Janis, I.T.   *(Not Including Freedmen)*   FIELD NO. **1143**

Dawes' Roll No.		NAME		Relationship to Person First Named	AGE	SEX	BLOOD	TRIBAL ENROLLMENT		
								Year	County	No.
DEAD	1	Wilson, Siltema			54	F	Full	1896	Red River	13660
3098	2	", Smith	31	Son	28	M	"	1896	" "	13667
3099	3	DIED PRIOR TO SEPTEMBER 25, 1908 ", Beckie		Dau	25	F	"	1896	" "	13661
3100	4	", Michael	25	Son	22	M	"	1896	" "	13659
3101	5	DIED PRIOR TO SEPTEMBER 25, 1924 ", David		"	21	"	"	1896	" "	13662
14640	6	", Charley	20	"	17	"	"	1896	" "	13664
	7									
	8	ENROLLMENT OF NOS. 2 3 4 and 5 HEREON								
	9	APPROVED BY THE SECRETARY								
	10	OF INTERIOR Dec. 12, 1902								
	11	For child of No6 see NB(March 3,1905) #922								
	12	No5 died in Jail at So. McAlester, get Proof from								
	13	Jailor. Sent up April 28, 1900.								
	14									
	15	ENROLLMENT OF NOS. 6 HEREON			No. 1 hereon dismissed under order					
	16	APPROVED BY THE SECRETARY			of the Commission to the Five					
	17	OF INTERIOR May 20, 1903			Civilized Tribes of March 31, 1905.					

TRIBAL ENROLLMENT OF PARENTS

	Name of Father	Year	County	Name of Mother	Year	County
1	Achinota	Ded	Red River	Nancy Wade	Ded	Red River
2	Reuben Wilson	"	" "	No 1		
3	" "	"	" "	No 1		
4	" "	"	" "	No 1		
5	" "	"	" "	No 1		
6	" "	"	" "	No 1		
7						
8	No3 died in 1899 or 1900: No5 died in 1899: Enrollment cancelled by Department May 2, 1906.					
9	No2 died November 5, 1901: Enrollment cancelled by Secretary					
10	of Interior, October 4, 1905" (I.T.D. 12694-1905)					
11	No1 on 1896 roll as Sallitrina Wilson					
12	No4 " " " Mike					
13	No5 " " " " Stephen "					
14	No6 " " " " Sallie "					
15	No1 Died April 24,1900. Evidence of death filed April 25, 1901					
16	and letter written in reference to the given name.			Date of Application for Enrollment.		
17	Letter received and filed May 10, 1901, stating that No1 was known by name of Estermer as well as that of Siltema: Certificate of death reads Estemer May 10, 1901			Apr. 29"99		

Choctaw By Blood Enrollment Cards 1898-1914

RESIDENCE: Towson COUNTY.
POST OFFICE: Fowlersville I.T.

Choctaw Nation

Choctaw Roll
(Not Including Freedmen)

CARD NO.
FIELD NO. 1144

Dawes' Roll No.	NAME	Relationship to Person	AGE	SEX	BLOOD	TRIBAL ENROLLMENT		
						Year	County	No.
3102	₁ Parsons, Susan ³⁴	First Named	31	F	1/2	1896	Towson	10330
	2							
	3	ENROLLMENT						
	4	OF NOS. 1 HEREON APPROVED BY THE SECRETARY						
	5	OF INTERIOR DEC 12 1902						
	6							
	7							
	8							
	9							
	10							
	11							
	12							
	13							
	14							
	15							
	16							
	17							

TRIBAL ENROLLMENT OF PARENTS

	Name of Father	Year	County	Name of Mother	Year	County
1	Jerry Gardner	Ded	Towson	Becky Austin	Ded	Towson
2						
3						
4						
5	No1 is the guardian of Sarah James Choc #514 11/28/02					
6	" 1 " " " Carrie Gardner " #974 "					
7						
8						
9						
10						
11						
12						
13						
14						Date of Application for Enrollment.
15						
16						Apr. 29 "99
17						

Choctaw By Blood Enrollment Cards 1898-1914

Choctaw Nation

Choctaw Roll
(Not Including Freedmen)

CARD No.
FIELD NO. 1145

Dawes' Roll No.		NAME	Relationship to Person First Named	AGE	SEX	BLOOD	TRIBAL ENROLLMENT		
							Year	County	No.
3103	1	McKinney McGowan 42	First Named	39	M	Full	1896	Red River	9367
	2								
	3								
	4	ENROLLMENT							
	5	OF NOS. 1 HEREON APPROVED BY THE SECRETARY							
	6	OF INTERIOR DEC 12 1902							
	7								
	8								
	9								
	10								
	11								
	12								
	13								
	14								
	15								
	16								
	17								

TRIBAL ENROLLMENT OF PARENTS

	Name of Father	Year	County	Name of Mother	Year	County
1	Atuklantubbi	Ded	Red River		Ded	Red River
2						
3						
4						
5						
6						
7						
8						
9						
10						
11						
12						
13						
14						
15						
16						
17						

Date of Application for Enrollment.

Apr. 29 "99

Choctaw By Blood Enrollment Cards 1898-1914

| RESIDENCE: Towson COUNTY. POST OFFICE: Garvin, I.T. | **Choctaw Nation** | Choctaw Roll (Not Including Freedmen) | CARD NO. FIELD NO. 1146 |

Dawes' Roll No.	NAME	Relationship to Person	AGE	SEX	BLOOD	TRIBAL ENROLLMENT		
						Year	County	No.
3104	1 Homer, Sopha ⁴⁶	First Named	43	F	Full	1896	Kiamitia	5763
3105	2 " Wilson ¹¹	Son	8	M	"	1896	"	5764
	3							
	4							
	5	ENROLLMENT						
	6	OF NOS. 1 and 2 HEREON APPROVED BY THE SECRETARY						
	7	OF INTERIOR DEC 12 1902						
	8							
	9							
	10							
	11							
	12							
	13							
	14							
	15							
	16							
	17							

TRIBAL ENROLLMENT OF PARENTS

Name of Father	Year	County	Name of Mother	Year	County
1 Chas Morrison	1896	Towson	Sathe Morrison	1896	Skullyville
2 Impson Homer	Dead	Kiamitia	No 1		
3					
4					
5					
6	No 1 is wife of Wilburn McAfee on Choc #1073				
7					
8					
9					
10					
11					
12					
13					
14			Date of Application for Enrollment.		
15					
16			Apr. 29/99		
17					

Choctaw By Blood Enrollment Cards 1898-1914

RESIDENCE: Red River COUNTY.
POST OFFICE: Goodwater, I.T.

Choctaw Nation

Choctaw Roll
(Not Including Freedmen)

CARD No.
FIELD NO. 1147

Dawes' Roll No.	NAME	Relationship to Person First Named	AGE	SEX	BLOOD	TRIBAL ENROLLMENT Year	TRIBAL ENROLLMENT County	TRIBAL ENROLLMENT No.
3106	1 McKinney, Watson 46	First Named	43	M	Full	1896	Red River	9346
3107	2 " Betsy 41	Wife	38	F	"	1896	" "	332
3108	3 " Linnie 12	Dau	9	"	"	1896	" "	9347
3109	4 Amos, Ainsworth 18	S.Son	15	M	"	1896	" "	333
	5							
	6	ENROLLMENT						
	7	OF NOS. 1 2 3 and 4 HEREON APPROVED BY THE SECRETARY						
	8	OF INTERIOR DEC 12 1902						
	9							
	10							
	11							
	12							
	13							
	14							
	15							
	16							
	17							

TRIBAL ENROLLMENT OF PARENTS

	Name of Father	Year	County	Name of Mother	Year	County
1	Jacob	Dead	Sans Bois	A-la-teach-e	Dead	Red River
2	Sampson Bully	"	Eagle		"	Eagle
3	No 1			Missie Watson	"	Red River
4	John Amos	Dead	Eagle	No 2		
5						
6						
7	No2 on 1896 roll as Betsy Amos					
8	No3 " 1896 " " Lena McKinney					
9						
10						
11						
12						
13						
14						
15					Date of Application for Enrollment.	
16					Apr. 29/99	
17						

Choctaw By Blood Enrollment Cards 1898-1914

RESIDENCE:	Cedar	COUNTY.
POST OFFICE:	Doaksville, I.T.	

Choctaw Nation

Choctaw Roll (Not Including Freedmen) FIELD NO. 1148

Dawes' Roll No.	NAME		Relationship to Person First Named	AGE	SEX	BLOOD	TRIBAL ENROLLMENT		
							Year	County	No.
3110	1 Wesley, Joseph	56	First Named	53	M	Full	1896	Cedar	13149
3111	2 " Eliza	26	Wife	23	F	"	1896	"	13150
3112	3 " Charlie	7	Son	4	M	"	1896	"	13151
~~3113~~	4 ~~Biny~~ DIED PRIOR TO SEPTEMBER 25, 1902		Dau	1	F	"			
3114	5 Peter, Sibbie	21	Ward	18	"	"	1896	Cedar	10329
3115	6 Wesley, Jackson	3	Son	4mo	M	"			
3116	7 " , James	1	Son	1mo	M	"			
	8								
	9	ENROLLMENT OF NOS. 1 2 3 4 5 6 and 7 HEREON APPROVED BY THE SECRETARY OF INTERIOR DEC 12 1902							
	10								
	11								
	12								
	13								
	14								
	15								
	16								
	17								

TRIBAL ENROLLMENT OF PARENTS

	Name of Father	Year	County	Name of Mother	Year	County
1	Me-shun-ta-ta	Dead	Cedar	Isabelle	Dead	Cedar
2	James Lowman	"	"	Elizabeth Lowman	1896	Nashoba
3	No1			No2		
4	~~No1~~			~~No2~~		
5	Joel Peter	Dead	Cedar	Famie[sic] Peter	Dead	Cedar
6	No.1			No.2		
7	No.1			No.2		
8						
9	No7 born Jany 12, 1902: Enrolled Feby. 4th, 1902					
10	No4 died August 3, 1900: proof of death filed Dec. 11, 1902					
11	No 4 died Aug. 3 1900: Enrollment cancelled by Department July 8, 1904					
12						
13	For child of Nos 1&2 see NB (Apr 26-06) #488					
14	" " " " " " (Mar 3-05) #1081				#1 to 5 inc	
15					Date of Application for Enrollment.	
16				No.6 Enrolled May 24, 1900	Apr 29/99	
17	P.O. Fort Towson I.T. 7/12/03					

Choctaw By Blood Enrollment Cards 1898-1914

Dawes' Roll No.	NAME	Relationship to Person First Named	AGE	SEX	BLOOD	TRIBAL ENROLLMENT Year	County	No.
3117	1 Tushka, Wallace ~~DIED PRIOR TO SEPTEMBER 25, 1902~~		59	M	Full	1896	Red River	12262
3118	2 " Lizzie 37	Wife	34	F	"	1896	" "	12263
Void.	3 " Missie	Dau	24	"	"	1896	" "	12264
3119	4 Jones, Littie 25	"	22	"	"	1896	" "	12265
3120	5 Tushka, Sallie 23	"	20	"	"	1896	" "	12266
3121	6 " Silas 21	Son	18	M	"	1896	" "	12267
3122	7 " Willis 18	"	15	"	"	1896	" "	12268
IW701	8 Jones, George W. (43)	HUSBAND OF NO 4	43	M	I.W.			
	9							
	10	ENROLLMENT OF NOS. 1 2 4 5 6 and 7 HEREON APPROVED BY THE SECRETARY						
	11	OF INTERIOR DEC 12 1902						
	12	Sept 4/99 No3 has been placed						
	13	upon Card No 4453 with husband Robert S. Harrison			No 7 is husband of No 2 Choc 704			
	14	~~No. 1 died April 30, 1901: Enrollment~~						
	15	~~cancelled by Department July 8, 1904~~						
	16				No6 Husband of Louisa Thomas 7-#1110 (Choctaw card)			
	17				No1 died April 30, 1901; proof of death filed Dec 3, 1902			

TRIBAL ENROLLMENT OF PARENTS

	Name of Father	Year	County	Name of Mother	Year	County
1	Tushka	Dead	Red River	Maley Tuska[sic]	Dead	Red River
2	Kone-et-obe	"	" "	E-mi-l-tona	"	" "
3	No 1			Kissie Tushka	1896	" "
4	No 1			" "	1896	" "
5	No 1			" "	1896	" "
6	No 1			" "	1896	" "
7	No 1			" "	1896	" "
8	Jackson Jones	dead	non-citizen	Charlotte Jones	dead	non-citizen
9						
10				ENROLLMENT		
11				OF NOS. ~~8~~ HEREON APPROVED BY THE SECRETARY		
12	No1 on 1896 roll as Wallace Tashka			OF INTERIOR MAY -7 1904		
13	No2 " 1896 " " Lizzie "					
14	No4 " 1896 " " Lydie Tushka					
15	~~No.4 is now the wife of George W. Jones on Choctaw card #D.693~~ Dec 20,1901			Date of Application for Enrollment.		
16	No1 died April 30, 1901; proof of death filed Dec 3, 1902			Apr. 29/99		
17	No.8 transferred from Choctaw card #D.695: See decision of Feby 27, 1904			1 to 7 inc		

249

Choctaw By Blood Enrollment Cards 1898-1914

RESIDENCE: Bok Tuklo   COUNTY.   **Choctaw Nation**   **Choctaw Roll**   CARD NO.
POST OFFICE: Lukfata, I.T.   *(Not Including Freedmen)*   FIELD NO.   1150

Dawes' Roll No.		NAME	Relationship to Person First Named	AGE	SEX	BLOOD	TRIBAL ENROLLMENT		
							Year	County	No.
3123	1	Sylvester, James ~~DIED PRIOR TO SEPTEMBER 25, 1902~~		18	M	Full	1896	Bok Tuklo	14424
	2								
	3								
	4	ENROLLMENT OF NOS. 1 HEREON							
	5	APPROVED BY THE SECRETARY							
	6	OF INTERIOR DEC 12 1902							
	7								
	8								
	9								
	10								
	11								
	12								
	13	No. 1 died before Sept. 25, 1902; Enrollment cancelled by Department May 2, 1906							
	14								
	15								
	16								
	17								

TRIBAL ENROLLMENT OF PARENTS

	Name of Father	Year	County	Name of Mother	Year	County
1	Sylvester Davis	1896	Bok Tuklo	E lan te ma	Dead	Bok Tuklo
2						
3						
4						
5						
6						
7						
8						
9						
10						
11						
12						
13						
14						
15						
16				Date of Application for Enrollment.		Apr. 29/99
17						

Choctaw By Blood Enrollment Cards 1898-1914

RESIDENCE: Red River COUNTY. **Choctaw Nation** **Choctaw Roll** CARD No.
POST OFFICE: Janis, I.T. (Not Including Freedmen) FIELD No. 1151

Dawes' Roll No.	NAME	Relationship to Person	AGE	SEX	BLOOD	TRIBAL ENROLLMENT		
						Year	County	No.
IW 1206	1 Walker, Martha 28	First Named	24	F	I.W.			
	2							
	3	ENROLLMENT						
	4	OF NOS. – 1 – HEREON						
		APPROVED BY THE SECRETARY						
	5	OF INTERIOR DEC 13 1904						
	6							
	7							
	8							
	9							
	10							
	11							
	12							
	13							
	14							
	15							
	16							
	17							

TRIBAL ENROLLMENT OF PARENTS

	Name of Father	Year	County	Name of Mother	Year	County
1	Thomas Aynes	1896	Non Citz	Liza Aynes	1896	Non Citz
2						
3						
4						
5		No.1 formerly wife of Stephen Walker, 1893 Pay roll,				
6		Red River County, No. 736, and 1896 Census Roll,				
7		Red River County, No. 13700 Said Stephen Walker				
8		died in 1899.				
9						
10						
11						
12						
13						
14						
15						
16				Date of Application for Enrollment. Apr. 29/99		
17	[Illegible]	4/27/06				

Choctaw By Blood Enrollment Cards 1898-1914

| RESIDENCE: Red River COUNTY.
 POST OFFICE: Goodwater, I.T. | **Choctaw Nation** | | | | Choctaw Roll
 (Not Including Freedmen) | | CARD NO.
 FIELD NO. 1152 | |

Dawes' Roll No.	NAME		Relationship to Person First Named	AGE	SEX	BLOOD	TRIBAL ENROLLMENT		
							Year	County	No.
3124	1 Sampson, Noel	24	First Named	21	M	Full	1896	Red River	11459
3125	2 " Lucy	28	Wife	25	F	"	1896	" "	7589
3126	3 " Peter	5	Son	1	M	"	1896	" "	
3127	4 King, Sernia	8	S.Dau	5	F	"			7594
3128	5 Sampson, Silena	1	Dau.	7mo	F	"	1896	Red River	
	6								
	7	ENROLLMENT							
	8	OF NOS. 1 2 3 4 and 5 HEREON APPROVED BY THE SECRETARY							
	9	OF INTERIOR DEC 12 1902							
	10								
	11								
	12								
	13								
	14								
	15								
	16								
	17								

TRIBAL ENROLLMENT OF PARENTS

	Name of Father	Year	County	Name of Mother	Year	County
1	Levi Sampson	1896	Red River	No-wa-te-ma	Dead	Red River
2	Millwit King	Dead	" "	Sallie King	1896	" "
3	No 1			No 2		
4	Hogan Jefferson	1896	Red River	No 2		
5	No.1			No.2		
6						
7			No2 on 1896 roll as Lucy King			
8			No4 " 1896 " " Cerny "			
9			No.5 born April 13, 1901: Enrolled Nov. 30, 1901.			
10			For child of Nos 1&2 see NB (March 3, 1905) #1039			
11			No 5 said to have died Sept 26, 1902			
12			more evidence desired			
13						
14					#1 to 4	
15					Date of Application for Enrollment.	
16					Apr. 29/99	
17						

252

Choctaw By Blood Enrollment Cards 1898-1914

RESIDENCE: Red River COUNTY.
POST OFFICE: Shawneetown, I.T.

Choctaw Nation

Choctaw Roll CARD NO.
(Not Including Freedmen) FIELD NO. 1153

Dawes' Roll No.	NAME	Relationship to Person First Named	AGE	SEX	BLOOD	TRIBAL ENROLLMENT		
						Year	County	No.
3129	1 Harley, Michael 29	First Named	26	M	Full	1896	Red River	5671
3130	2 " Salena 29	Wife	26	F	"	1896	" "	4214
3131	3 " Florence 2	Dau	1½	F	"			
	4							
	5	ENROLLMENT						
	6	OF NOS. 1 2 and 3 HEREON APPROVED BY THE SECRETARY						
	7	OF INTERIOR DEC 12 1902						
	8							
	9							
	10							
	11							
	12							
	13							
	14							
	15							
	16							
	17							

TRIBAL ENROLLMENT OF PARENTS

	Name of Father	Year	County	Name of Mother	Year	County
1	Calvin Harley	Dead	Red River	Phoebe Tushka	1896	Red River
2	Hicks Fisher	1896	" "	Susie Fisher	Dead	" "
3	No. 1			No. 2		
4						
5						
6						
7						
8						
9		No 2 on 1896 roll as Serena Fisher				
10		No. 3 Enrolled Oct. 10, 1901.				
11		For child of Nos 1&2 see NB (Apr 26-06) Card #489				
12						
13						
14						#1&2
15					Date of Application for Enrollment.	
16					Apr. 29/99	
17						

Choctaw By Blood Enrollment Cards 1898-1914

RESIDENCE: Bok Tuklo   COUNTY. **Choctaw Nation**   **Choctaw Roll**   CARD NO.
POST OFFICE: Lukfata, I.T.   *(Not Including Freedmen)*   FIELD NO. 1154

Dawes' Roll No.		NAME		Relationship to Person First Named	AGE	SEX	BLOOD	TRIBAL ENROLLMENT		
								Year	County	No.
3132	1	Willis, Tom H.	40	First Named	37	M	Full	1896	Bok Tuklo	13428
	2									
	3	ENROLLMENT								
	4	OF NOS. 1 HEREON APPROVED BY THE SECRETARY								
	5	OF INTERIOR DEC 12 1902								
	6									
	7									
	8									
	9									
	10									
	11									
	12									
	13									
	14									
	15									
	16									
	17									

TRIBAL ENROLLMENT OF PARENTS

	Name of Father	Year	County	Name of Mother	Year	County
1	Hick-e-tambe	Dead	Bok Tuklo	Nah-yoh-ke	Dead	Bok Tuklo
2						
3						
4						
5						
6	No 1 is now husband of Mela Joseph Choc #720 11/28/02					
7						
8						
9						
10						
11						
12						
13						
14						
15						
16				Date of Application for Enrollment	Apr. 29/99	
17						

254

Choctaw By Blood Enrollment Cards 1898-1914

RESIDENCE: Nashoba COUNTY.
POST OFFICE: Octava[sic], I.T.

Choctaw Nation

Choctaw Roll (Not Including Freedmen)

CARD NO.
FIELD NO. 1155

Dawes' Roll No.	NAME		Relationship to Person First Named	AGE	SEX	BLOOD	TRIBAL ENROLLMENT		
							Year	County	No.
IW224	1 Nichols, Levi	38		32	M	I.W.			
3133	2 " Emma	23	Wife	20	F	1/4	1896	Nashoba	7950
3134	3 " Unie	7	S.Son	4	M	1/8	1896	"	7958
3135	4 " Roy	2	Son	4mo	M	1/8			
3136	5 " Buel	1	Son	4mo	M	1/8			
	6								
	7	ENROLLMENT							
	8	OF NOS. 2 3 4 and 5 HEREON APPROVED BY THE SECRETARY							
	9	OF INTERIOR DEC 12 1902							
	10	ENROLLMENT							
	11	OF NOS. 1 HEREON APPROVED BY THE SECRETARY							
	12	OF INTERIOR SEP 12 1903							
	13								
	14								
	15								
	16								
	17								

TRIBAL ENROLLMENT OF PARENTS

	Name of Father	Year	County	Name of Mother	Year	County
1	M. Nichols	Dead	Non Citz	Sarah Nichols	1896	Non Citz
2	Houston Labor	1896	" "	Permelia Labor	1896	Nashoba
3	Unie Hancock	Dead	" "	No 2		
4	No 1			No 2		
5	No 1			No 2		
6						
7						
8	No2 on 1896 roll as Emma Labor					
9	No3 " " " " Unie Labor					
10	No4 Enrolled December 21, 1900					
11	No5 Born Feb 12th 1902; Enrolled June 25th 1902					
	For child of Nos1 and 2 see NB (March 3 1905) #1248					
12						
13						
14					#1 to 3	
15					Date of Application for Enrollment.	
16					Apr. 29/99	
17	P.O. Antlers I.T.					

12/2/02

Choctaw By Blood Enrollment Cards 1898-1914

RESIDENCE: Nashoba COUNTY. **Choctaw Nation** **Choctaw Roll** CARD No.

POST OFFICE: Octava[sic], I.T. (Not Including Freedmen) FIELD No. 1156

Dawes' Roll No.	NAME	Relationship to Person	AGE	SEX	BLOOD	TRIBAL ENROLLMENT		
						Year	County	No.
3137	₁ Watson, Betsy ⁷⁸	First Named	75	F	1/2	1896	Nashoba	13239
3138	₂ " Sanders ⁸	G.Son	5	M	1/4	1896	"	13238
	3							
	4	ENROLLMENT						
	5	OF NOS. 1 and 2 HEREON APPROVED BY THE SECRETARY						
	6	OF INTERIOR DEC 12 1902						
	7							
	8							
	9							
	10							
	11							
	12							
	13							
	14							
	15							
	16							
	17							

TRIBAL ENROLLMENT OF PARENTS

	Name of Father	Year	County	Name of Mother	Year	County
1	Louis Robinson	Dead	Non Citz		Dead	Nashoba
2	Ben Watson	"	Nashoba	Eveline Watson	"	Non Citz
3						
4						
5						
6	The guardian of No2 is William Labor Choc card #3915					
7						
8						
9						
10						
11						
12						
13						
14						
15						
16				Date of Application for Enrollment	Apr 29/99	
17						

256

Choctaw By Blood Enrollment Cards 1898-1914

RESIDENCE: Bok Tuklo   COUNTY.   **Choctaw Nation**   Choctaw Roll   CARD NO.
POST OFFICE: Lukfata, I.T.   *(Not Including Freedmen)*   FIELD NO.   1157

Dawes' Roll No.	NAME	Relationship to Person First Named	AGE	SEX	BLOOD	TRIBAL ENROLLMENT Year	TRIBAL ENROLLMENT County	TRIBAL ENROLLMENT No.
3139	1 Willis, Soyo 48	First Named	45	F	Full	1896	Bok Tuklo	13424
3140	2 James, Benjamin ED PRIOR TO SEPTEMBER 25, 1902	Son	20	M	"	1896	" "	6910
3141	3 " Mary 13	Dau	10	F	"	1896	" "	6912
	4							
	5 ENROLLMENT							
	6 OF NOS. 1 2 and 3 HEREON APPROVED BY THE SECRETARY							
	7 OF INTERIOR DEC 12 1902							
	8							
	9							
	10							
	11							
	12							
	13							
	14							
	15							
	16							
	17							

TRIBAL ENROLLMENT OF PARENTS

Name of Father	Year	County	Name of Mother koke	Year	County
1 Hick-a-tomby	Dead	Bok Tuklo	Ish-te-mo-na ^	Dead	Bok Tuklo
2 Alfred James	"	" " "	No 1		
3 " "	"	" " "	No 1		
4					
5					
6					
7					
8		No2 died in 1900; proof of death filed Dec 3, 1902			
9		No2 died – –, 1900" Enrollment cancelled by Department July 8, 1904			
10					
11					
12					
13					
14					
15					
16				Date of Application for Enrollment	Apr. 29/99
17					

RESIDENCE: Red River COUNTY. **Choctaw Nation** Choctaw Roll CARD NO.
POST OFFICE: Garvin, I.T. *(Not Including Freedmen)* FIELD NO. **1158**

Dawes' Roll No.	NAME	Relationship to Person First Named	AGE	SEX	BLOOD	TRIBAL ENROLLMENT		
						Year	County	No.
3142	1 Charles, William ³⁵	First Named	32	M	Full	1896	Red River	2652
15970	2 " Martin	Son	7	M	"	1896	" "	2647
	3 ENROLLMENT							
	4 OF NOS. 1 HEREON APPROVED BY THE SECRETARY							
	5 OF INTERIOR Dec. 12, 1902							
15969	6 Charles, Sally	Dau	12	F	Full			
	7 ENROLLMENT							
	8 OF NOS. 2&3 HEREON APPROVED BY THE SECRETARY							
	9 OF INTERIOR Mar 14, 1906							
	10							
	11	Correct name of father of No.1 is Charles James and						
	12	Correct name of Mother is Sallie Jackson						
Nos 2 and 3		For child of No1 see NB (March3'05) #976 Dec 10,1900						
	14 GRANTED							
	15 Dec. 27, 1905.							
	16							
	17							

TRIBAL ENROLLMENT OF PARENTS

	Name of Father	Year	County	Name of Mother	Year	County
1	William Charles	Died	in Louisiana	Cealy Charles	1896	Red River
2	Charles James			Sallie Jackson		
3	No 1			Mary Charles		Choctaw
4						
5						
6	No 1			Sealy Charles	Dead	Choctaw
7						
8						
9				No1 admitted as a Mississippi Choctaw by Act of		
10				Council, approved, October 16ᵗʰ, 1895.		
11				on Dec 10,1900 & age was 6		
12	No2 originally listed on Choctaw card #D597 ∧ Transferred					
13	to this card September 22,1905. See testimony of April 11,1905					
14	Application for enrollment of No3 received					
15	April 11, 1905, under Act of Congress approved March 3, 1905.			Date of Application for Enrollment.		
16				Apr. 29/99		
17						

Choctaw By Blood Enrollment Cards 1898-1914

RESIDENCE: Red River   COUNTY.
POST OFFICE: Janis, I.T.

Choctaw Nation

Choctaw Roll *(Not Including Freedmen)*

CARD NO.
FIELD NO. 1159

Dawes' Roll No.	NAME	Relationship to Person First Named	AGE	SEX	BLOOD	TRIBAL ENROLLMENT		
						Year	County	No.
3143	1 Jefferson, Hogan 43	First Named	40	M	Full	1896	Red River	7045
	2							
	3	ENROLLMENT						
	4	OF NOS. 1 HEREON APPROVED BY THE SECRETARY						
	5	OF INTERIOR Dec 12 1902						
	6							
	7							
	8							
	9							
	10							
	11							
	12							
	13							
	14							
	15							
	16							
	17							

TRIBAL ENROLLMENT OF PARENTS

	Name of Father	Year	County	Name of Mother	Year	County
1	Josie Jefferson	Dead	Red River	Maggie Jefferson	Dead	Red River
2						
3						
4						
5						
6						
7						
8						
9						
10						
11						
12						
13						
14						
15				Date of Application for Enrollment.		
16				Apr. 29/99		
17	Goodwater I.T.					

11/27/02

Choctaw By Blood Enrollment Cards 1898-1914

RESIDENCE: Red River   COUNTY.   **Choctaw Nation**   **Choctaw Roll**   CARD NO.

POST OFFICE: Goodwater, I.T.   *(Not Including Freedmen)*   FIELD NO. **1160**

Dawes' Roll No.	NAME	Relationship to Person First Named	AGE	SEX	BLOOD	TRIBAL ENROLLMENT Year	County	No.
3144	1 James, Mimey ³³	First Named	30	F	Full	1896	Red River	7010
3145	2 James, Hudson (DIED PRIOR TO SEPTEMBER 25, 1902)	Son	16	M	"	1896	" "	7011
3146	3 " , Charlison ¹⁴	"	11	"	"	1896	" "	7012
3147	4 " , Mary ¹¹	Dau	8	F	"	1896	" "	7013
3148	5 " , Lena ⁸	"	5	"	"	1896	" "	7014
3149	6 McClure, Louis ⁵	Son	2	M				
3150	7 Harley, Ansie ¹⁷	Sister	14	F	"	1896	Red River	5666
	8							
	9	ENROLLMENT OF NOS. 123456and7 HEREON APPROVED BY THE SECRETARY OF INTERIOR Dec 12, 1902						
	10							
	11							
	12							
	13							
	14							
	15							
	16							
	17							

TRIBAL ENROLLMENT OF PARENTS

	Name of Father	Year	County	Name of Mother	Year	County
1	Calvin Harley	Dead	Red River	Mollie Harley	Dead	Red River
2	Womsley James	"	" "	No 1		
3	" "	"	" "	No 1		
4	" "	"	" "	No 1		
5	" "	"	" "	No 1		
6	Dickson McClure	1896	" "	No 1		
7	Calvin Harley	Dead	" "	Amy Harley	Dead	Red River
8						
9	No1 on 1896 roll as Mimy James					
10	No2 died June 26, 1900: Proof of death filed Dec 3, 1902.					
11	No1 now wife of Thomas A. Byington on Choc #852					
12	No2 died June 26, 1900: Enrollment cancelled by Department July 8, 1904					
13						
14						
15				Date of Application for Enrollment.		
16				Apr. 29/99		
17						

260

Choctaw By Blood Enrollment Cards 1898-1914

Dawes' Roll No.	NAME		Relationship to Person First Named	AGE	SEX	BLOOD	TRIBAL ENROLLMENT		
							Year	County	No.
3151	1	Frazier, Ben DIED PRIOR TO SEPTEMBER 25, 1902		41	M	Full	1896	Cedar	4082
3152	2	" , Susan 30	Wife	27	F	"	1896	"	4083
3153	3	" , Isaac DIED PRIOR TO SEPTEMBER 25, 1902	Son	20	M	"	1896	"	4084
3154	4	" , Thompson DIED PRIOR TO SEPTEMBER 25, 1902	"	18	"	"	1896	"	4085
3155	5	" , Davis 19	"	16	"	"	1896	"	4086
3156	6	" , Billy 10	"	7	"	"	1896	"	4087
3157	7	" , Lizzie 6	Dau	3	F	"	1896	"	4088
3158	8	" , James 3	Son	4mo	M	"			
	9								
	10								
	11								
	12								
	13								
	14								
	15								
	16								
	17								

ENROLLMENT
OF NOS. 1234567and8 HEREON
APPROVED BY THE SECRETARY
OF INTERIOR Dec. 12, 1902.

TRIBAL ENROLLMENT OF PARENTS

	Name of Father	Year	County	Name of Mother	Year	County
1	Smith Frazier	Dead	Cedar		Dead	Cedar
2	Wallace McAlester	1896	Nashoba	Elizabeth McAlester	"	"
3	No 1			Susie Frazier	"	"
4	No 1			" "	"	"
5	No 1			" "	"	"
6	No 1			No 2		
7	No 1			No 2		
8	No 1			No 2		
9						

No3 died Dec 19, 1900. No4 died Aug 12, 1900. Enrollment cancelled by Department May 2, 1906

No5 on 1896 roll as Lewie Frazier

For child of No2 see NB (Apr 26,06) No 536
    "   "   "   "   "   " 677

No8 enrolled Dec 19/99. Affidavit
irregular and returned for correction
Returned corrected and filed Oct 16th 1900.

No1 died in 1901: Proof of death filed Dec 10, 1902.

No1 died — — 1901: Enrollment cancelled by Department July 8, 1904

Date of Application for Enrollment.

Apr. 29/99

Choctaw By Blood Enrollment Cards 1898-1914

RESIDENCE: Red River COUNTY.   **Choctaw Nation**   Choctaw Roll   CARD NO.
POST OFFICE: Janis, I.T.   (Not Including Freedmen)   FIELD NO. **1162**

Dawes' Roll No.	NAME	Relationship to Person First Named	AGE	SEX	BLOOD	TRIBAL ENROLLMENT		
						Year	County	No.
3159	₁ Alexander, Henry ²⁶	First Named	23	M	Full	1896	Red River	329
3160	₂ ~~Kizzie~~ DIED PRIOR TO SEPTEMBER 25, 190?	~~Wife~~	~~17~~	F	"	~~1896~~	" "	~~7032~~
3161	₃ Winship, Stewart ¹³	Bro	10	M	"	1896	" "	13682
3162	₄ Alexander, Ellen ³	Dau	2mo	F	"			
	₅							
	₆							
	₇	ENROLLMENT OF NOS. 1 2 3 and 4 HEREON APPROVED BY THE SECRETARY OF INTERIOR Dec. 12, 1902						
	₈							
	₉							
	10							
	11							
	12							
	13							
	14							
	15							
	16							
	17							

TRIBAL ENROLLMENT OF PARENTS

	Name of Father	Year	County	Name of Mother	Year	County
₁	Milton Alexander	Dead	Red River	Liza Winship	Dead	Red River
₂	~~Thos Jefferson~~	"	" "	~~Mary Jefferson~~	1896	" "
₃	Jamison McKinney	1896	" "	Liza Winship	Dead	" "
₄	No 1			No 2		
₅						
₆			No 2 on 1896 roll as Kissy Jefferson			
₇			No 3 " 1896 " " Stuart Winship			
₈						
₉			No 2 died March 14, 1900: Proof of death filed Dec. 3, 1902			
10			No 1 husband of No 2 on 7-940			
11			No.2 died March 14, 1902; Enrollment cancelled by Department July 8, 1904.			
12			For child of No1 see N.B. (March 3, 1905) #959			
13			" " " " " " (April 26, 1906) #387			
14						
15				Date of Application for Enrollment.	No 4 enrolled Nov. 24/99	
16					Apr. 29/99	
17					#1 to 3	

Choctaw By Blood Enrollment Cards 1898-1914

Dawes' Roll No.	NAME		Relationship to Person First Named	AGE	SEX	BLOOD	TRIBAL ENROLLMENT		
							Year	County	No.
3163	1 Billy, Willie	ED PRIOR TO SEPTEMBER 25, 1902	First Named	25	M	Full	1893	Nashoba	P.R. 108
3164	2 Phoebe	ED PRIOR TO SEPTEMBER 25, 1902	Wife	20	F	"	1896	Wade	10285
3165	3 " Marry 2		Dau	4mo	"	"			
	4								
	5	ENROLLMENT							
	6	OF NOS. 1 2 and 3 HEREON APPROVED BY THE SECRETARY							
	7	OF INTERIOR DEC 12 1902							
	8								
	9								
	10								
	11								
	12								
	13								
	14								
	15								
	16								
	17								

TRIBAL ENROLLMENT OF PARENTS

	Name of Father	Year	County	Name of Mother	Year	County
1	Daniel Billy	1896	Nashoba	Man-te-hu-na	1896	Cedar
2	Calvin Anderson	1896	Jacks Fork	Salema[sic] Anderson	Dead	Jacks Fork
3	No 1			No 2		
4						
5			No1 on 1893 Pay roll as Willy Bally			
6			No2 " 1896 " " Phoebe Pitchlynn			
7						
8			No1 died January 22, 1901; proof of death filed Dec 5, 1902			
9			No2 " October 28, 1901; " " " " " 5, 1902			
10						
11			No. 3 lives with Solomon Uehka Choc #893			
12	No.1 died Jan.22,1901; No.2 died Oct.28,1901; Enrollment cancelled by Department July 8, 1904					
13						
14						
15						
16					Date of Application for Enrollment. Apr. 29/99	
17					No 3 enrolled Nov 24/99	

263

Choctaw By Blood Enrollment Cards 1898-1914

RESIDENCE: Towson   COUNTY.

POST OFFICE: Doaksville, I.T.

Choctaw Nation

Choctaw Roll
(Not Including Freedmen)

CARD NO.

FIELD NO. **1164**

Dawes' Roll No.	NAME	Relationship to Person First Named	AGE	SEX	BLOOD	TRIBAL ENROLLMENT		
						Year	County	No.
3166	1 Nanomantube, Wilmon ³³	First Named	30	M	Full	1896	Towson	9657
3167	2 " Lucinda ²⁶				3/4	1896	Kiamitia	2723
3168	3 " Jonathan ⁴				7/8			
3169	4 " Silvester ²				7/8			
	5							
	6	ENROLLMENT OF NOS. 1 2 3 and 4 HEREON						
	7	APPROVED BY THE SECRETARY OF INTERIOR Dec 12, 1902						
	8							
	9							
	10							
	11							
	12							
	13							
	14							
	15							
	16							
	17							

TRIBAL ENROLLMENT OF PARENTS

	Name of Father	Year	County	Name of Mother	Year	County
1	Nanomantube	Dead	Towson	Mary	1896	Towson
2	Louis Crowder	1896	Jackson	Nancy Ward	Dead	Jackson
3	No 1			No 2		
4	No 1			No 2		
5						
6						
7						
8	No1 on 1896 roll as Wᵐ Nanomantube					
9	No2 " 1896 " " Lucinda Crowder					
10	No.2 also on 1896 Choctaw roll as Lucinda Cole, page 65, 2729.					
	No.4 Enrolled April 6, 1901					
11						
12	For child of No2 see N.B. (Act Apr 26-06) Card #311					
13						
14					#1 to 3	
15				Date of Application for Enrollment.	Apr. 29/99	
16						
17						

Choctaw By Blood Enrollment Cards 1898-1914

RESIDENCE: Eagle   COUNTY.   **Ch**_____   **Choctaw Roll**   CARD No.

POST OFFICE: Eagletown, I.T.   *(Not Including Freedmen)*   FIELD No. 1165

Dawes' Roll No.	NAME	Relationship to Person First Named	AGE	SEX	BLOOD	TRIBAL ENROLLMENT		
						Year	County	No.
3170	1 Fobb, Willie ³²		29	M	Full	1896	Eagle	
	2							
	3							
	4							
	5							
	6							
	7							
	8							
	9							
	10							
	11							
	12							
	13							
	14							
	15							
	16							
	17							

ENROLLMENT
OF NOS. 1 HEREON
APPROVED BY THE SECRETARY
OF INTERIOR DEC 12 1902

TRIBAL ENROLLMENT OF PARENTS

	Name of Father	Year	County	Name of Mother	Year	County
1	Joe Fobb	Dead	Eagle	Hate Fobb	1896	Eagle
2						
3						
4						
5						
6						
7						
8						
9	No					
10						
11						
12						
13						
14						
15						
16				Date of Application for Enrollment.	Apr. 29/99	
17						

RESIDENCE: Nashoba   COUNTY. **Choctaw Nation**   **Choctaw Roll** CARD NO.
POST OFFICE: Alikchi, I.T.   (Not Including Freedmen)   FIELD NO. **1166**

Dawes' Roll No.	NAME	Relationship to Person First Named	AGE	SEX	BLOOD	TRIBAL ENROLLMENT		
						Year	County	No.
3171	1 Wilson, Carlo A. 41	First Named	38	M	Full	1896	Nashoba	13300
3172	2 " Margaret 25	Wife	22	F	"	1896	"	5537
3173	3 " Thompson 20	Son	17	M	"	1896	"	13229
3174	4 " Noah 12	"	9	"	"	1896	"	13301
3175	5 " Gardner 8	"	5	"	1/2	1896	"	13302
3176	6 " Eve 6	Dau	2	F	1/2			
3177	7 " Abbott 4	Son	1	M	Full			
3178	8 Holmes, Sissy 14	Ward	11	F	"	1896	Nashoba	5538
3179	9 Wilson, Greenwood 2	Son	5mo	M	"			
	10							
	11	ENROLLMENT						
	12	OF NOS.12345678and9 HEREON APPROVED BY THE SECRETARY						
	13	OF INTERIOR Dec. 12 1902						
	14							
	15							
	16							
	17							

TRIBAL ENROLLMENT OF PARENTS

	Name of Father	Year	County	Name of Mother	Year	County
1	Alexander Wilson	1896	Nashoba	Lige Wilson	1896	Nashoba
2	James Holmes	Dead	"	Susan Holmes	Dead	"
3	No 1			Sarah Wilson	"	Eagle
4	No 1			Celistia Wilson	1896	Jacks Fork
5	No 1			Laura Wilson	Dead	Non Citz
6	No 1			" "	"	" " "
7	No 1			No 2		
8	Wallace Carney	Dead	Nashoba	Silly A. Holmes	Dead	Nashoba
9	No 1			No 2		
10	No 2 on 1896 roll as Margaret Holmes					
11	No 3 " 1896 " " Thomas Wilson					
12	No.9 Enrolled Aug 27, 1901					
13	For child of Nos 1&2 see N.B. (Apr 26-06) Card #661					
14	" " " " " " " (Mar 3-05) " #1298			#1 to 8		
15	Date of application for enrollment			Date of Application for Enrollment.		
16				Apr. 29/99		
17						

Choctaw By Blood Enrollment Cards 1898-1914

Choctaw Nation

POST OFFICE: Fowlerville, I.T.

Choctaw Roll *(Not Including Freedmen)*

CARD NO. FIELD NO. **1167**

	NAME		Relationship to Person First Named	AGE	SEX	BLOOD	TRIBAL ENROLLMENT		
							Year	County	No.
3180	1 Christie, Jesse L	35	First Named	32	M	Full	1896	Towson	2476
DEAD	2 " Milan		Wife	28	F	"	1896	"	2477
3181	3 " Nelson	7	Son	4	M	"	1896	"	2478
3182	4 " Adeline	5	Dau	1	F	"			
	5								
	6		ENROLLMENT						
	7		OF NOS. 1, 3, and 4 HEREON APPROVED BY THE SECRETARY						
	8		OF INTERIOR DEC 12 1902						
	9								
	10	No. 2 HEREON DISMISSED UNDER							
	11	ORDER OF THE COMMISSION TO THE FIVE CIVILIZED TRIBES OF MARCH 31, 1905.							
	12								
	13								
	14								
	15								
	16								
	17								

TRIBAL ENROLLMENT OF PARENTS

	Name of Father	Year	County	Name of Mother	Year	County
1	Louis Christie	Dead	Towson	Mary Christie	Dead	Towson
2	Chicca	"	"	Amy Chicca	"	"
3	No 1			No 2		
4	No 1			No 2		
5						
6						
7						
8	Nº2 Died May 25, 1899, proof of death filed Oct. 13, 1902					
9	For child of No1 see NB (March 3 1905) #1259					
10						
11						
12						
13						
14					Date of Application for Enrollment.	
15						
16					Apr. 29/99	
17	Chula I.T. 10/13/02					

Choctaw By Blood Enrollment Cards 1898-1914

RESIDENCE: Bok Tuklo   COUNTY. Choctaw Nation   Choctaw Roll (Not Including Freedmen)

POST OFFICE: Lukfata, I.T.   FIELD NO. 1168

Dawes' Roll No.	NAME	Relationship to Person Named	AGE	SEX	BLOOD	TRIBAL ENROLLMENT		
						Year	County	No.
3183	1 Ishtonake, Gibson ³²	First Named	29	M	Full	1896	Bok Tuklo	6288
3184	2 " Sis ³⁴	Wife	31	F	"	1896	" "	6289
3185	3 Lheohtambi, Sophia ¹⁵	S.Dau	12	"	"	1893	" "	P.R. 61
	4							
	5	ENROLLMENT OF NOS. 1 2 and 3 HEREON APPROVED BY THE SECRETARY OF INTERIOR DEC 12 1902						
	6							
	7							
	8							
	9							
	10							
	11							
	12							
	13							
	14							
	15							
	16							
	17							

TRIBAL ENROLLMENT OF PARENTS

Name of Father	Year	County	Name of Mother	Year	County
1 Ish-to-nake	Dead	Bok Tuklo	Ba-che-hu-na	Dead	Bok Tuklo
2 Isin Thlitambi	"	" "	Ellen Thlitambi	"	" "
3 Sans Lheohtambi	1896	Eagle	No 2		
4					
5					
6					
7	No 3 on 1893 Pay roll as Sophia Tithlitambe also on				
8	1896 roll as Sophy Tithitombe Page 317, No 12197,				
9	Bok Tuklo Co.				
	No 2 wife of Keith Shaw #3 on 7 – 1309				
10	No 1 and 2 divorced				
11	No 3 is now wife of No1.				
12					
13					
14					
15				Date of Application for Enrollment.	
16				Apr. 29/99	
17					

Choctaw By Blood Enrollment Cards 1898-1914

RESIDENCE: Red River COUNTY. **Choctaw Nation** **Choctaw Roll** CARD NO.
POST OFFICE: Goodwater, I.T. *(Not Including Freedmen)* FIELD NO. 1169

Dawes' Roll No.	NAME		Relationship to Person First Named	AGE	SEX	BLOOD	TRIBAL ENROLLMENT		
							Year	County	No.
3186	1 Dyer, Louis	37	First Named	34	M	Full	1896	Red River	3448
DEAD.	2 " Raymond DEAD.		Son	6	"	1/2	1896	" "	3449
	3								
	4	ENROLLMENT							
	5	OF NOS. 1 HEREON APPROVED BY THE SECRETARY							
	6	OF INTERIOR DEC 12 1902							
	7								
	8	No. 2 HEREON DISMISSED UNDER ORDER OF THE COMMISSION TO THE FIVE							
	9	CIVILIZED TRIBES OF MARCH 31, 1905.							
	10								
	11								
	12	For child of No1 see NB (Mar 3-05) #878							
	13	" " " " " " (Apr 26-06) #525							
	14								
	15								
	16								
	17								

TRIBAL ENROLLMENT OF PARENTS

	Name of Father	Year	County	Name of Mother	Year	County
1	Billis Dyer	Dead	Eagle	Maha Jones	Dead	Eagle
2	No 1			Melvina Dyer	"	"
3						
4						
5						
6						
7	Evidence of marriage of parents of Raymond Dyer whose					
8	mother was a Mexican – waived by Commissioner					
9	McKennon.					
10						
11	No 2 also on 1896 roll, Page 82, No 3410, Eagle Co					
12	No 1 " " 1896 " " 83, " 3443, Red River Co					
13	No 1 " " 1896 " " 82, " 3422, Eagle Co					
14	No2 died May 28, 1900: proof of death filed Dec 3 1902					
15	No1 is now husband of Maggie Harley, Choctaw card #1217					
16					Date of Application for Enrollment. Apr. 29/99	
17	Norwood I.T. 11/28/02					

269

Choctaw By Blood Enrollment Cards 1898-1914

	NAME		Relationship to Person First Named	AGE	SEX	BLOOD	TRIBAL ENROLLMENT		
							Year	County	No.

Red River COUNTY. **Choctaw Nation** Choctaw Roll (Not Including Freedmen) FIELD NO. 1170
Goodwater, I.T.

	NAME		Relationship to Person First Named	AGE	SEX	BLOOD	Year	County	No.
3187	Billy, John	52	First Named	49	M	Full	1896	Red River	1394
3188	" Sallie	36	Wife	33	F	"	1896	" "	1395
3189	" Wilkin	20	Son	17	M	"	1893	" "	P.R. 77
3190	" Siney	10	Dau	7	F	"	1896	" "	1397

ENROLLMENT
OF NOS. 1 2 3 and 4 HEREON
APPROVED BY THE SECRETARY
OF INTERIOR DEC 12 1902

TRIBAL ENROLLMENT OF PARENTS

	Name of Father	Year	County	Name of Mother	Year	County
1		Died	in Mississippi	Okla-e-ma	Dead	Red River
2	Edmond Jones	Dead	Red River	A-no-ha	"	" " "
3	No 1			Ulsey Billy	"	Eagle
4	No 1			No 2		
5						
6						
7						
8			For child of No3 see NB (March 3 1905) #1068			
9						
10						
11						
12						
13						
14						
15		No 3 is now husband of Emily Moore Choc #1177 11/25/02				
16				Date of Application for Enrollment.	Apr. 29/99	
17						

Choctaw By Blood Enrollment Cards 1898-1914

RESIDENCE: Bok Tuklo	COUNTY. **Choctaw Nation**				**Choctaw Roll** (Not Including Freedmen)	CARD NO.		
POST OFFICE: Lukfata, I.T.						FIELD NO. 1171		

Dawes' Roll No.	NAME	Relationship to Person First Named	AGE	SEX	BLOOD	TRIBAL ENROLLMENT		
						Year	County	No.
3191	1 Tokabe, Lena 24		21	F	Full	1896	Bok Tuklo	12111
	2							
	3	ENROLLMENT						
	4	OF NOS. 1 HEREON APPROVED BY THE SECRETARY						
	5	OF INTERIOR DEC 12 1902						
	6							
	7							
	8							
	9							
	10							
	11							
	12							
	13							
	14							
	15							
	16							
	17							

TRIBAL ENROLLMENT OF PARENTS

Name of Father	Year	County	Name of Mother	Year	County
1 Billy Tokabe	Dead	Bok Tuklo	Ista Tokabe	Dead	Bok Tuklo
2					
3					
4					
5	For child of No1 see NB (Apr 26-06) Card #928				
6					
7					
8					
9					
10					
11					
12					
13					
14			Date of Application for Enrollment.		
15					
16			Apr. 29/99		
17					

Choctaw By Blood Enrollment Cards 1898-1914

RESIDENCE: Red River   COUNTY.

POST OFFICE: Goodwater, I.T.

Choctaw Nation

Choctaw Roll

(Not Including Freedmen)   FIELD NO. **1172**

Dawes' Roll No.	NAME	Relationship to Person First Named	AGE	SEX	BLOOD	Year	County	No.
3192	1 Kemp, Nelson ²⁴		21	M	Full	1896	Red River	7602
3193	2 Melvina DIED PRIOR TO SEPTEMBER 25, 1902	Wife	16	F	"	1896	" "	13695
	3							
	4							
	5	ENROLLMENT						
	6	OF NOS. 1 and 2 HEREON APPROVED BY THE SECRETARY						
	7	OF INTERIOR DEC 12 1902						
	8							
	9							
	10							
	11							
	12							
	13							
	14							
	15							
	16							
	17							

TRIBAL ENROLLMENT OF PARENTS

	Name of Father	Year	County	Name of Mother	Year	County
1	William Kemp	Dead	Red River	In-sorry	1896	Red River
2	Aaron Wade	"	" "	Liza Wade	Dead	" "
3						
4						
5						
6		No1 on 1896 roll as Nancy Kemp, also on 1893 Pay roll as				
7		Nelson Camp, Page 13, No 108.				
8		No2 on 1896 roll as Mary Wade				
9		For child of No.1 see NB (March 3, 1905) #1184				
		No2 died in Aug. 1900: proof of death filed Dec 3 1902				
10		No.2 died Aug – , 1900: Enrollment cancelled by Department July 8, 1904				
11						
12						
13						
14						
15						
16				Date of Application for Enrollment	Apr. 29/99	
17						

272

Choctaw By Blood Enrollment Cards 1898-1914

RESIDENCE: Red River	COUNTY.	**Choctaw Nation**	**Choctaw Roll** *(Not Including Freedmen)*	CARD NO.	
POST OFFICE: Janis, I.T.				FIELD NO.	1173

Dawes' Roll No.	NAME		Relationship to Person First Named	AGE	SEX	BLOOD	TRIBAL ENROLLMENT		
							Year	County	No.
3194	1 Brown, Sarah	47	First Named	44	F	Full	1896	Red River	1393
	2								
	3	ENROLLMENT							
	4	OF NOS. 1	HEREON						
		APPROVED BY THE SECRETARY							
	5	OF INTERIOR DEC 12 1902							
	6								
	7								
	8								
	9								
	10								
	11								
	12								
	13								
	14								
	15								
	16								
	17								

TRIBAL ENROLLMENT OF PARENTS

Name of Father	Year	County	Name of Mother	Year	County
1 Isht-noah	Dead	Red River		Dead	Red River
2					
3					
4					
5					
6					
7					
8					
9					
10					
11					
12					
13					
14					
15			Date of Application for Enrollment.		
16			Apr. 29/99		
17					

Choctaw By Blood Enrollment Cards 1898-1914

RESIDENCE: Red River COUNTY.								
POST OFFICE: Goodwater, I.T.	**Choctaw Nation**		Choctaw Roll (Not Including Freedmen)			CARD NO.		
						FIELD NO. 1174		

Dawes' Roll No.	NAME	Relationship to Person	AGE	SEX	BLOOD	TRIBAL ENROLLMENT		
						Year	County	No.
3195	1 Brown, Adolphus 21	First Named	18	M	Full	1896	Red River	1408
	2							
	3							
	4							
	5							
	6							
	7							
	8							
	9							
	10							
	11							
	12							
	13							
	14							
	15							
	16							
	17							

ENROLLMENT
OF NOS. 1 HEREON
APPROVED BY THE SECRETARY
OF INTERIOR DEC 12 1902

TRIBAL ENROLLMENT OF PARENTS

	Name of Father	Year	County	Name of Mother	Year	County
1	Joshn[sic] Brown	Dead	Red River	Susie Brown	Dead	Red River
2						
3						
4						
5						
6						
7						
8						
9						
10						
11						
12						
13		No 1 now in Jail at Atoka 11/21/02				
14						
15						
16					Date of Application for Enrollment Apr 29/99	
17						

Choctaw By Blood Enrollment Cards 1898-1914

RESIDENCE: Cedar
POST OFFICE: Doaksville, I.T.

COUNTY: **Choctaw Nation**

Choctaw Roll (Not Including Freedmen) CARD NO. FIELD NO. 1175

Dawes' Roll No.	NAME		Relationship to Person First Named	AGE	SEX	BLOOD	TRIBAL ENROLLMENT		
							Year	County	No.
3196	1 Thomas, Josiah	28	First Named	25	M	Full	1896	Cedar	12174
3197	2 " Elbina	23	Wife	20	F	"	1896	"	12175
3198	3 " Lixan	5	Son	1	M	"			
3199	4 " Impson	3	"	6mo	M	"			
3200	5 " Joe	1	"	1mo	M	"			
	6								
	7	ENROLLMENT							
	8	OF NOS. 1 2 3 4 and 5 HEREON APPROVED BY THE SECRETARY							
	9	OF INTERIOR DEC 12 1902							
	10								
	11								
	12	Correct given name of N⁰5 is "Billy"							
	13	N⁰5 was born in August 1901 and died							
	14	about one year thereafter. See testimony of N⁰1 of May 23, 1903.							
	15								
	16								
	17								

TRIBAL ENROLLMENT OF PARENTS

	Name of Father	Year	County	Name of Mother	Year	County
1	Ish-te-me-lachuby	Dead	Cedar	Sillin Ishtemelgchuby	1896	Cedar
2	Adam Narlett	1896	Nashoba		Dead	Nashoba
3	No1			No2		
4	No1			No2		
5	No1			No2		
6						
7						
8						
9						
10	For child of Nos 1&2 see NB (March 3 1905) #1337					
11	No2 on 1896 roll as Bainie Thomas					
12	For child of Noˢ 1&2 see NB (Apr 26,1906) Card No. 51.					
13	No3 Affidavit received. Irregular and returned for correction Dec 19/99.					
14	No4 enrolled Dec 19/99. Affidavit irregular and returned for correction				Date of Application for Enrollment. #1 to 4	
15	No.3 Returned corrected and filed Feby. 20, 1900.					
16	No.4 Returned corrected and filed Feby. 20, 1900.			Apr. 29/99		
17	No.5 Enrolled Sept 23, 1901.					

Choctaw By Blood Enrollment Cards 1898-1914

RESIDENCE: Towson	COUNTY.				**Choctaw Nation**	**Choctaw Roll** (Not Including Freedmen)		CARD NO.	
POST OFFICE: Fowlersville I.T.								FIELD NO. 1176	

Dawes' Roll No.	NAME	Relationship to Person First Named	AGE	SEX	BLOOD	TRIBAL ENROLLMENT		
						Year	County	No.
3201	1 Bobb Ellis		31	M	Full	1896	Towson	1092
	2							
	3							
	4							
	5							
	6							
	7							
	8							
	9							
	10							
	11							
	12							
	13							
	14							
	15							
	16							
	17							

DIED PRIOR TO SEPTEMBER 25, 1902

ENROLLMENT
OF NOS. 1 HEREON
APPROVED BY THE SECRETARY
OF INTERIOR DEC 12 1902

TRIBAL ENROLLMENT OF PARENTS

Name of Father	Year	County	Name of Mother	Year	County
1 Bob Hliohtubbi	Ded	Towson	Hochefo	Ded	Towson
2					
3					
4 No. 1 died before Sept. 25, 1902; Enrollment cancelled by Department May 2, 1906					
5					
6					
7					
8					
9					
10					
11					
12					
13					
14					
15					
16				Date of Application for Enrollment	Apr. 29-99
17					

276

Choctaw By Blood Enrollment Cards 1898-1914

RESIDENCE: Red River   COUNTY.   **Choctaw Nation**   **Choctaw Roll** (Not Including Freedmen)   CARD No.
POST OFFICE: Goodwater I.T.   FIELD No. **1177**

Dawes' Roll No.	NAME	Relationship to Person First Named	AGE	SEX	BLOOD	TRIBAL ENROLLMENT Year	TRIBAL ENROLLMENT County	TRIBAL ENROLLMENT No.
DEAD	1 Moore James	First Named	48	M	Full	1896	Red River	8694
3202	2 King Lina ²¹	Dau	18	F	"	1896	" "	8697
3203	3 Moore Emily ¹⁹	"	16	"	"	1896	" "	8696
3204	4 King, Jenney ¹	Dau of Nº 2	1/2	F	"			
	5							
	6							
	7	ENROLLMENT OF NOS. 2 3 and 4 HEREON APPROVED BY THE SECRETARY OF INTERIOR Dec 12, 1902						
	8							
	9							
	10							
	11	No 1 Hereon dismissed under order of						
	12	the Commission to the Five Civilized						
	13	Tribes of March 31, 1905.						
	14							
	15							
	16							
	17							

TRIBAL ENROLLMENT OF PARENTS

	Name of Father	Year	County	Name of Mother	Year	County
1	Achinota	Ded	Red River	Nancy Moore	1896	Red River
2	No 1			Nancy Moore		
3	No 1			" "		
4	Harris King	1896	Red River	No 2		
5						
6	No.1 Died May 9, 1900 Evidence of death filed April 25, 1901.					
7	No.2 is the wife of Harris King on Choc. card 1194. Evidence of marriage filed Feb. 17, 1902					
8	No.4 born Aug. 7, 1901: Enrolled Feby. 17, 1902.					
9	No3 is now wife of Wilkin Billy Choc #1170 11/25/02					
10						
11	For child of No2 see N.B. (Apr 26-06) Card #462					
12	" " " No3 " " (Mar 3-05) " #1068					
13						
14					Date of Application for Enrollment.	
15						
16					Apr. 29"99	
17						

Choctaw By Blood Enrollment Cards 1898-1914

RESIDENCE: Towson COUNTY.　　**Choctaw Nation**　　Choctaw Roll　CARD NO.
POST OFFICE: Fowlersville I.T.　　　　　　　　(Not Including Freedmen)　FIELD NO. **1178**

Dawes' Roll No.	NAME	Relationship to Person First Named	AGE	SEX	BLOOD	TRIBAL ENROLLMENT Year	TRIBAL ENROLLMENT County	TRIBAL ENROLLMENT No.
14641	1 Le Flore Morris 41	First Named	38	M	3/4	1896	Towson	7923
I.W. 1092	2 "　" Puss 34	Wife	28	F	I.W.	1896	"	14765
14642	3 "　" Wilburn 16	Son	13	M	3/8	1896	"	7924
14643	4 "　" Forbis 13	"	10	"	3/8	1896	"	7925
	5							
	6 ENROLLMENT							
	7 OF NOS. 1, 3 and 4 HEREON APPROVED BY THE SECRETARY							
	8 OF INTERIOR May 20, 1903							
	9							
	10							
	11 ENROLLMENT OF NOS. ___ 2 ___ HEREON							
	12 APPROVED BY THE SECRETARY							
	13 OF INTERIOR Nov 16 1904							
	14							
	15							
	16							
	17							

TRIBAL ENROLLMENT OF PARENTS

	Name of Father	Year	County	Name of Mother	Year	County
1	Forbus Le Flore	De'd	Kiamitia	Tuna Le Flore	Ded	Bok Tuklo
2	Norman Runnell	"	Non citz	Eliza Runnell		Non citizen
3	No 1			No 2		
4	No 1			No 2		
5						
6	For information as to Choctaw blood see affidavit					
7	of Morris Leflore filed October 13, 1902					
8						
9						
10						
11						
12						
13						
14						
15					Date of Application for Enrollment.	
16					Apr. 29 "99	
17	P.O. Parsons 7/15/04					

Choctaw By Blood Enrollment Cards 1898-1914

RESIDENCE: Towson COUNTY. **Choctaw Nation** Choctaw Roll CARD No.
POST OFFICE: Fowlersville I.T. *(Not Including Freedmen)* FIELD No. 1179

Dawes' Roll No.	NAME	Relationship to Person	AGE	SEX	BLOOD	TRIBAL ENROLLMENT		
						Year	County	No.
3205	1 Nelson Bettie 23	First Named	20	F	Full	1896	Towson	9680
	2							
	3	ENROLLMENT						
	4	OF NOS. 1 HEREON APPROVED BY THE SECRETARY						
	5	OF INTERIOR DEC 12 1902						
	6							
	7							
	8							
	9							
	10							
	11							
	12							
	13							
	14							
	15							
	16							
	17							

TRIBAL ENROLLMENT OF PARENTS

	Name of Father	Year	County	Name of Mother	Year	County
1	Gabrael Nelson	1896	Kiamatia[sic]	Nancy Nelson	Ded	Jacks Fork
2						
3						
4						
5		No 1 on 1893 pay roll Jack Fork Co page 65 No 583.				
6						
7	No 1 now wife of R. M. Edwards, Choctaw D-168; Evidence of marriage filed Dec 10, 1902					
8						
9						
10						
11						
12						
13						
14						Date of Application for Enrollment.
15						
16						Apr. 29"99
17						

Choctaw By Blood Enrollment Cards 1898-1914

RESIDENCE: Red River COUNTY.

POST OFFICE: Fowlersville I T

Choctaw Nation

Choctaw Roll
(Not Including Freedmen)

CARD NO.

FIELD NO. 1180

Dawes' Roll No.	NAME	Relationship to Person First Named	AGE	SEX	BLOOD	TRIBAL ENROLLMENT		
						Year	County	No.
3206	1 Christie Isaac ³⁵	First Named	32	M	Full	1896	Red River	2653
3207	2 Bicy ~~DIED PRIOR TO SEPTEMBER 25, 1902~~	Wife	29	F	"	1896	" "	13574
3208	3 Jackson George ¹⁸	Nep.	15	M	"	1896	" "	7001
	4							
	5 ENROLLMENT							
	6 OF NOS. 1 2 and 3 HEREON APPROVED BY THE SECRETARY							
	7 OF INTERIOR DEC 12 1902							
	8							
	9							
	10							
	11							
	12							
	13							
	14							
	15							
	16							
	17							

TRIBAL ENROLLMENT OF PARENTS

	Name of Father	Year	County	Name of Mother	Year	County
1	Louisa Christie	Ded	Towson	Mary Christie	Ded	Towson
2	~~Sampson Williams~~	~~1896~~	~~Red River~~	~~Betsy Williams~~	~~Ded~~	~~Red River~~
3	James Jackson	Ded	" "	Mary Jackson	"	" "
4						
5			No 2 on 1896 roll as Bicy Williams			
6						
7						
8			No2 died Sept. 15, 1902; proof of death filed Dec. 3, 1902			
9			No.2 died Sept. 15, 1902: Enrollment cancelled by Department July 8 1904			
10						
11						
12						
13						
14					Date of Application for Enrollment.	
15						
16					Apr. 29-99	
17	P.O. Garvin I.T. 11/26/02					

Choctaw By Blood Enrollment Cards 1898-1914

RESIDENCE: Bok Tuk lo   COUNTY.   **Choctaw Nation**   **Choctaw Roll**   CARD No.
POST OFFICE: Luk-fa-tah I.T.   *(Not Including Freedmen)*   FIELD No.   1181

Dawes' Roll No.	NAME	Relationship to Person First Named	AGE	SEX	BLOOD	TRIBAL ENROLLMENT		
						Year	County	No.
3209	1 Ischomer Monroe ²⁵	First Named	22	M	Full	1896	Bok Tuklo	6280
	2							
	3							
	4	ENROLLMENT OF NOS. 1 HEREON						
	5	APPROVED BY THE SECRETARY OF INTERIOR DEC 12 1902						
	6							
	7							
	8							
	9							
	10							
	11							
	12							
	13							
	14							
	15							
	16							
	17							

TRIBAL ENROLLMENT OF PARENTS

	Name of Father	Year	County	Name of Mother	Year	County
1	Nelson Ischomer	Ded	Bok Tuklo	Ish-la-yo-ke	Ded	Bok Tuklo
2						
3						
4						
5						
6		No1 on Choctaw roll as Monroe Ishcomer				
7						
8						
9						
10						
11						
12						
13						
14						
15						
16						Apr. 29-99
17						

Choctaw By Blood Enrollment Cards 1898-1914

RESIDENCE: Red River   COUNTY.   **Choctaw Nation**   **Choctaw Roll** *(Not Including Freedmen)*   CARD NO.

POST OFFICE: ~~Cerro Gorda, Ark.~~   FIELD NO. **1182**

Dawes' Roll No.	NAME	Relationship to Person First Named	AGE	SEX	BLOOD	TRIBAL ENROLLMENT		
						Year	County	No.
3210	₁ Billy David ²⁹	First Named	26	M	Full	1896	Red River	1392
DEAD	₂ " Lizzie	Wife	24	F	"	1896	" "	8067
	₃ " Levisa	Dau	2	"	"			
DEAD Dead	₄ Logan Louina	S. "	6	"	"	1896	Red River	8068
3211	₅ Simon	S.Son	4	M	"	1896	" "	8069
	₆							
	₇							
	₈							
	₉							
	₁₀							
	₁₁							
	₁₂							
	₁₃							
	₁₄							
	₁₅							
	₁₆							
	₁₇							

DIED PRIOR TO SEPTEMBER 25, 1902 (overlay near line 5)

ENROLLMENT OF NOS. 1 and 5 HEREON APPROVED BY THE SECRETARY OF INTERIOR Dec. 12, 1902

No.5 died Feb. – 1900: Enrollment cancelled by Department Sept. 16, 1904

No 3 is duplicate of No 9 on Choctaw card #585

Enrollment hereon cancelled August 24, 1905.

No. 2&4 Hereon dismissed under order of the Commission to the Five Civilized Tribes of March 31, 1905.

TRIBAL ENROLLMENT OF PARENTS

	Name of Father	Year	County	Name of Mother	Year	County
₁	John Billy	1896	Red River	Elsie Billy	Dead	Eagle
₂	Jino Hunter	Ded	" "	Lila Hunter	"	Red River
₃	No 1			No 2		
₄	Franklin Logan			No 2		
₅	" "			No 2		
₆						
₇						
₈						
₉						
₁₀	Evidence of birth of No3 requested 3 times: no response Nov 20 '03					
₁₁	No 2 on 1896 roll as Lizzie Logan					
₁₂	No 4 " 1896 " " Louiana "					
₁₃	No 4 died about the 28th of November, 1899 Evidence of death filed May 2, 1901.					
₁₄	No.2 Died March 4-1900. Evidence of death filed June 3, 1901.					
₁₅	No 5 died February, 1901, proof of death filed December 3, 1902.			Date of Application for Enrollment.		
₁₆				Apr. 29 "99		
₁₇						

Choctaw By Blood Enrollment Cards 1898-1914

NAME: Kiamatia[sic]

RESIDENCE: Goodland I.T.

COUNTY

Choctaw Nation

Choctaw Roll (Not Including Freedmen)

CARD NO.

FIELD NO. 1183

	NAME		Relationship to Person First Named	AGE	SEX	BLOOD	TRIBAL ENROLLMENT		
							Year	County	No.
3213	1 Wallace Dixon W.	54	DIED PRIOR TO SEPTEMBER 25, 1902	54	M	Full	1896	Kiamatia[sic]	13709
3214	2 " Serena	48	Wife	45	F	"	1896	"	9754
3215	3 " Sweny	20	Son	17	M	"	1896	"	13710
3216	4 " Ida	11	Dau	8	F	"	1896	"	13711
3216	5 " Lina	14	"	11	"	"	1896	"	13712
3217	6 " Charlie	10	Son	7	M	"	1896	"	13713
3218	7 " Felisela	DIED PRIOR TO SEPTEMBER 25, 1902	Dau	5	F	"	1896	"	13714
3218	8 Reeves Rachel	14	S "	11	"	"	1896	"	11020
	9								
	10 ENROLLMENT OF NOS. 1234567and8 HEREON APPROVED BY THE SECRETARY								
	11 OF INTERIOR DEC 12 1902	For child of No4 see NB (Apr 26-06) Card No 719							
			(Mar 3-05) " " 965						
	12 No1 died Aug, 1900; proof of death filed Dec 5,1902.		" " " " "						
	13 No7 " Jany,1901; " " " " " 5,1902.								
	14 No2 wife of Charley Winston on 7-1521								
	15 No8 " " No1 on 7-1125								
	16 No.1 died Aug - 1900; No.7 died Jan. - 1901 Enrollment								
	17 cancelled by Department July 8, 1904.								

TRIBAL ENROLLMENT OF PARENTS							
Name of Father	Year	County	Name of Mother	Year	County		
1 John Wallace	De'd	Skullyville	Yok-oh-tima	Ded	Eagle		
2 Nicholus Hampton	"	Wade		"	Cedar		
3 No 1			Becky Wallace	"	Nashoba		
4 No 1			" "	"	"		
5 No 1			" "	"	"		
6 No 1			Clarissa Wallace	Ded	Kiamatia[sic]		
7 No 1			" "	"	"		
8 Henry Reeves	De'd	Kiamatia[sic]	No 2				
9							
10							
11	No 2 on 1896 roll as Serena Nelson						
12	No 5 " " " "Lynnie Wallace						
13	No 7 " " " "Falichi "						
14	No 8 " " " " Rachel Reaves						
15	No 4 also on 1896 roll No 13265						
16	No 5 " " 1896 " No 13266 as Lean Wallace					Date of Application for Enrollment.	
17	" 3 " " " " " " Sweny "					Apr. 29"99	

283

Choctaw By Blood Enrollment Cards 1898-1914

RESIDENCE: Red River COUNTY. **Choctaw Nation** Choctaw Roll *(Not Including Freedmen)* CARD NO.
POST OFFICE: Goodwater I.T. FIELD NO. 1184

Dawes' Roll No.	NAME	Relationship to Person First Named	AGE	SEX	BLOOD	TRIBAL ENROLLMENT		
						Year	County	No.
3220	1 Logan Calvin 23	First Named	20	M	Full	1896	Red River	8065
	2							
	3							
	4							
	5							
	6							
	7							
	8							
	9							
	10							
	11							
	12							
	13							
	14							
	15							
	16							
	17							

ENROLLMENT
OF NOS.   1   HEREON
APPROVED BY THE SECRETARY
OF INTERIOR DEC 12 1902

TRIBAL ENROLLMENT OF PARENTS

	Name of Father	Year	County	Name of Mother	Year	County
1	Frank Logan	Ded	Red River	Luey Logan	Ded	Red River
2						
3						
4						
5	For child of No.1 see N.B. (Apr. 26 '06) card #267.					
6						
7						
8						
9						
10						
11						
12						
13						
14						
15						Date of Application for Enrollment.
16						Apr. 29"99
17						

Choctaw By Blood Enrollment Cards 1898-1914

RESIDENCE: Red River COUNTY.
POST OFFICE: Goodwater I.T.

Choctaw Nation

Choctaw Roll *(Not Including Freedmen)*
CARD NO.
FIELD NO. 1185

Dawes' Roll No.	NAME	Relationship to Person First Named	AGE	SEX	BLOOD	TRIBAL ENROLLMENT Year	County	No.
3221	1 Jefferson Jincy 26	23	F	Full	1896	Red River	7019
3222	2 " Loston 9	Son	6	M	"	1896	" "	7020
14644	3 Billy, William 1	Son	1	M	"			
	4	ENROLLMENT OF NOS. 1 and 2 HEREON APPROVED BY THE SECRETARY OF INTERIOR DEC 12 1902						
	5							
	6							
	7	ENROLLMENT OF NOS 3 HEREON APPROVED BY THE SECRETARY OF INTERIOR MAY 20 1903						
	8							
	9							
	10							
	11							
	12							
	13							
	14							
	15							
	16							
	17							

TRIBAL ENROLLMENT OF PARENTS

Name of Father	Year	County	Name of Mother	Year	County
1 Israel Jefferson	Ded	Red River	Sally Sampson	Ded	Red River
2 Foston Jefferson	"	Eagle	No 1		
3 Simon Billy	1896	"	No 1		
4					
5					
6 No 1 is now wife of Simon Billy on 7-1010					
7 Nº3 Born Nov. 30, 1901, application first received Nov 25 1902 proof of birth filed Feby 28 1903					
8					
9					
10					
11					
12					
13					
14					
15					
16					
17			Date of Application for Enrollment. Apr. 29/99		

Choctaw By Blood Enrollment Cards 1898-1914

| RESIDENCE: Red River | COUNTY. | **Choctaw Nation** | Choctaw Roll | CARD NO. |
| POST OFFICE: Kullituklo, I.T. | | | *(Not Including Freedmen)* | FIELD NO. 1186 |

Dawes' Roll No.	NAME	Relationship to Person First Named	AGE	SEX	BLOOD	TRIBAL ENROLLMENT		
						Year	County	No.
3223	1 Jacob, Jack	DIED PRIOR TO SEPTEMBER 25, 1902	60	M	Full	1896	Red River	7036
	2							
	3	ENROLLMENT						
	4	OF NOS. 1 HEREON APPROVED BY THE SECRETARY						
	5	OF INTERIOR DEC 12 1902						
	6							
	7							
	8							
	9							
	10							
	11							
	12							
	13							
	14							
	15							
	16							
	17							

TRIBAL ENROLLMENT OF PARENTS

	Name of Father	Year	County	Name of Mother	Year	County
1	O-ba-tambe	Dead	Red River	Hannah	Dead	Red River
2						
3						
4						
5	No. 1 died Sept 1901; proof of death filed Dec. 3, 1902					
6	No.1 died Sept – 1901: Enrollment cancelled by Department July 8, 1904					
7						
8						
9						
10						
11						
12						
13						
14						
15						
16			Date of Application for Enrollment.		Apr. 29/99	
17						

Choctaw By Blood Enrollment Cards 1898-1914

RESIDENCE: Bok Tuklo   COUNTY.   **Choctaw Nation**   **Choctaw Roll**   CARD NO.
POST OFFICE: Lukfata, I.T.   *(Not Including Freedmen)*   FIELD NO. **1187**

Dawes' Roll No.	NAME	Relationship to Person First Named	AGE	SEX	BLOOD	TRIBAL ENROLLMENT Year	County	No.
3224	1 Ishcomer, Phillip N. 42	First Named	39	M	Full	1896	Bok Tuklo	6278
3225	2 " Nicie 43	Wife	40	F	"	1896	" "	6279
	3							
	4							
	5							
	6							
	7	ENROLLMENT						
	8	OF NOS. 1 and 2 HEREON APPROVED BY THE SECRETARY						
	9	OF INTERIOR Dec. 12, 1902						
	10							
	11							
	12							
	13							
	14							
	15							
	16							
	17							

TRIBAL ENROLLMENT OF PARENTS

	Name of Father	Year	County	Name of Mother	Year	County
1	Nelson Ishcomer	Dead	Bok Tuklo	Ah-le-ho-ke	Dead	Nashoba
2	Parker	"	" "	Susan Parker	"	Bok Tuklo
3						
4						
5						
6	No 1 on 1896 roll as P.N. Ishcomer.					
7						
8						
9						
10						
11						
12						
13						
14						
15						
16				Date of Application for Enrollment		
17				Apr. 29/99		

287

Choctaw By Blood Enrollment Cards 1898-1914

ICE: Fowlerville, I.T.   **Choctaw Nation**   **Choctaw Roll**   CARD NO.
(Not Including Freedmen)   FIELD NO.   **1188**

NAME	Relationship to Person First Named	AGE	SEX	BLOOD	TRIBAL ENROLLMENT		
					Year	County	No.
1 McKinney, Ephraim ²¹	First Named	18	M	Full	1893	Blue	P.R. 49
2							
3	ENROLLMENT						
4	OF NOS. I HEREON APPROVED BY THE SECRETARY						
5	OF INTERIOR DEC 12 1902						
6							
7							
8							
9							
10							
11							
12							
13							
14							
15							
16							
17							

TRIBAL ENROLLMENT OF PARENTS

	Name of Father	Year	County	Name of Mother	Year	County
1		Dead	Kiamitia		Dead	Kiamitia
2						
3						
4						
5	On Page 120 No 49, 1893 Pay roll, Blue County as Ephranis					
6	McKinney					
7	Came from Kiamitia County, when an infant, Claims never to have known father or mother					
8						
9						
10						
11						
12						
13						
14						
15						
16				Date of Application for Enrollment	Apr. 29/99	
17						

288

Choctaw By Blood Enrollment Cards 1898-1914

RESIDENCE: Red River COUNTY.
POST OFFICE: Goodwater, I.T.

Choctaw Nation

Choctaw Roll
(Not Including Freedmen)

CARD No.
FIELD No. 1189

Dawes' Roll No.	NAME		Relationship to Person First Named	AGE	SEX	BLOOD	TRIBAL ENROLLMENT		
							Year	County	No.
3227	1 Logan, Joel	38	First Named	35	M	Full	1896	Red River	8079
3228	2 " Tennessee	DIED PRIOR TO SEPTEMBER 25, 1902	Wife	29	F	"	1893	Bok Tuklo	P.R. 89
Dead	3 " John DEAD		Son	1	M	"			
	4								
	5	ENROLLMENT							
	6	OF NOS. 1 and 2 HEREON APPROVED BY THE SECRETARY							
	7	OF INTERIOR DEC 12 1902							
	8								
	9	No. 2 HEREON DISMISSED UNDER							
	10	ORDER OF THE COMMISSION TO THE FIVE CIVILIZED TRIBES OF MARCH 31, 1905.							
	11								
	12								
	13								
	14								
	15								
	16								
	17								

TRIBAL ENROLLMENT OF PARENTS

	Name of Father	Year	County	Name of Mother	Year	County
1	Bob Logan	Dead	Red River		Dead	Red River
2	Dixon Pickens	"	Bok Tuklo	Siney Pickens	"	Bok Tuklo
3	No 1			No 2		
4						
5						
6			No2 on 1893 Pay roll as Tennessee Picken, Page 11.			
7			No.3 Died October 29, 1900. Evidence of death filed April 9, 1901.			
8			No2 died August 20, 1902; proof of death filed Dec 3 1902.			
9			No.2 died Aug. 20, 1902; Enrollment cancelled by Department Sept 16, 1904			
10						
11						
12						
13						
14						
15						
16				Date of Application for Enrollment.	Apr. 29/99	
17						

289

Choctaw By Blood Enrollment Cards 1898-1914

RESIDENCE: Red River COUNTY.
POST OFFICE: Goodwater, I.T.

Choctaw Nation

Choctaw Roll
(Not Including Freedmen)

CARD NO.
FIELD NO. 1190

Dawes' Roll No.	NAME	Relationship to Person First Named	AGE	SEX	BLOOD	TRIBAL ENROLLMENT		
						Year	County	No.
3229	1 Camp, Lima 59		56	F	Full	1893	Red River	P.R. 109
	2							
	3	ENROLLMENT						
	4	OF NOS. 1 HEREON APPROVED BY THE SECRETARY						
	5	OF INTERIOR DEC 12 1902						
	6							
	7							
	8							
	9							
	10							
	11							
	12							
	13							
	14							
	15							
	16							
	17							

TRIBAL ENROLLMENT OF PARENTS

	Name of Father	Year	County	Name of Mother	Year	County
1	Jack McKinney	Dead	Red River	Sukey McKinney	Dead	Red River
2						
3						
4						
5	On 1893 Pay roll as Antsarah Camp, Page 13.					
6						
7						
8						
9						
10						
11						
12						
13						
14						
15						
16				Date of Application for Enrollment.	Apr. 29/99	
17						

290

Choctaw By Blood Enrollment Cards 1898-1914

RESIDENCE: Red River   COUNTY.   **Choctaw Nation**   **Choctaw Roll**   CARD No.
POST OFFICE: Kullituklo, I.T.   *(Not Including Freedmen)*   FIELD No.   1191

Dawes' Roll No.	NAME	Relationship to Person First Named	AGE	SEX	BLOOD	TRIBAL ENROLLMENT Year	County	No.
3230	1 Frazier, Frances ²⁸	First Named	25	F	Full	1896	Red River	4222
	2							
	3	ENROLLMENT						
	4	OF NOS. 1 HEREON APPROVED BY THE SECRETARY						
	5	OF INTERIOR Dec 12 1902						
	6							
	7							
	8							
	9							
	10							
	11							
	12							
	13							
	14							
	15							
	16							
	17							

TRIBAL ENROLLMENT OF PARENTS

Name of Father	Year	County	Name of Mother	Year	County
1 Louis Frazier	Dead	Bok Tuklo	Sophia Watson	Dead	Red River
2					
3					
4					
5	No 1 now wife of No1 on 7-1222. Evidence of marriage				
6	requested 11/28/02				
7					
8					
9					
10					
11					
12					
13					
14					
15					
16			Date of Application for Enrollment.	Apr. 29/99	
17					

Choctaw By Blood Enrollment Cards 1898-1914

Dawes' Roll No.	NAME	Relationship to Person First Named	AGE	SEX	BLOOD	TRIBAL ENROLLMENT		
						Year	County	No.
3231	1 Hickman, James 27	First Named	24	M	Full	1896	Bok Tuklo	5567
	2							
	3							
	4							
	5							
	6							
	7							
	8							
	9							
	10							
	11							
	12							
	13							
	14							
	15							
	16							
	17							

ENROLLMENT
OF NOS. 1 HEREON
APPROVED BY THE SECRETARY
OF INTERIOR DEC 12 1902

TRIBAL ENROLLMENT OF PARENTS

Name of Father	Year	County	Name of Mother	Year	County
1 Coleman Hickman	1896	Bok Tuklo	Selin Hickman	Dead	Bok Tuklo
2					
3					
4					
5			Hickman 2/26/02		
6			No. 1 is the husband of Winie Henderson on Choctaw card #1013.		Nov. 15, 1901
7					
8					
9					
10					
11					
12					
13					
14					
15					
16				Date of Application for Enrollment	Apr. 29/99
17					

Choctaw By Blood Enrollment Cards 1898-1914

RESIDENCE: Bok Tuklo   COUNTY.   **Choctaw Nation**   Choctaw Roll   CARD No.
POST OFFICE: Alikchi, I.T.   (Not Including Freedmen)   FIELD No.   1193

Dawes' Roll No.	NAME	Relationship to Person First Named	AGE	SEX	BLOOD	TRIBAL ENROLLMENT Year	County	No.
3232	1 Nakishi, David 30	First Named	27	M	Full	1896	Bok Tuklo	9719
3233	2 " Mary 23	Wife	20	F	"	1893	" "	P.R. 74
	3							
	4							
	5	ENROLLMENT OF NOS. 1 and 2 HEREON APPROVED BY THE SECRETARY OF INTERIOR DEC 12 1902						
	6							
	7							
	8							
	9							
	10							
	11							
	12							
	13							
	14							
	15							
	16							
	17							

TRIBAL ENROLLMENT OF PARENTS

	Name of Father	Year	County	Name of Mother	Year	County
1	Lewis Nakishi	Dead	Bok Tuklo	Mayah Nakishi	Dead	Bok Tuklo
2	Jacoway Hickman	"	" "	Rosie Hickman	"	" "
3						
4						
5						
6	No 2 on 1893 Pay roll as Mary Cobb, Page 10, Bok Tuklo County also					
7	on 1896 roll as Mary, Page 216, No 8643 " " "					
8						
9						
10						
11						
12						
13						
14						
15						
16				Date of Application for Enrollment	Apr. 29/99	
17						

293

Choctaw By Blood Enrollment Cards 1898-1914

Choctaw Nation

Choctaw Roll
(Not Including Freedmen)

CARD NO.
FIELD NO. 1194

Dawes' Roll No.	NAME	Relationship to Person First Named	AGE	SEX	BLOOD	TRIBAL ENROLLMENT		
						Year	County	No.
3234	1 King, Harris 22		19	M	Full	1896	Red River	7590
	2							
	3							
	4							
	5							
	6							
	7							
	8							
	9							
	10							
	11							
	12							
	13							
	14							
	15							
	16							
	17							

ENROLLMENT
OF NOS. 1 HEREON
APPROVED BY THE SECRETARY
OF INTERIOR DEC 12 1902

TRIBAL ENROLLMENT OF PARENTS

Name of Father	Year	County	Name of Mother	Year	County
1 Milurt King	Dead	Red River	E-yah-hoke	1896	Red River
2					
3					
4					
5	No.1 is the husband of Lina Moore on Choc. Card #1177. Feby. 17, 1902.				
6					
7					
8					
9					
10					
11					
12					
13					
14				Date of Application for Enrollment.		
15						
16				Apr. 29/99		
17						

Choctaw By Blood Enrollment Cards 1898-1914

RESIDENCE: Red River   COUNTY.   **Choctaw Nation**   Choctaw Roll   CARD No.
POST OFFICE: Kully Tuklo I.T.   (Not Including Freedmen)   FIELD NO. **1195**

Dawes' Roll No.	NAME	Relationship to Person First Named	AGE	SEX	BLOOD	TRIBAL ENROLLMENT Year	County	No.
DEAD.	1 Juzan Jackson DEAD	First Named	53	M	Full	1896	Red River	7002
3235	2 " Sela 46	Wife	43	F	"	1896	" "	7003
3236	3 Fisher Winston 14	Ward	11	M	"	1896	" "	4200
	4							
	5	ENROLLMENT OF NOS. 2 and 3 HEREON APPROVED BY THE SECRETARY OF INTERIOR DEC 12 1902						
	6							
	7							
	8	No. 1 HEREON DISMISSED UNDER ORDER OF THE COMMISSION TO THE FIVE CIVILIZED TRIBES OF MARCH 31, 1905.						
	9							
	10							
	11							
	12							
	13							
	14							
	15							
	16							
	17							

TRIBAL ENROLLMENT OF PARENTS

	Name of Father	Year	County	Name of Mother	Year	County
1	Louis Juzan	Ded	Red River	Amy Juzan	1896	Red River
2	Ish-ta-na-bi	"	" "	Po-shi-ma	Ded	" "
3	Stephen Fisher	"	" "	Silva Watkins	1896	" "
4						
5						
6						
7		No 2 on roll as Silie Josund				
8		No 1 " " " Jackson "				
9	No 1 Died Feby. 15, 1901: Proof of death filed Nov. 9, 1901.					
10						
11						
12						
13						
14						
15						
16				Date of Application for Enrollment. Apr. 29"99		
17						

Choctaw By Blood Enrollment Cards 1898-1914

RESIDENCE: Red River   COUNTY.   **Choctaw Nation**   Choctaw Roll *(Not Including Freedmen)*   CARD No. FIELD NO. **1196**
POST OFFICE: Goodwater I.T.

Dawes' Roll No.	NAME	Relationship to Person First Named	AGE	SEX	BLOOD	TRIBAL ENROLLMENT Year	County	No.
3237	₁ Dyer, Sallie ³⁵	First Named	32	F	Full	1896	Red River	3444
3238	₂ Louis Mary ¹⁴	Dau	11	"	"	1896	Eagle	8017
3239	₃ Louis Winey ¹²	"	9	"	"	1896	Red River	3445
3240	₄ " Louisa ⁹	"	6	"	"	1896	" "	3446
14645	₅ Byington, David ¹	Son of Nº 2	5mo	M	"			
	6	ENROLLMENT						
	7	OF NOS. 1 2 3 and 4 HEREON						
	8	APPROVED BY THE SECRETARY OF INTERIOR DEC 12 1902						
	9							
	10	ENROLLMENT						
	11	OF NOS. 5 HEREON						
	12	APPROVED BY THE SECRETARY OF INTERIOR MAY 20 1903						
	13							
	14							
	15							
	16							
	17							

TRIBAL ENROLLMENT OF PARENTS

	Name of Father	Year	County	Name of Mother	Year	County
1	George Nelson	Ded	Red River	Mary Nelson	Ded	Red River
2	Jacob Lewis[sic]	Ded	Eagle	No 1		
3	" "			No 1		
4	" "			No 1		
5	Simeon Byington	1896	Red River	Nº2		
6						
7						
8			No 3 on 1896 roll as Weley Dyer			
9			No 4 " " " " Louisa "			
10		No 1 is now wife of Eastman Fobb on 7-1341				
11		No 2 " " " " Simeon Byington on 7-1035 Evidence of				
12		marriage filed Dec. 24, 1902				
		Nº5 Born July 7, 1902, enrolled Dec. 24, 1902.				
13		For child of No.1 see NB (March 3 1905) #1266.				
14					#1 to 4 inc Date of Application for Enrollment.	
15						
16					Apr. 29"99	
17						

Choctaw By Blood Enrollment Cards 1898-1914

RESIDENCE: Bok-Tuk-lo   COUNTY.   **Choctaw Nation**   Choctaw Roll   CARD NO.
POST OFFICE: Fowlersville I.T.   *(Not Including Freedmen)*   FIELD NO.   1197

Dawes' Roll No.	NAME	Relationship to Person First Named	AGE	SEX	BLOOD	TRIBAL ENROLLMENT Year	County	No.
3241	1 Kanashambe Forbis ⁴⁷	First Named	44	M	Full	1896	Kiamatia[sic]	7546
3242	2 " Basin ³⁹	Wife	36	F	"	1896	"	7547
	3							
	4 ENROLLMENT							
	OF NOS. 1 and 2 HEREON							
	5 APPROVED BY THE SECRETARY							
	6 OF INTERIOR DEC 12 1902							
	7							
	8							
	9							
	10							
	11							
	12							
	13							
	14							
	15							
	16							
	17							

TRIBAL ENROLLMENT OF PARENTS

Name of Father	Year	County	Name of Mother	Year	County
1 Kanashambe	Ded	Bok Tuk lo	Ela-ima	Ded	Bok Tuklo
2 Robert M. Byer	"	" " "	Liza	"	" " "
3					
4					
5					
6					
7					
8		No 2 on 1896 roll as Bisson Kanashambe			
9					
10					
11					
12					
13					
14					
15					
16			Date of Application for Enrollment	Apr. 29"99	
17					

Choctaw By Blood Enrollment Cards 1898-1914

RESIDENCE: Red River COUNTY **Choctaw Nation** Choctaw Roll CARD NO.
POST OFFICE: Goodwater I.T. (Not Including Freedmen) FIELD NO. 1198

Dawes' Roll No.	NAME	Relationship to Person First Named	AGE	SEX	BLOOD	TRIBAL ENROLLMENT Year	County	No.
3243	1 McClure Dixon 36	First Named	33	M	Full	1896	Red River	9317
3244	2 " " Betsy 28	Wife	25	F	"	1896	" "	9318
3245	3 " " Walter 10	Son	7	M	"	1896	" "	9319
3246	4 DIED PRIOR TO SEPTEMBER 25, 1902 " " Agnes	Dau	2	F	"			
3247	5 " " Mary Belle 3	"	2wks	"	"			
3248	6 " " Jourdan 1	Son	1mo	M	"			
	7							
	8 ENROLLMENT							
	9 OF NOS. 1 2 3 4 5 and 6 HEREON APPROVED BY THE SECRETARY							
	10 OF INTERIOR DEC 12 1902							
	11							
	12							
	13							
	14							
	15							
	16							
	17							

TRIBAL ENROLLMENT OF PARENTS

Name of Father	Year	County	Name of Mother	Year	County
1 Isom McClure	De'd	Red River	Eliza Going	1896	Red River
2 Israel Jefferson	"	" "	Kan-chi-hoke	Ded	" "
3 No 1			No 2		
4 No 1			No 2		
5 No 1			No 2		
6 No.1			No.2		
7					
8		No.6 born Oct. 28th 1901: Enrolled Nov. 21st 1901			
9		No4 died June 1900: proof of death filed Dec. 3 1902			
10		No.4 died June – 1900: Enrollment cancelled by Department Sept 16, 1904.			
11					
12					
13					
14					
15					#1 to 4 inc
16				Date of Application for Enrollment	Apr. 29-99
17					No 5 May 12/99

298

Choctaw By Blood Enrollment Cards 1898-1914

RESIDENCE: Red River COUNTY.
POST OFFICE: Goodwater I.T.

Choctaw Nation

Choctaw Roll (Not Including Freedmen)

CARD NO.
FIELD NO. **1199**

Dawes' Roll No.	NAME		Relationship to Person First Named	AGE	SEX	BLOOD	TRIBAL ENROLLMENT Year	County	No.
3249	1	Brown, Alle ~~DIED PRIOR TO SEPTEMBER 25, 1902~~	First Named	29	F	Full	1896	Red River	1406
3250	2	" Willard	Son	12	M	"	1896	" "	1409
3251	3	" Victor	"	9	"	"	1896	" "	1410
3252	4	" Ephraim	"	7	"	"	1896	" "	1411
3253	5	" Chloe	Dau	5	F	"	1896	" "	1412
14646	6	" Ida	Dau	3	F	Full			
	7	ENROLLMENT OF NOS. 1 2 3 4 and 5 HEREON APPROVED BY THE SECRETARY OF INTERIOR Dec 12, 1902							
	8								
	9								
	10								
	11	ENROLLMENT OF NOS. ~6~ HEREON APPROVED BY THE SECRETARY OF INTERIOR May 20, 1903							
	12								
	13								
	14								
	15								
	16								
	17								

TRIBAL ENROLLMENT OF PARENTS

	Name of Father	Year	County	Name of Mother	Year	County
1	Isom McClure	Ded	Red River	Eliza Going	1896	Red River
2	J. J. Brown	"	" "	No 1		
3	" " "			No 1		
4	" " "			No 1		
5	" " "			No 1		
6	Mike J. Brown			No 1		
7						
8						
9						
10						
11	No1 died June 1900: proof of death filed Dec 3, 1902					
12	application made for enrollment of No6 Nov. 28, 1902, see sworn statement of Elliston McClure and others of that date.					
13	Guardianship papers issued County Court Red River Co to Esabelle McClure dated Sept 2, 1901 filed Jany. 17, 1903.					
14						
15	See copy of letter from W.J. Whiteman relative to parentage of No6, filed Jany 17, 1903.			Date of Application for Enrollment.		
16	No6 Born in Aug. 1899. Affidavits as birth filed Feby. 17, 1903			Apr. 29"99		
17	No.1 died June – 1900: Enrollment cancelled by Department Sept. 16, 1904.					

RESIDENCE: Red River COUNTY.								
POST OFFICE: Goodwater I.T.	**Choctaw Nation**				Choctaw Roll (Not Including Freedmen)		CARD NO. FIELD NO.	**1200**

Dawes' Roll No.	NAME		Relationship to Person First Named	AGE	SEX	BLOOD	TRIBAL ENROLLMENT		
							Year	County	No.
3254	1 Harley Stiles	24	First Named	21	M	Full	1896	Red River	5664
3255	2 " Sissy	27	Wife	24	F	"	1893	Eagle	286
3256	3 " Preston	4	Son	5mo	M	"			
14647	4 " Mattie	1	Dau	1½	F	"			
	5								
	6	ENROLLMENT OF NOS. 1 2 and 3 HEREON APPROVED BY THE SECRETARY OF INTERIOR Dec. 12, 1902							
	7								
	8								
	9								
	10	ENROLLMENT OF NOS. 4 HEREON APPROVED BY THE SECRETARY OF INTERIOR May 20, 1903							
	11								
	12								
	13								
	14								
	15								
	16								
	17								

TRIBAL ENROLLMENT OF PARENTS

	Name of Father	Year	County	Name of Mother	Year	County
1	Nixon Harley	Ded	Red River	Jinsy Wallin	Ded	Red River
2	Onnahabbi	Ded	" "	Nicey Onnahabbi	"	Eagle
3	No 1			No 2		
4	No 1			No 2		
5						
6						
7						
8	No 2 is mother of Mima Going on Choctaw card #669					
9	See testimony in Choctaw allotment Jacket Nº 1603.					
10						
11			No2 on 1893 pay roll as Cissy drawing pay with			
12			Alexon Going in Eagle Co			
13			No4 born June 1 1901; enrolled Dec. 13, 1902			
14	For child of Nos 1&2 see N.B. (Apr. 26-06) Card #334				#1 to 3 inc Date of Application for Enrollment.	
15						
16					Apr. 28, 1899	
17						

307

317

Eveline....256
Missie....247
Sanders....256
Sophia....291
Wm....232
WAY-TUBBEE....153
WEBSTER
Daniel....186
David....186
Ida May....186
Josiah....186
Lizzie....186
Maggie....186
Melvina....186
Nannie W....186
Pliny....186
Robert....186
Susie....186
Wood Kirk....186
WESLEY
Biny....248
Charlie....248
Colbert....9
Edward....15
Eliza....248
Jackson....248
James....248
Johnson....96
Joseph....248
Konchee....25
Moses....15,25
Sam....9
WHEELER
John....213
Sibby....213
WHITE
Artin....58
Charlie Phillips....236
WHITEMAN
D C....183
Maggie E....183
Mary E....183
Mary Lena....183
Mattie J....183
W J....183,299
WILISTON, Elizabeth....55
WILLIAMS
Ansby....37
Betsy....280
Bicy....280
Billy....37
Edmund....37
Edward....37
Ella....54
Ellis....48
Emma....48,54
George....142
John....37
Levicy....37
Lonena....37
Lottie....54
Lucy....37
Mike....37
Nora....48
Osby....37
Sallie....48
Sampson....280
Sillen....37
Sol....158
Sophie....37
Thomas....37
Tom....54
Wicey....158
WILLIE
Ansie....10
Edmond P....42
Harriet....42
Hodges....10
Liza....42
Nelson....42
Sina....10
Thomas....10
William A....10
Williamson....10
Wm Amos....10
WILLIS....101
Alisse....140
Allen....140
E H....200
Eastman H....200
Ed P....42
Emma....101
Frances....200
Garben....237

www.ingramcontent.com/pod-product-compliance
Lightning Source LLC
Chambersburg PA
CBHW030236030426
42336CB00009B/123